Ransome in Russia

Arthur's Adventures in Eastern Europe

Ted Alexander
&
Tatiana Verizhnikova

Portchester Publishing

Also by Ted Alexander

Ransome at Home (1996)
Ransome in the Baltic (2002)
Ransome in Estonia (2003)

Front Cover Painting. The Litovsky Castle on fire during the 1917 spring uprising. Commissioned from Mitrokhin as the cover picture for Ransome's own proposed book on the Revolution. From UA Rysakov's Collection, St Petersburg.
Front and Back Cover Portrait. Ransome wearing Russian cap bearing his initials in Russian, AK for Artur Kirrilovich [Ransom]. From Special Collections, Leeds University.

Published by Portchester Publishing
7 Camelot Crescent, Portchester, Fareham, Hampshire PO16 8ER

Copyright CE Alexander 2003
CE Alexander has asserted his right under the Copyright, Designs and Patents Act 1988 to be identified as the author of this work.

ISBN: 0-9545554-0-6

Design and layout Claire Kendall-Price, Wild Cat Publishing.
The Greenwood Cottage, Lower Bockhampton,
Dorchester, Dorset DT2 8PZ

Printed by The Friary Press, Bridport Road, Dorchester, Dorset DT1 1JL

CONTENTS

1 The Early Years — 1

2 Journey to the Moon — 24

3 Where East Meets West — 47

4 Year of the Revolution — 74

5 Dissatisfaction at Home — 93

6 Ransome as Diplomatic Emissary — 112

7 Correspondent in the Baltic States — 139

8 Evgenia Shelepina and the October Revolution — 166

Acknowledgements — 186

Illustrations — 188

Bibliography — 189

Index — 192

PHOTOGRAPH OF BEARER.

SIGNATURE OF BEARER.

INTRODUCTION

Arthur Ransome lived a long, interesting and fruitful literary life. He died in 1967 aged 83 having spent a large part of his life fulfiling his dreams – writing in one form or another, fishing and sailing.

While his writing before 1913 was mixed, the time subsequently spent in Eastern Europe was to be very important in helping him to fashion and hone his writing skills. Working as a correspondent for the *Daily News* and later the *Manchester Guardian*, Ransome developed a descriptive and easy reading style, which made him such an attractive author when writing the *Swallows and Amazon* series of books in middle age.

Although providing a brief biography of Ransome from birth to 1913, the main thrust of this book concerns the period Ransome spent in Russia and the Baltic States. For much of the time from 1913 to 1924 there were major events such as the First World War and the Russian Revolution to contend with but also some minor events, all of which he reported. Much of the daily task of visiting Government offices, attending interviews and press briefings and telegraphing reports was a boring, tiring and repetitious affair.

Hundreds of books recording aspects of the First World War and the Russian Revolution have been written, and a fairly comprehensive account of Ransome's reporting of these events and involvement in their politics has been set out in Brogan's excellent biography *The Life of Arthur Ransome*. It seemed appropriate to us therefore, to concentrate on Ransome's time generally, sketching in some of the places he visited, mentioning those people who were important to him, and how he spent some of his spare time. This book has been written to provide an overview of these years, touching on the major events only where it is a necessary part of the story. It does not however cover a day-by-day, blow-by-blow account of everything that he did.

In 1919, Ransome made an amazing and quite important journey across the Russian civil war lines from Reval to Moscow and back. With the aid of new information, including Ransome's own notes, this journey has been reconstructed and covered at some length.

Finally, there is an account fashioned by Evgenia intended as information for Ransome about her involvement with the Bolsheviks, her subsequent employment as Trotsky's secretary and the trip she made to the Brest-Litovsk peace negotiations.

All of this, it is hoped, will afford a better understanding of Ransome and give as much pleasure to the reader as we have had in putting it all together.

CEA & TV

Chapter I
The Early Years

Arthur Ransome embarked on a journey to Russia at the end of May 1913. He went with the express object of learning the language. Some accomplishment of which, it was hoped, would enable him to read Russian folk tales at first hand. He had been interested in this aspect of literature for a few years and wanted to research enough 'tales' to publish a book on the subject for English readers.

By the middle of 1913, Ransome had been married for a little over four years. The marriage, however, had been unhappy almost since the start. It was a big mistake, and was a drain on Ransome emotionally in trying to cope, as well as having a debilitating effect on his ability to produce enough writing work. Ransome had got to the point where he was looking for a 'way out' from this marriage, and thought that by going to Russia, where there were still entry restrictions, he could achieve his writing objective and at the same time find a haven far away from his demanding wife.

Having established himself in Russia, a 'chance' opportunity a few years later presented itself and Ransome became a newspaper correspondent there. In due course, he would witness the Russian Revolution at first hand. As part of his correspondent's duties, he would also become well acquainted with all the leaders of the new Russia, and help in the birth of independence for the fledgling state of Estonia.

In his final years in Eastern Europe spent living in the Baltic States, he commissioned a seagoing yacht to sail in those waters. The resulting voyages culminated in a book which became a classic nautical tale – titled, *Racundra's First Cruise*. In his last year as Special Correspondent for the *Manchester Guardian*, Ransome finally got a divorce from his wife and remarried.

His second wife had been Trotsky's first secretary in Petrograd after the Bolsheviks came to power in October 1917. At the end of 1924, Ransome gave up the life of a foreign correspondent and came home to live permanently in England. The whole East European experience including the dealings he had had with Russia's new leaders had been unique, and contributed in no small way to the accomplishment and fame that would eventually come as author of the famous Swallows and Amazon series of books for children.

Before we get to these episodes, however, it seems appropriate to look at the sort of family that Ransome came from, how he developed, and how he came to be interested in writing and going to Russia in the first place.

The Early Years

Arthur Ransome was already into the latter half of his sixties when he commenced writing his autobiography. This time interval from when he was very young, meant that recollections and details from the early years were a bit hazy, to say the least, but such details as have been published, both in the *Autobiography* and Hugh Brogan's biography, *The Life of Arthur Ransome*, together with more recent research, provide enough information about this remarkable man to be able to account for most of the important features of his early life fairly accurately.

Arthur Michell Ransome (the Michell was rarely used) was born to Cyril and Edith Ransome on the 18 January 1884 at 6 Ash Grove, Headingly – a district on the north side of Leeds. In those days it was semi rural, but is now in the heart of the university bed-sit area. Eventually he would be joined by two sisters and a brother, Cecily, Joyce and Geoffrey.

Although Ransome's early life was unremarkable, even mundane, a closer look at those who were there to influence him has left us with sufficient clues to his nature and why he developed the way he did.

Ransome came from a huge family. Both his grandfathers married twice and both had large families. On his father's side were the Ransomes with a Quaker background, including a large number of parsons, as well as north country connections such as the Butterworths, Jacksons, Remingtons and Binyons. On his mother's side there were the Boultons, the Boutflowers and Tailleurs, as well as connections in New South Wales, with which his mother's step brothers and sisters were more intimately linked. There was an uncle who lived in British Colombia to a great age, and another uncle who, when he was a young man, went to live in a lighthouse near the entrance to the Mersey. This same uncle eventually became involved in the cotton trade in India, was fond of horses, won the Bombay Hunt Cup, and finally died there of a fever.

Thomas Ransome, the grandfather, was a man of ideas. He developed one scheme after another to make money, but none of these enterprises achieved much except debts. These losses eventually fell to his eldest son, Cyril Ransome, who was clearly affected by this set of circumstances, and ended up in adulthood having to shoulder these debts himself. It is hardly surprising then, that he was determined to succeed in life to ensure that a similar fate did not befall him also.

Cyril gained an MA at Oxford, became an academic as professor of history at the Yorkshire College (now Leeds University), and contributed much to the City of Leeds, sitting on various interest committees. During his time there he wrote a number of authoritative books on world history. It was also a period when a disciplinarian attitude began to emerge, which he was not adverse to exercising on his own family from time to time. He was very fond of the outdoors and loved fishing. Cyril had aspirations of becoming a conservative MP, but an accident, which subsequently caused his death, prevented him from achieving it.

Edward Baker Boulton, the other grandfather, was a completely different character. He grew up in Bridgnorth, Shropshire and inherited the family banking flair for business. Of a pleasant disposition, he was articulate, enterprising, bold on decisions and very spirited. All in all, he was a kindly man, with a more understanding and less rigid attitude to life. He came from a family of comfortable means and had emigrated to New South Wales aboard the sailing ship *Ellen* in 1836. Together with his brothers, he acquired an area totalling at least a quarter of a million acres in the Wellington Valley for sheep farming. This estate was situated to the west of Sydney, and by any standards, was enterprise on a huge scale.

This arrangement was a partnership between brothers. George and Thomas ran the sheep station, while Edward took care of the export side of the business from Sydney, with the occasional visit to Wellington to consult. His share of the profits provided the funds by which he could live in some style in the city and enjoy the life of a gentleman, while indulging in his real interest – a passion for water-colour painting. These skills developed with age, enabling him to paint pictures which would one day hang in such places as Government House, Canberra; in the Art Gallery of New South Wales and Windsor Castle. Edward had a similar artistic style to Conrad Martens, another Australian artist, but he was not so prolific nor would he become as famous.

The brothers separated after about ten years, and Edward, together with another partner, Mr Bell, purchased the 'Bergen-op-Zoom' sheep station at Walcha in New South Wales – some 300 miles to the north of Sydney. The Walcha region was noted for its high quality wool, and appealed to Edward because of its convenient size and availability. This purchase made Edward independent of his brothers and helped him to consolidate his position, although he had to do some financial juggling to accomplish it.

In the 1840s, the New South Wales Government became concerned about the huge tracts of land being controlled by a relatively small number of 'squatters'. These huge squats had been largely taken up in the 1830s, but as they were mostly gentlemen's agreements, the boundaries were vague and undefined. Governor Gibbs made himself enormously unpopular, but he had to do something – the land-grab was totally out of control. To ensure a fairer use of the territory, new Government legislation followed. This resulted in the breakup of the large estates. The Boulton brothers were gazetted in 1848 as proprietors of Cardington, Billabong and Weirguari near Wellington – a total

The Bergen-op-Zoom sheep station, Walcha, New South Wales, Australia. Periodic home and centre of Edward Baker Boulton's sheep interests for the last 35 years of his life.

of 228,400 acres, but this appears to have been quickly reduced to their core 22,400 acre Cardington property. By the time Edward bought the Bergen-op-Zoom Estate in 1853, the 'war' with the Government was over and the squatters had lost. Edward's partnership with his brothers was not dissolved until 1859, when presumably his financial share in the sale of Cardington allowed him to consolidate his position at Bergen-op-Zoom.

In 1850, Edward married Mary Atkinson, the daughter of Irish entrepreneur James Atkinson in Sydney. With this marriage, Edward started his first family, that within a few years was to become quite large. In 1859, leaving the Walcha estate in the care of his partner, he transported his entire family home to England on the sailing ship *Camperdown*. The voyage lasted an exhausting four months, and shortly after arrival, his wife Mary, having gone to Dublin to visit her parents, died. She was only 29. Although financially sound and able to pay for a governess to look after the children, being alone wasn't in keeping with Edward's style.

In 1861, Edward married again. His second bride was Rachel Emma Gwynne, a 33 year old spinster. She was living with a relative in Shrewsbury at the time, but her father was a solicitor, who was a friend and neighbour of the Boulton families living in the small town of Wem. The wedding was held in Shrewsbury Abbey and was conducted by his brother, the Rev. William Boulton M.A., headmaster of Wem Grammar School and Curate of the parish of Lee Brockhurst. Ten children would grace this second family, the first of whom would be Rachel Edith (for some reason she was always known as

Edith), who would later become the mother of Arthur Ransome. Edith received an above-average education for a girl at the time, and in later years, wrote a very readable and popular History of England, as well as developing, like her father, artistic skills as an excellent water-colourist. She married Cyril Ransome in Wem Parish Church on 28 December 1882.

The 'Australian' Boultons remained in Wem, Shropshire for many years, occupying first the 'Tilley House' until the early seventies, then the 'Old Hall', before finally taking up residence in Clifton, Bristol. Occasional painting commissions kept Edward occupied, but he also served as a county magistrate for many years and kept an eye on the wool market for the British end of his New South Wales business. In the early 1870s, the Eastern Regions of the continent suffered from drought, which affected wool production. With the prospect of an economic downturn, Edward decided to make a return visit to Walcha to take control of matters. After many months of worry, the situation eased and he returned to England. During the next twenty years he made a number of voyages back and forth between the two countries.

This commuting became necessary to oversee business affairs and to keep relations going between his two families – the 'first family' children having returned to New South Wales, as did two from the second marriage. His wife, however, is thought to have remained in England throughout their marriage except for a short two year visit to New South Wales starting in 1890. The strain of the business, long voyages back and forth, and the suicide of his son Nithsdale (from his first marriage) in 1893, all became too much. Edward died in Walcha at the grand age of 83 in October 1895.

It is interesting to note that a number of the brothers and sisters of Edith also had artistic skills; and this aptitude, which in a broad sense the family appears to have inherited, would one day blossom forth in the young Arthur as well. It was also the Boulton grandmother, Rachel, who introduced Arthur at an early age to the mysteries of chess, as she was an excellent player. He records in a draft document,

> 'Grandmother was fairly good at chess, for players in the county matches at Bristol and Shropshire used to think it worthwhile to come to her for practice.'

RANSOME AT SCHOOL

Most children from a middle class home would have expected, in those days, to start their education at a kindergarten. Arthur however, was sent to a private tutor, whom he shared with a friend, Ric Eddison. There were a number of tutors; some good, some not so good, but in time, he was sent to his first school on Headingley Hill. This day school was situated half way between Headingley and the college where his father lectured. As a rule he would go by tram, but could, by running, save the penny fare! Evidence, that Arthur already understood the benefits of saving money for other things. He was not at this school very long, but was extremely happy there.

His father, feeling that he wanted his son to have as much as possible of a lake-country background/upbringing, decided to change his school and sent him instead to a boarding school at Windermere. It was an environment which Arthur did not fit into and did not like. He was lonely there, had no friends and made only modest progress. Of course, he never told his parents how he was feeling about this situation, believing that if he mentioned it in his letters home, it would bring him into conflict with the school. In order to survive Arthur, like most resilient little boys, kept his head down and got on with it.

A saving grace in this unfortunate situation, was his kindly great-aunt Susan, who lived up the hill from the school at 2 The Terrace, just above the railway station. She lived alone and quite liked the smoke and noise of the trains, which was all to the good, as her income was derived from dividends and shares in the London & North Western Railway. A lover of nature, she kept a tortoise and hedgehog for company. Her home was always a haven, especially on Sunday mornings when Arthur, after the school church service, would be given permission to visit her – visits he records as always being a great pleasure.

The whole family spent the summers in the late 1880s/early 1890s at a farmhouse at Nibthwaite, a delightful village at the south end of Coniston, in the Lake District. When it rained, Cyril wrote books and the children drew or played with transfers, but when the weather was fine, it was fishing on Coniston Water for Cyril, with the children playing outside or on the nearby fells. It was while he was at the Old College Windermere in 1897 aged 13, that his father died. Cyril had been fishing some years earlier and climbed from the water carrying a heavy basket. He slipped and fell, catching his foot under a large stone. At first, Cyril assumed his foot was just sprained, but it turned out to be much worse and over time, his foot, then his lower leg, and finally his upper leg had to be amputated. Cyril struggled on with an artificial limb, but finally died aged 46, leaving Arthur as the senior male of the family.

An attempt at a scholarship for Rugby, one of England's premier public schools, was unsuccessful. However, with help from her family, Mrs Ransome succeeded in getting Arthur a place there to follow in his father's footsteps. Entry was into the Lower Middle II of the school. Arthur records this as being fortuitous, because in passing in at such a low level, he came under the

Old College Windermere at the turn of the century.

watchful eye of a remarkable teacher, Dr. W.H.D. Rouse. Dr. Rouse was a classical scholar who helped and supported the young Ransome through his early period in the school. They were to remain friends for over half a century.

The importance of getting Arthur into this, or a similar school should the application fail, was 'respectability'. In late Victorian Britain, 'respectability' was the means by which the middle classes survived. It was the currency of attending the right schools; getting a good education; having qualifications; being professional; and having the right address and circle of friends. Such factors as these were sometimes more important in selecting the occupation or career of a young person than aptitude or suitability. Arthur already had aspirations to being a writer, which Rouse was happy to encourage, but this was in conflict with the sort of career Mrs Ransome had in mind for her son. Given the Ransome grandfather's propensity for being unable to organise and co-ordinate his affairs and the loss of his father, the last thing the family wanted was that Arthur would adopt some inappropriate or insecure means of earning a living. With approval from Mrs. Ransome, every effort was made by the next housemaster, Robert Whitelaw, to steer the young pupil towards a more acceptable career.

It was to Rouse and a mathematics master, however, that Arthur owed the discovery that he was short-sighted. Hitherto, he had had great difficulty in seeing the classroom blackboard, as well as being poor at sport. Not surprising, when half the time he could not see the ball or what was being written on the blackboard. Progress through the school was slow and Arthur finally left from the lower fifth. He sat the matriculation for The Yorkshire College, Leeds, expecting to fail, but to his great surprise, passed in the first division.

THE EMERGING WRITER

To satisfy the family demands of a respectable career, Ransome commenced a science degree course in the autumn of 1901. Although he enjoyed the study up to a point, he always considered it second best to the real business of writing. The emancipating effect of attending a university, failed to tempt Ransome into joining in social activities or becoming involved with an interest group. Nor did he pursue any scientific research connected with his study, but instead, devoted his time to scouring the second-hand bookshops of Leeds for suitable literary books with which to build a library. This mixture of career obligation and literary disposition was ever-present, making it difficult for him to properly concentrate on the course. As Ransome recalls in the *Autobiography*, events were to take a hand in helping him out of this impasse:

> The decisive moment found me in the college library. I had gone there from the laboratory to consult a book on measurement or magnetism, and happening on some shelves where the books were classified not by their subject but by the names of their authors I saw two tall brown volumes with richly gilt lettering and decoration on their backs: J.W. Mackail's Life of William Morris. I began dipping into them and never went back to the laboratory that day... From that moment, I suppose, my fate was decided,and any chance I ever had of a smooth career in academic or applied science was gone forever.

His natural disposition, which was inclined more towards the Boulton temperament than to the Ransome's, made him susceptible to the easy life-styles portrayed in J.W. Mackail's Life of William Morris. The life-style portrayed, of course, was for Ransome, a wonderful idea, but without means, it was just a dream. Things dragged on for nearly two terms. Ransome also experimented in visiting many different denominations of worship, deciding in the end to give them all a miss!

In early 1902, with the course not going at all well, Ransome realised that there was probably no chance of getting through the impending Intermediate Examinations. His first thought was to protect his father's rightly respected name from disgrace by deciding to leave. He would need a job. Enquiries amongst Leeds booksellers revealed the most enterprising publisher of the day to be a firm called Grant Richards. Ransome carefully drafted a letter setting out his education and something about himself, and quickly posted it before having second thoughts! He wrote to tell his mother what he had done, expecting her to explode, but she didn't, although she cannot have been pleased.

Being a perceptive woman, she may have realised that her eldest son was not cut out to be an academic, and supported his initiative by advancing him the train fare for the London interview.

Mrs Ransome later visited the offices of Grant Richards, and reluctantly accepted that her son would become an office boy on eight shillings a week. Resignation, was to become a way of life for her so far as Ransome was concerned, but she bore it all in true spirit, always hoping that one day things would change – they never did! Forty years later, when Ransome was on the last few volumes of the twelve book series, Edith did privately concede that she was secretly pleased with his achievements, and was happy to show him the odd letter of approval that had come her way from admirers of the books. It was some sort of acceptance – at last!

Lodgings were found in the Clapham area of South London, from where he would commute daily by horse-drawn bus into the City. His room was shared with others, a position which was not ideal, but one which would suffice, pending his mother's arrangements to rent a property for all the family somewhere in south London.

The job was instructive and very useful, and Ransome learnt a considerable amount about the business of publishing. In early August he left Grant Richards after only five months and joined the Unicorn Press, a small publishing firm under Ernest Oldmeadow. He was offered double the salary for doing less work; a situation he couldn't refuse. Reading took up much of his spare time, even at work, as there was sometimes very little to do. The library was slowly increasing, partly funded by a few commissions and some freelance work, and partly by spending his lunch money on bargain offers from stalls in the London streets.

Late in the year, Mrs Ransome set up a home for her family at 67 Huron Road, Balham, and Arthur was pleased to join her there. The *Autobiography* records this house as being small, but it had 13 rooms and was, in practical terms, quite spacious. This move restored the comforts of home life, especially meals, enabling him to eat a good breakfast and supper which he hoped, would last him for the whole day. It also enabled his sister Cecily to have a studio in which to paint.

Living at home clearly had its' benefits, but it also had its drawbacks. His mother was able to keep a watchful eye on his activities and occasionally, to cast a disapproving look over his choice of friends and acquaintances; a situation which sometimes had Arthur irritated. His brother Geoffrey, and sisters Cecily and Joyce, were quite busy with their own activities, but during their spare time produced a small magazine called *The Huron Weekly* – a publication to which Arthur was pleased to contribute from time to time.

Thirteen copies are known to survive. When contributions got less, it became *The Huron Monthly* and so on... Travelling for Ransome was up-graded from a horse-drawn bus to a season ticket on the train from Balham to Victoria in London.

In 1903, Ransome was due a weeks holiday. He dashed straight north on the night train to spend the whole of it at Coniston. This was the important week in July when he met W.G. Collingwood. A desire to write some poetry found him lying on some large boulders in the middle of the beck at Miner's Bridge up Coppermines Valley. W.G. was passing and noticed a still body. He hailed and the body came to life! Having got to the footpath at the side of the beck, the two men then walked down to the village together with Ransome talking about poetry and writing. This chance meeting led to an invitation to visit Lanehead, the Collingwood's home on the east side of the lake, opposite Coniston village. Although initially, the meeting was as strangers, both the Ramsomes and Collingwoods had met in 1895 while on a picnic on Peel Island on Coniston Water. The Collingwoods may also have known the Ransomes from earlier correspondence.

Ransome was too shy to visit immediately, but summed up enough courage to call on his last day before returning to London. On this visit, Ransome was shown into the Collingwood's dining room, where W.G. Collingwood listened to his thoughts and aspirations, and offered his guidance and support. He reassured Ransome that writing was an honourable vocation and offered a sympathetic ear, but more importantly, an understanding of his situation, something which up until this point, Arthur had not experienced before.

During the autumn of 1903, believing that he could support himself by the growing amount of paid writing, he gave his notice to leave the Unicorn Press for fresh pastures – a departure engendered by the fact that it was, as he recorded in the *Autobiography*, 'showing clear signs of mortality'. Sadly, a few weeks later, it went into liquidation.

It was during this year that Ransome records meeting the poet and writer Edward Thomas, 'a man with a fine-cut, sad face, looking very unlike a townsman', during one of his frequent trips to the St. Martin's Lane coffee-houses. They eventually became firm friends and often visited each other; Thomas to Ransome's lodgings and Ransome to Thomas's home in Kent.

Early on in the relationship, Ransome was slightly in awe of Edward Thomas, partly because of his age (Thomas was almost six years older) and partly because of his greater maturity and experience. In addition, Thomas was married with a family, and was reviewing books – an activity which Ransome would eventually take up.

RANSOME THE BOHEMIAN

Ransome's aspirations started to grow in line with his increasing income. Feeling that he could support himself, and with the desire to be independent again and free from maternal displeasure, he set about trying to find somewhere to live. Chelsea beckoned – it was the heart of London's Bohemia on the north bank of the Thames. A morning was spent hunting for an affordable flat, which he eventually found in Hollywood Road, two floors up above a grocer. A boy with a horse-drawn van was hired for seven shillings (plus a shilling tip for the boy) to transport his books and few possessions from Balham across Albert Bridge to Chelsea. 'Of this I am now ashamed,' he writes in the *Autobiography*. 'I should have thought of my mother's feelings and not mounted the tailboard of the van in full view of all our neighbours who were watching from behind their lace curtains and aspidistras.'

Ransome's Hollywood Road top floor, corner flat today.

By late afternoon, Ransome was settled into his top floor corner flat. He was now back in the position of having to do everything for himself, including the purchase and preparation of food. 'I never starved but I was always hungry,' he writes in the *Autobiography*. 'A solid meal could be made from a haddock and the cooking of it wasted no time. Haddocks could be bought in the King's Road. I used to buy my haddock and take it home, then boil a kettle of water on the fire, and pour the boiling water over the haddock in a saucepan, put the lid on, read for another ten minutes, when a meal would be ready that would last for twenty-four hours.'

All this was fine, but Ransome often didn't eat enough of the right foods to sustain himself properly. The day-to-day business of shopping, eating and just looking after himself was inconvenient; taking up, as he thought, too much of his valuable writing time. He wanted to perfect the art of living on

The Early Years

as little food as possible in order to buy books, but in the end, all he got were the foundations for the almost continuous stomach problems that plagued him for much of the rest of his life.

During this period in Hollywood Road, Ransome was introduced by Yoshio Markino, a Japanese artist friend, to the home of Miss Pamela Coleman-Smith. Weekly evening meetings were held in Pamela's studio in the Boltons for actors, actresses, authors and artists. At these meetings Ransome met W.B. Yeats, and Masefield amongst others, and it was also the time when he first heard the Anansi stories. Life was reasonably good; he was meeting people, writing plenty, with the hope of some small commissions and enjoying himself. But access to his flat was two floors down, and the landlord had been unfriendly and an irritant since the commencement of the tenancy.

After only eight months, and with a view to bettering his situation, he moved in the spring of 1904 to another room close by at One Gunter Grove. Life here was easier. The landlord, who was a postman, lived in the basement, while Ransome occupied the ground floor front room. Rent was ten shillings per week and included breakfast, but there were extra charges for the use of light, coal, and for washing. Later, rents were offered at one pound a week 'full board', but it is not known whether this offer was ever taken up. At the turn of the twentieth century, cereals as we know them today were not being produced, which meant that breakfast was a substantial cooked meal. Large quantities of porridge, bacon, eggs and other cooked products were consumed for the first meal of the day. By getting a substantial breakfast, Ransome thereby improved his chances of lasting out until the evening meal. The money saved, of course, went on books!

Shortly after establishing himself at this new address, Ransome decided to move north to Coniston for the summer season. The idea was to continue his work there. Initially, he stayed for a few days at Bank House in the village, but later, at the invitation of Mrs Collingwood, stayed in her son's room at Lanehead until he came home from boarding school for the summer holidays. There were four children to this family: Dora, who was eighteen; Barbara, who was seventeen, plus Robin and Ursula, both of whom were that much younger.

This was an idyllic period. Each day, Mrs Collingwood would herald the morning by playing a piece on the piano. Perhaps her family needed rousing, but these morning serenades were always appreciated, as it seemed to set the tone for the day to come. Following breakfast, everybody in the house would spend the morning at work or study. Ransome did likewise, but spent the afternoons sailing, picnicking on the lake or exploring the nearby fells. What a wonderful time he had! It was an experience which would remain in his memory forever, and help him through those difficult times to come when, years later, he felt alone as a correspondent in Russia.

The effect this family had on Ransome and his affection for them, cannot be overstated. They were terribly important to him in many ways, but as a surrogate family, provided that understanding and balance to life that had been missing in his own. His attachment to them can be gauged by the return visits that he made to the Lakes when home on leave. In all his eleven years abroad, he never once missed them out!

In the middle of July, Ransome returned to London and Gunter Grove, 'leaving a gap', as Dora said, in the Collingwood household, but not before showing an interest in Barbara, the second of the Collingwood daughters. Two weeks after he had left, Dora recorded in her journal:

> ... and then – well, it was rather unexpected, but anyone could see that something had been going on between them for weeks before Arthur left. Barbara and I were having tea together – the others were out, and she told me. She pretends not to care in the least, but I have my doubts!

He also had a commission from Mrs Collingwood to find them a lodging, which they could use for the winter season in London, as both the elder girls were expecting to attend an art school near Chelsea. With the assistance of Peggotty Cole, a nearby artist friend, a flat on the fourth floor of a nearly new block of flats was found in Edith Grove, which the Collingwoods accepted and occupied in late September.

Shortly after they took up occupancy at Editha Mansions, Ransome asked Barbara to marry him. She considered his proposal, but erring on the side of caution, said, 'NO'! It was hardly surprising; at an age of only 17, her education yet to complete it's course, and Ransome with barely enough money to keep himself, let alone take on the responsibilities of a wife. He was upset enough with this reply though, to take himself off into Surrey; only returning after receiving a letter from Mrs. Collingwood. The situation, however, soon assumed some normality once Ransome was back and the position had been talked through.

As Edith Grove is next but one and parallel to Gunter Grove it follows that Ransome was a frequent visitor to the girls, and they to his flat. The subjects they discussed were invariably writing and poetry, with Ransome reading passages from his latest work. In 1904, the first fruits of his labours resulted in the publishing of *The ABC of Physical Culture* and *The Souls of the Streets*.

Towards the end of September, however, Ransome's friend Edward Thomas rented the rear room at the same address for one month. The two men had a rather rowdy and not very studious time together. On one occasion

Thomas received a cheque, and in order to get the money rushed round to a bank before closing time to cash it. This windfall was celebrated by the two of them going for a meal at a nearby restaurant. Having completed the meal, they paid, left, walked across the road into another restaurant and had a second meal. Ransome records that no comment passed between them as they entered the second restaurant to gorge themselves. At the end of the month Thomas left, and returned to his wife Helen and the family in Kent.

The summer of 1905 saw Ransome returning to the Lakes again for his summer season. Feeling that he might wear his welcome out with the Collingwoods, he opted instead for a nice first floor bedroom, with the use of a sitting room at Wall Nook Farmhouse at Cartmel. This choice location, that had been found for him by Gordon Bottomley, a poet friend, provided stimulating views of the surrounding fells from his bedroom window. Ransome so enjoyed this peaceful place that he made it his summer home each year until 1907. It was also the place where he made one of his most important friendships. Another guest was standing by the front door one day and Ransome bumped into him. It was none other than Lascelles Abercrombie, another budding writer and poet, who was staying at the farmhouse while courting his future wife Catherine. The two men struck up a conversation and instantly hit it off. They became life-long friends.

Ransome published this year his third book and first novel, *The Stone Lady*. He also decided, as a result of his improved financial position, to move again to better lodgings. In the autumn, Gunter Grove was given up in favour of a two roomed arrangement at the Carlyle Studios, 296 King's Road, Chelsea. The property was owned by two charming and friendly spinster sisters, who were much more agreeable as landlords than Ransome's previous ones. He was very free here, and much enjoyed having both a bedroom and a study, the latter having a fashionable Adam fireplace. Soon after moving in, he wrote to his mother telling her that the landladies did not supply blankets, and asking her if she could send him some. Whether this request was ever met, is not known, but Ransome, even at the age of nearly 22, was not adverse to making requests to his mother if he thought she would oblige. On another occasion, when his three sets of pyjamas gave out, a word to his mother brought a replacement parcel almost by return of post.

1906 saw Ransome gaining in confidence, partly as a result of increasing success with paid writing, and partly due to the approval, acceptance and encouragement of the Collingwood family. This productive period, which included a second summer at Wall Nook Farm, resulted in the publication of four works – *A Child's Book of the Garden*, *Pond and Stream*, *Things in Season*, and a contribution to *Temple Bar Magazine*.

Ransome wrote to his mother on 5 March 1906; the last paragraph of which reflects his high spirits and self confidence – arrogance even.

My love to the kids and company. Tell 'em to write me a letter, and I'll send 'em a collective, individualistic, rhetorical, imaginative, superlatively beautiful, impassioned and intellectual little piece of four short verses.

Goodbye AR.

Above and right: Edith Ransome in the greenhouse Kemsing, Kent

Towards the end of the year, Ransome signed a contract and began the writing of *Bohemia in London*. This work was to occupy a large part of 1907, including his last summer season at Wall Nook Farm and five weeks spent with his mother in Edinburgh. Bohemia was Ransome's first major success and was published on his return from the Lakes in September. Also published this year was *Highways and Byways in Fairyland*.

Towards the end of the year, he closed up his flat, paid advance rent to his landladies and set off for Paris. In the spring of 1908, he returned to London having been away six months researching introductions to French writers that he was compiling for the A.&C. Black, World's Best Storytellers series at the National Library. Unfortunately for Ransome, he was greeted on his return by news that the landladies wished to retire and wanted to sell the property. This was rather a set-back, especially as life with the ladies had been most agreeable, and what with the desirable location it was altogether a disappointment.

In characteristic style, however, he looked around and found even better accommodation at Owen Mansions, Queen's Club Gardens, near Baron's Court. The property consisted of three rooms (opulently decorated), a separate bathroom, electric light and coal-fired ranges with back boilers. He officially occupied the premises on 1 September. It is clear that Ransome was now earning enough to support a considerably improved life-stile. He describes his new flat with some pride:

> I had there a good work-room, plenty of bookshelves, the first of the big tables I have always liked, two armchairs, one given by my mother, a kitchen, airy bedroom, a bathroom and a 'daily woman' who used to come in the mornings to tidy up, though I did most of my own cooking (*Autobiography*, p127).

ENTANGLEMENTS

Shortly after returning from Paris, Ransome headed north to the Lakes for his summer season. Having exhausted the area around Wall Nook, he decided on a room at Low Yewdale farmhouse much nearer Coniston. In periods of fine weather, he camped on a bit of high ground in an adjacent field alongside Yewdale Beck, but when the weather was disagreeable, retreated to the farmhouse. Ransome had spent some years thinking that it was about time he got married, but 1908 must be the year that he seriously considered doing something about it. A number of his friends were either courting or getting married, and he thought he ought to do the same. Having been turned down by Barbara in 1904, he still thought that his best bet was to persist with the Collingwood girls in the hope that the position might turn in his favour. After a decent interval Arthur's affections shifted to Dora. He had always been fond of Beetle (his nickname for her), and they spent much of that summer in each others company. In one of her journals, Dora records one of their late July outings together:

> Arthur came to lunch, and afterwards I went to Low Yewdale with him where he read me various things that he had written... And then we packed the tea basket and went up past Shepherd's Bridge, and got over the wall and down into the beck and picnicked in a lovely spot in the bottom of the gorge... The water made a continuous rush and rumble and there was no other sound; it was most delightful. We boiled a kettle – Arthur has a new tea basket of which he is immensely proud - it is certainly very 'Tweaky'. I cut the bread and butter while he boiled the water, and then played about dropping stones into the water and fishing them out again, and rushing about enjoying myself... I did enjoy it so much. He was very nice, he is so utterly different from any other man I know – indeed he is the only one I know well, and in spite of his many eccentricities he is really a dear. Then we came home; he came as far as Boon Crag with me – I don't wonder that our neighbours talk about us and AR, and I equally don't care. The other day a neighbour asked mother, 'is it true that it's Miss Collingwood Mr. R's after?' and that is not the first or second time.

Just a month later, Ransome was in the Lanehead studio 'sitting' for a sketch she was doing of him, when he took her quite by surprise. With his time in the Lakes drawing to a close, he saw his chance and asked her to marry him. She did not, however, take him seriously and declined the offer almost out-of-hand. In her perceptive way, she felt he was someone who was looking for anyone and everyone – anything for a wife! It is also clear that Dora was now looking on him more from a sisterly point of view, rather than perhaps, from a romantic one. Ransome was, however, very serious and deeply hurt with this negative response. On the following day, the day he was due to go home, Dora walked over to Low Yewdale to help him pack up, but found him in despair and very melancholy. Eventually his packing was done and he left, leaving his lodgings looking very distrait.

But Ransome was not one to give up easily. A couple of months after this major setback, he entertained both Dora and Barbara to tea in London at his new Owen Mansions flat, when the subject of marriage cropped up again. Not necessarily to Dora, although it is clear he was still harbouring thoughts that she might change her mind. Instead, Dora advised him to pursue another lady whom he had mentioned back in the summer – a lady, real or imagined for the purposes of the conversation. There is no doubt that Dora loved Ransome for part of this year, but she still declined his offers! Why? We may never know the whole story but it is interesting to observe, that he remained life-long friends with both Collingwood girls (and outlived both of them).

Ransome, like most other men of his age did not have physical relationships with females – such was the pattern of social behaviour at the time. Instead, it was normal and accepted practice to wait until one was either married or very much older before becoming involved. This behaviour may seem strange in today's climate of 'gym-slip' mothers, and a 'free-for-all', but it was so.

The quest to find a wife took an unexpected turn for the better, when an acquaintance in London, Ralph Courtney, whom he had first met at the office of Curtis Brown, the literary agent who had sold *Bohemia in London*, took him to an art studio in Chelsea. There he met a crowd of art students who were in the habit of roller-skating at Earls Court or Olympia, and after a long day at his typewriter he was often pleased to join them there for skating sessions in the evening. One day, a couple of them together with Courtney, went to Ransome's flat at Owen Mansions bringing with them one of Courtney's friends – a Miss Ivy Walker.

Shortly after arriving, Ivy implied 'she was not a barmaid', alluding no doubt to the impropriety of visiting a young mans rooms. To which Ransome says that he replied in jest along the lines of, 'Well we could solve that by getting married', or something similar. Not that he would have thought of her in those terms, having often entertained the Collingwood girls at his various Chelsea addresses.

The result of this meeting was that Ransome was quite taken with Ivy and began to fall in love, not in a plain straightforward way as he had with each of the Collingwood girls, but in a rather haphazard manner, learning that she had an amazing imagination, could fantasise, and surround the simplest act with secrecy and excitement. Ivy was a very attractive woman, not just to Arthur, but to all men, and he was soon swept off his feet. In the new year (1909) they became engaged. Ransome dutifully wrote to Dora telling her all about Ivy. On hearing the news she made some astute notes in her journal for 23 January:

> On Saturday I heard from Arthur – who tells me that he is nearly engaged to a lady called Ivy who apparently is very charming and writes. It's all very sudden – a very short time ago his heart was in a very different place but won't think it ever stays in the same place long. I wonder what will be the end of this. I wrote to him congratulating him on having asked her at last, as I told him in the summer – tho' privately I much doubt if it is the same she.

They were married by special licence in St Andrew's Church, Fulham on March 13th where Edward Thomas's wife Helen was a witness. A church blessing followed on April 1. Ivy was the elder by two years and four days. Ransome sub-let his flat and they moved to their first married home; a pleasant cottage found for them by Edward Thomas and delightfully situated some 800 feet up on top of the Hangers (the collective name for separately named hills to the north of Petersfield), with views over Petersfield to the South Downs. It was very convenient for Ransome getting to London, as well as for Ivy, who had her parents at Bournemouth.

In meeting Ivy's parents, Ransome was introduced to a family vastly different from his own. The Walkers were descended from landed gentry (Pochin of Barkby – a family of great antiquity: they also had cousins with direct decent from Edward III), and although Mr. Walker was a qualified solicitor, he rarely, if ever, practiced, being able to exist on his assets or private means alone. He had married a woman who was partly Portuguese, and Ivy was their only child. To some extent she was 'played off' between her parents in their desire to hold her affections, which may account for the subterfuge, tantrums and manipulation she found necessary in order to survive as a child.

The Walker family had not wanted this marriage: Ivy was already engaged to a cousin, with the wedding dress made and all the arrangements in place when Ransome appeared on the scene. Ivy, for most of her life, loved her mother dearly – the feelings were mutual, so Mrs. Walker, in order not to upset her relationship with her daughter, found it convenient for grandmother Walker to write the appropriate stiff 'Victorian missive' imploring her not to proceed. 'It is not for you and you should remember the mistakes made by other members of our family in the past', she wrote. But it was to no avail. Perhaps in Ransome, she thought she had found someone who would jazz up her life a little, as well as giving her a home of her own.

If observations of friends are to be believed, Ivy was devoted to Arthur and loved him very much – she gave up everything for him, but whether there was any thought of 'getting back' at her parents by staying the course with Arthur, may never be known.

If Mr. Walker was undecided where Arthur was concerned, his wife most certainly was not. She very much disapproved of him and gave him a hard time every moment they had the misfortune to meet. He in turn, loathed her, kept out of her way as far as possible and detested her prying visits. Mrs Walker was a discerning woman who only wanted the best circumstances for her daughter. It can be assumed that she judged Arthur to be an inappropriate match and unsuitable in some way. Marriage for many women before the First World War was still very much a career, that meant that the parents of the bride were bound to examine the credentials of any prospective suitor (particularly where a family has an illustrious pedigree) with more than a 'passing' interest.

A little over a year later on 9 May 1910, Ivy gave birth to a daughter Tabitha. She was born in a rooming house at 15 Frances Road, Bournemouth, just a few minutes walk from her parents. The couple had moved there some weeks earlier in order that Ivy could be near her mother for the confinement, having spent the winter at Peake's Farm, just to the north of Shaftesbury. The event was to prove a strain for Ransome, and as soon as practicable they left, and headed north with the child to spend a few weeks with Mrs. Ransome in Edinburgh.

A couple of months later, Ivy and the baby were settled 'in rooms' near Godalming. Ransome decided that he needed a break from his domestic circumstances, and set off to spend a few days visiting the Lake District. It would be unnatural for him not to visit the Collingwoods, so for a few nights he camped in their garden at Lanehead. Within a few days, they asked him if he would like to house-sit for them, as they were going to be away for the autumn term at Reading University. He jumped at the chance, and rushed south to organise the family and collect some work. He quickly returned, followed by Ivy and the nurse with baby Tabitha, to join him there. Seizing the opportunity, Ransome decided to give his daughter a bit of Lakeland heritage by having her Christened in Coniston church. The ceremony was on 7 November, to which the dreaded mother-in-law was invited. Ransome's misery was also reflected in his diary entry for the 12th: 'evening spoilt by Ivy's mother. Night ditto: by the sheer ugliness of remembering her!'

They vacated Lanehead in mid-December as the Collingwoods were due to return for the holiday period. Arthur and Ivy crossed to France and spent Christmas and the New Year in Paris. In the previous September, both Dora and Barbara had gone to Paris to continue their art studies. It was inevitable then, that an opportunity would present itself whereby Ransome could introduce his wife to Dora. The meeting, when it came, was very difficult. Dora was terribly shy, she could hardly speak and didn't know what to say. She recorded in her journal, that she felt 'for no apparent reason' as if she wanted to cry. But, she got over it, and during the next few weeks joined the Ransomes on several outings. On one such night, the three of them went out to visit a street café, and while Arthur was engaged in a lengthy game of billiards in a back room, she and Ivy had a long conversation lasting an hour and a half – mostly about Arthur!

Following an unsettled period in the spring of 1911 (there were a couple of moves to different addresses) they rented a mediaeval farmhouse at Hatch,

Ivy Ransome née Walker

near Tisbury in Wiltshire. This gave Ransome a direct train service to London, and Ivy convenient access to Bournemouth to visit her parents.

A notable event occurred in late May 1912, when Ransome took part in a donkey cart trek with his friend Ivar Campbell. A donkey, together with a green cart showing yellow roses on the side, had been bought for five pounds. They carried a tent and cooking utensils on the cart, as well as a sack full of books for review. The official start took place at the British Museum, but they got off very late in the day and decided to spend the first night at Campbell's family home in Bryanston Square. The real start was at 5 am next morning, and ended at Hatch ten days later, with the intrepid walkers having passed near Guildford, Four Marks, Winchester, Salisbury, Wilton and along the Downs to the farm at Hatch.

Three weeks after this event, Lascelles Abercrombie visited Hatch. He and Ransome rode around Dorset on bicycles. Abercrombie knocked on Thomas Hardy's front door near Dorchester hoping to obtain information for a possible biography, while Ransome lay on the grass nearby. Unfortunately Hardy thought him a reporter and slammed the door in his face. Much later, Hardy was contrite when he realised he had made a mistake, but by then it was too late.

During the early months at Hatch the cracks, already apparent in Arthur's relationship with Ivy, began to open up. She craved attention and was unhappy at being left alone for so much of the time in what was quite a lonely place. Her behaviour could be quite demanding, theatrical and unreasonable, just when he wanted to sit at his desk and write, or go fishing. Ransome for his part, did not always appreciate Ivy's needs, nor the fact that when he was away, which was often, she was isolated, stuck in a large house out in the country with few neighbours. His needs, however, which were quite the opposite of hers, required the solitary peace and quiet necessary to contemplate the writing in hand, and those works he would like to write. Time spent on his own playing billiards in a Shaftesbury club, or days spent quietly at a river's bank fishing, were all essential in nourishing his spirit to accomplish this task. Ivy wanted to be the traditional wife, running the home with her husband at her side for the benefit of the family as a whole. But Ransome was often away. He would journey to Leeds to see his mother; the Lakes to see the Collingwoods, or go to London on business. Sometimes having come home, he would go off on a long walk or fish at the stream at the bottom of the village. Their personalities were not in harmony either and their mutual presence was enough to spark antagonisms and arguments between them. On one occasion, they both sat down and talked out their differences, 'long intimate talk – both very happy', Arthur records, but it didn't last.

The Early Years

In order to provide the family income, Ransome was seriously committed to writing, writing and writing, and nothing in their relationship, or her behaviour was going to get in the way. From his point of view, she was too possessive and would not leave him alone to get on with his work. In the end, it became one of the factors which persuaded him to leave England and travel to Russia to pursue his writing interests.

It had taken just a little over four years, for the prediction of friends and the worst fears of Mrs. Walker, to come to fruition. Commentators have found it convenient to blame one side or the other, but both were at fault, not to mention being quite unsuited. Domestic troubles aside, Ransome spent much of 1911 working on a number of short stories and articles for new books, and in particular on a biography of Oscar Wilde: a critical study, a work which was published in 1912, along with a translation of Remy de Gourmont's *A Night in Luxembourg*.

The biography of Oscar Wilde was an important book, having been commissioned by the publisher, Martin Secker. Wilde's literary executor, Robert Ross, arranged for Michael Likiardopoulos of the Moscow Arts Theatre to visit Ransome at Hatch with a view to arranging the translation of the work into Russian. As it happens, publication in Russia was postponed by the outbreak of war, and because of the Revolution, ultimately cancelled.

The proofs of Oscar Wilde were read and approved by Ross before publication, which occurred in the third week of February. In the middle of March, Lord Alfred Douglas, who had had a relationship with Wilde, issued a writ for libel against Ransome, Secker, and The Times Book Club. This action was quite unexpected and took Ransome by surprise. To help Ransome in his original appraisal of all aspects of Wilde's work, Ross had allowed him to see the unpublished parts of the De Profundis letter. Having treated the subject sympathetically, Ransome did not think he had written anything to which anybody could take offence. However, what he did not know, was that this skirmish would turn out to be only part of the story for Ross and Douglas who were engaged in a private feud

Ransome spent a miserable year waiting for the case to come to trial in April 1913 before Mr.Justice Darling. He had wanted to keep Ivy out of it, but she insisted on attending the court. By all accounts, she revelled in the proceedings and publicity, which somewhat annoyed Ransome. The trial lasted four days, and might have gone on for longer, but for the intervention of counsel for The Times Book Club, who spoke up for him. The jury found in favour of the defendants – Ransome was acquitted. The whole affair was a debilitating business and Ransome was left exhausted, fed up and determined not to embark on any more 'critical' books, however tempting the offer.

Chapter II
Journey to the Moon

The Lord Alfred Douglas case had occupied his thoughts and energies for nearly a year, just wondering what the outcome would be, but in walking out of the court cleared of all charges, he was now free to focus on his work, plans for the future and his family. By the end of May 1913 Ransome had reached an impasse in his relationship with Ivy. A relationship aggravated by her behaviour over the court case, and marred by quarrels and disagreements for most of the time they had been married. This led him to feel that this situation could not go on, especially if he was to produce enough published material to provide an adequate family income.

It is not clear precisely when the decision to 'run away' was made, and in all probability it would have been difficult to make, especially with Tabitha at such a tender age. Quietly mulling over the possibilities in private, he must have reached a decision within days of the court case ending because, there was only a five week gap between the end of the trial and his departure. He did not tell anybody and even his mother, his most trusted confidant, was not let into the secret. Before departure, however, he did consult his solicitor Sir George Lewis, who advised him not to remain in the house, particularly after

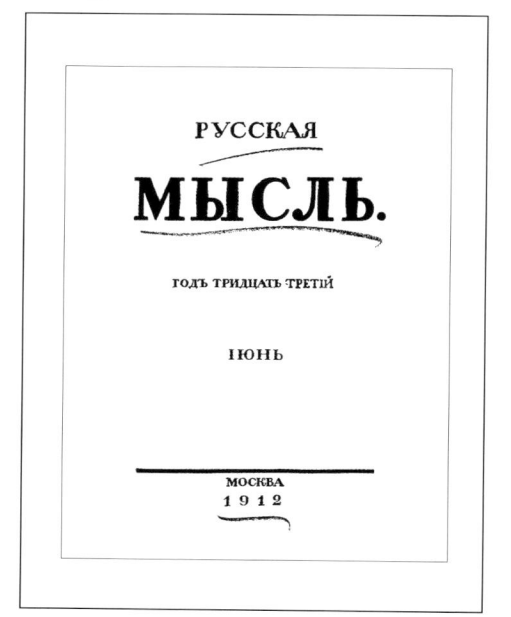

Title pages for *The Silver Snakes* published on behalf of Ransome by Michael Lykiardopoulos in Moscow 1912, the year prior to his visit. Other articles were also published in Russia that year.

Ivy had picked up two lighted lamps and smashed them to pieces. It was agreed that Sir George would try and arrange a peaceful separation, if only for a few months.

Ransome already knew about Russia; he had a contact in Michael Lykiardopoulos (Secretary of the Moscow Arts Theatre), and in 1912 had had *The Little Silver Snakes*, and other works, translated and published in Moscow. Moreover, his interest in Russian folk tales had been developing for some time. *Russian Wonder Tales*, of which Ransome could not have been unaware, had already been published in 1912, by A.&C. Black in London. A need therefore, to research some original material for himself, together with the desire to get away from Ivy was sufficient to point Ransome in the direction of where he should go.

Before the First World War, travel around most of Europe could be accomplished without papers, but Russia, where papers were needed, was different, so off he went believing that Ivy would be unlikely to follow him there. It is not clear whether he left England with the full intention of proceeding to Russia straight away, or not. In a hastily pencilled note to his mother before embarkation he says:

Dear Maw [May 1913]
   I am going for a short holiday to Stockholm. Address Post Restante, Stockholm, Sweden.
   No time for more before going on board. Please write to me at Stockholm. I wish I had a letter for/from you [illegible] could send Ivy, saying that you think I ought to stay away 2 or 3 months for the good of my health and work. As it is I am only going for three weeks which is useless...
                                                Goodbye Arthur.

No mention of Russia here! This suggests that the final decision may not have been made until sometime during the ten days that were subsequently spent in Stockholm.

When the gangway was raised, the mooring lines cast off, and the ship moved away from the quay with a blast on the whistle, it was a signal that Ransome had reached the beginning of the end of his marriage to Ivy. This was a turning point; one which he would savour in the ensuing days and months, and the mixed emotions and feelings of doubt would slowly ebb away, to be replaced with a growing determination to do something about his position.

The arrival off the Danish Coast the following morning, with the scent of lilac in the air and the mists stirring over the roofs of Elsinore Castle, helped to reawaken the life and freedom that he had known in earlier years at

Coniston and Cartmel. The memories of visiting the Collingwoods; a family living on the shores of Coniston Water who had befriended him when he was much younger, Lakeland sailing, and the Cartmel (Cumbria) meetings with Lascelles Abercrombie and Bottomley, were all too fresh in his mind. The taste of freedom was intoxicating! After spending some time on the ship in Copenhagen Harbour, he crossed by ferry to the port of Malmö on the Swedish mainland and completed the journey to Stockholm in a third class railway carriage. (See coloured map i)

Having arrived in Stockholm he had to decide on what to do next and whether to proceed further. It also provided a period of reflection to weigh up the 'running away' process so far. It must have been during this period that he decided to take advantage of the chance of a passage to St. Petersburg and abandoned the brief three week absence that he had planned. Having got over the initial hurdle of leaving England, the decision not to return but to proceed on the next stage to Russia, was in all probability not a difficult one, given his new found strength to see the job, once started, through to the end.

Whilst in Stockholm, Ransome was able to fulfil a promise made to the mother of Strindberg (famous Swedish dramatist and novelist) who was living in London, to deliver a letter to her daughter. The reasons for this letter and any subsequent outcome, would remain a mystery. They never met again.

Ransome finally left Stockholm late one afternoon aboard a steamer bound for St. Petersburg. It was a glorious day in the middle of June, which made the departing views of the sea approaches to Stockholm an enchanting sight, as he set out on the final stage of this 'Journey to the Moon' – Ransome's title for the trip. Later, cruising in calm weather along the rock-studded south coast of Finland, he was able to view an area of outstanding natural beauty, with many islands and beaches, which unknown to him then, would one day become a cruising ground on his own little ship. With the closing coastline of the Gulf of Finland, came distant views of the spires and guilded domes of the St. Petersburg skyline to herald his arrival to

A drosky - Ransome's first transport on arrival in Russia

Journey to the Moon

Finland Railway Station, St Petersburg c1900.
Frequently used by Ransome

a new and totally different world.

The first Russian port of call was Kronstadt, the island fortress guarding the eastern part of the Gulf of Finland. The stop was brief and there was insufficient time to go ashore, but his papers were dealt with by the officials who came on board for that purpose. The last part of the journey to the Neva River offered him, as it does to all visitors arriving by sea, spectacular views of the approaching majestic city of St. Petersburg. Immediately on arrival, he was met at the quayside by Edmund Gellibrand, a member of one of the earliest established Anglo-Russian families of timber merchants and a member of the local English Club. The introduction had been courtesy of one of his friends from his early Bohemian days in London.

They rode in a droskey, which is a horse-drawn carriage, over the cobbled streets and along the banks of the Neva River to the Finland Railway Station, (so named, because all the trains leaving this station would be destined for Finland – an autonomous province of Russia in those days). After admiring the icons in the booking hall, which were removed when the station was rebuilt after the Second World War, they set off by train on the 30 mile journey to the small town of Terioki, just a few miles inside the Finnish border (this town is now in Russia and named Zelenogorsk).

The Gellibrand family were well

Belovstrov Railway Station on Russian/Finnish border c1910.
Ransome crossed here every time he visited Terioki.

27

established in Russia, with other branches of the family scattered about the world in England, America, India and Australia. (There is a headland near Melbourne named after them). Their main business in Russia was in timber and pit props, with operations situated near Onega in the far north, but with a St.Petersburg connection handling the administration and export side of the business. In addition, their tentacles stretched far and wide with other interests, including another timber company in Latvia. They owned an impressive residence in the north part of St. Petersburg and had a large private estate out along the Gulf of Finland just to the west of Terioki.

Left, Russo-Finnish foot border crossing c1900. Right, Terioki Railway Station c1910. Ransome frequently used this station which is still operational.

It appears that the Gellibrand estate at Terioki (see map in colour section) probably consisted of three houses, two hidden in woods near the main road almost together, with a third about 200 metres to the north on higher ground. The lower two (one of which Ransome almost certainly stayed), have been reduced to rubble in a forest clearing. The area is now covered in low undergrowth, while the remains in the shape of bricks, timber, and bits of construction lie scattered about. Ransome records the dacha as being a pleasant wooden house among pine-trees, almost on the shore of the gulf. Standing in this mosquito-riddled clearing today (June 1996), one can admire the surrounding woodland, which in spite of the passage of time, still looks just as described all those years ago.

Ransome soon settled down and spent an idyllic few weeks living in this normal, but very Russian, household. He was able to relax, write letters, concentrate on some work, as well as walk the short distance through the forest to the shores of the Gulf of Finland. Here, the beautiful sweeping beaches offered swimming, picnics, sailing or just lazing about in the sun. He also rushed head-long into learning the Russian language to enable him to translate folk tales. He was happy at last.

Encouraged by all members of the family, and with the aid of children's early reading books, he was soon able to promote himself from beginner to infant, infant to junior, and so that by the time he went home in the autumn, he was able to read Russian in an elementary way. Ransome was always modest about his language achievements, but in spite of this and his comments upon how easy Russian is to learn (most would disagree), he became fluent in speech and reading, but perhaps less so with writing. These achievements were such, that within a couple of years, he was able to attend Government meetings to report on the politics and eventually, the Revolution that was to come. But this is jumping ahead.

Terioki beach c1900. A place of relaxation just ten minutes away from his lodgings.

A short distance to the west of Terioki there was (and still is) an unofficial art colony. It was operating mostly in summer, and was close enough for Ransome to visit by walking through the woods. There he would enjoy the

Page from Ransome's Russian notebook when he was learning the language.

occasional game of tennis, as well as meet other young Russians. In subsequent visits to Russia, Ransome would be a frequent visitor to both Terioki and this artistic colony, preferring them as places for peace, relaxation

Terioki Yacht Club c1910

and quiet contemplation, to the hustle and bustle of St. Petersburg.

After a few weeks in Terioki, he left and journeyed back round the head of the Gulf of Finland, through St. Petersburg, and down to Dorpat (Tartu) in the Baltic Provinces. Accommodation was provided by Norman Whishaw, who was almost certainly known to the Gellibrands, at Teichstrasse 39 (now Tiigi Street), in a house belonging to a firm of English flax merchants. His Russian studies, and work on a new project, a book on R.L. Stevenson, continued to occupy most of his time, but for light relief, he joined Norman Whishaw for long journeys into the flax growing countryside, often travelling day and night through endless forests in a carriage drawn by horses. His stay was relatively short with a decision to leave for London made half way through September. The route for his return journey was taken overland via Riga, Berlin and Paris.

A return to England permitted visits to his mother, the Collingwoods and various other friends. He also met Ivy in London to discuss their situation and, as a result, reluctantly agreed to return home and live at Hatch for the time being (he was always upset at being parted from his daughter). Quite what this period away achieved, other than three months of freedom and doing what he pleased, is difficult to quantify. Initially, when Ivy found out he had gone away, she was furious, and in her highly charged state accused Ransome of leaving her a deserted woman. She remained very emotional and highly distressed about the situation, and suffered continual anxiety throughout his absence, but thought that if she could get him home, he might be persuaded to stay. Ivy even thought that a period of a few months away might have given him enough time to get out of his system whatever it was that was giving him a problem, so that now he would settle down. If that was the case, she badly misjudged, as Ransome only ever saw returning home as a convenient stop-gap arrangement pending a resolution of their differences. As Ransome was to later realise, it was a grave mistake to return to Hatch, as having decided to leave, he should have stayed away so that Ivy could not be in any doubt about his actions. As it was, a sort of 'arms-length' relationship was carried on throughout the winter and into the spring. For a while they got along quite well. Ransome concentrated on *Blue Treacle* and *Stevenson*. Ivy helped a bit and they both went fishing. The strains, however, were never very far away and surfaced again in the new year. This period at home, unfortunately, failed to resolve anything.

GUIDE TO ST. PETERSBURG

Ivy's difficulties became a nightmare, particularly when she realised that Ransome had not given up the idea of leaving the married home. In the following spring of 1914, he received a commission from Douglas Goldring, a former editor of a magazine called *The Tramp*, to write a descriptive and historical Guide to St. Petersburg. Amongst other offers, such a commission was ideal and impossible to resist – it had also come at the right time. Almost immediately, he was on his way by train via Paris and Berlin, and arrived in St. Petersburg in the middle of May. He quickly settled himself into the Hermitage Hotel at 116 Nevsky Prospect and launched headlong into compiling the guide.

The hotel was of medium to large size, moderately expensive, and overlooked the Moscow Station. Such a quality hotel was likely to become a drain on his meagre financial resources, and he quickly realised that if he stayed too long he would run out of money. After exactly four weeks, he moved some miles to the western side of the city and rented a room in a large block of flats at 115 Ekateningofsky Pr kb5. This was cheap, self-catering type of accommodation, but had the benefit of a tram terminus

Hermitage Hotel - 116 Nevsky Prospect early 1900s. Large building centre top. Ransome stayed for the first four weeks while writing his Guide to St Petersburg.

Nevski Prospect - St Petersburg's main street. At more than 4km, Ransome walked some part of it daily while moving about the city. Top left, from Sadovaya towards the Admiralty c1912. The Gostiny dept store shown on the left is still there.
Top right, near Sadovaya junction c1910. Below left, lower section of the street.

outside the front of the building. Quite why he moved here, instead of staying within the central district, is a mystery. He immediately found himself at some distance from the places he needed to visit. So, whatever the merits of the room, he soon recognised the mistake, and after only four days moved again, renting a room in a side street near his previous hotel. This address, which he kept for the remaining time required to complete the guide, was at Nicholaerskaya 9, 12, kv23 (now the Ulitsa Marata, situated off the Nevsky Prospect. For photograph see colour section). The room was on the third floor (ground is 'first' in Russia), and reached via a stone staircase from the courtyard below. It was relatively small by Russian standards, had some furniture, and only enjoyed any brightness through the one small window when the sun was at its highest across the middle of the day. Soon after arriving at this last address, Ransome sent a letter to his mother bemoaning his moving problems: 'I am having a pretty awful time here. I have twice moved rooms, and much regret the hotel, where I was very comfortable. But I simply can't afford it.'

The completed guidebook covered all the principal attractions of St. Petersburg; the very many palaces (there were about twenty in the city, with yet another twenty in the surrounding countryside), numerous cathedrals, art galleries, museums and buildings of interest, as well as clubs and food – all about how to get it in Russian. Then there was entertainment, and numerous other items of interest such as The People's Fair, The Islands, Beggars and Funerals! Undoubtedly, it was a comprehensive and informative guide.

Flat 4, 115 Ekateningofsky access was gained through the archway. Ransome moved here from the Hermitage Hotel and stayed only four days.

With the room being rented for just one month, he vacated on 8 July and completed the guide the following day, having spent 57 hectic days pounding the city streets in search of information. Most unfortunately, the guide was never published due to the outbreak of the First World War; and such were the subsequent upheavals, that Ransome later destroyed the manuscript when it became obsolete from revolutionary and political changes. Ransome did concede, however, that writing the guide had been a wonderful way to explore and learn about the city. It had also taught him about focusing his effort to produce the 60,000 words necessary within the two month time frame, and overall the experience was to stand him in good stead when a couple of years later he became a correspondent.

Left, St Isaacs Cathedral which dominates the skyline. Built by Frenchman Richard de Montferrand between 1818 and 1858. Right, the Russian Museum, a vast art gallery housing only Russian art. Opened at the beginning of the 20th century.

Alexandro-Nevski Lavra (Superior Monestary). Early C18th. Contains the graves of some of Russias most celebrated artistic persons - Tchaicovsky, Borodin, Mussorgsky, Rubinshteyn, Glinka and Dostoevsky.

Having decided it was time for a rest, he moved out to the Gellibrands at Terioki, spending the remainder of the month playing tennis at the art colony nearby, swimming, fishing (at Pike Lake) taking time to relax, and his diary suggests he also took time out to visit Penarts (the nearby country estate of the famous Russian painter Repin).

As an Englishman coming to the great city of St. Petersburg, Ransome was carrying on a tradition stretching back over 200 years, 'St. Petersburg – The Russian Window to Europe', was how Peter the Great described it. From the beginning it was intended as an international city and harbour. Peter I decided that it would be a city open to foreigners, by guaranteeing them freedom of movement, export of capital, places of work and official protection.'

The British community were one of the first foreign groupings to take advantage of this opportunity, and in 1706 the registration of baptisms, marriages and deaths commenced in the local English church. The last entry before the records were returned to England, was dated 1918. Some of the earliest people who went to Russia came from noble families, such as the Bruces, Gordons and Hamiltons, to name but a few. They settled on the south bank of the Neva River before the Admiralty. The place was named the Angliyskaya Nab (English Embankment). It still is – the name was changed just after the Revolution, but was restored on the occasion of the visit of Her Majesty the Queen a few years ago.

Here the properties

Zarskoe Selo, Ekaterininsky Palace - west wing. Just one of the palaces Ransome visited in those hectic eight weeks.

occupied by the early settlers were quite large and enjoyed superb views over the river to the north. Those less opulent members of the group chose the Ulitsa Galernaya, a street behind and parallel with the English Embankment, while some merchants and sailors settled near the port on Vasilyevsky Island on the north side of the river.

Around the middle of the eighteenth century an outpost of the British community

'Penarts', the estate and country home of the Russian painter Repin situated on the train route to Terioki. Ransome visited both here and Pike Lake nearby for fishing.

was established in Kronstadt on Kotlin Island in the Gulf of Finland. The earliest entries in the register there are dated 1762.

The British Community in St. Petersburg developed very quickly, partly because of the favourable business climate, but partly because it was a genuinely attractive place in which to live and work. In the recollections of Elizabeth Justice, an early English governess in Russia who worked for a prominent person of the time, she wrote 'I'm sure in no part of the world English people can find a place better for living than St. Petersburg'. Three Years in Russia - London 1739

The most active period for the English Community began after Catherine the Great was enthroned in 1762. Large numbers of Britons went to Russia during her reign – English and Scottish of many professions – doctors, engineers, ship builders, military specialists, architects and painters etc. who began playing an important part in the development and life of the city. Many factories were owned or run by them. Contracts for the new Russian capital also came their way – many being distributed by the Imperial Court. Clark's factory made metal structures for the Winter Palace and many of the large buildings being erected in the city, while the dome of St Isaac's Cathedral was supplied by Bird's factory.

English specialist Thomas Telford was consulted over bridge construction across the Neva, while another area of influence was that of British gardeners. Many public gardens and those of a number of palaces were laid out by people such as Menelas, and William Gould, who was perhaps the most famous of them all. Then there was also Charles Cameron, who designed garden pavilions and a gallery in Tzarskoye Selo. He employed his own team of British craftsmen, constructors and painters – all 140 of them! Most of these artisans came from Scotland, complete with their families. An entire street, Anglkiskaya Street, was built in Tzarskoye Selo in order to accommodate them.

Pyramid water fountain in the gardens of Peterhof in St Petersburg, the Imperial family's summer residence.

The English propensity for trade also extended to the shops and department stores which lined the main streets. These became a symbol and the hallmark of quality and respectability. Intended for the sale of the latest products from leading British factories, they became very popular and their number gradually increased. One large store on the Nevsky Prospect became noted for its inviting interior, excellent service and the superb range of goods sold. For over a century, all the noble people of the city, including the Imperial family, were among its customers.

British trade became so developed that the English/Russian Chamber of Commerce had 900 members at the beginning of the 20th century. English merchants created the first club in the city in 1770. It was called 'The English Club' (Gellibrands were members) and allowed suitable Russians to join, although the membership had a ceiling of 400. This club became a meeting place for nobles and the famous, and counted amongst its members the poets Pushkin, Krylov and Nekrasov.

Another aspect over which there was some influence, was in the matter of education. English education became fashionable at the beginning of the 19th century and many famous Russians, including Vladimir Nabokov, were taught by English governesses. With such a large expatriate community (although it never went much above 2100 persons), it was not uncommon for English ladies to marry into Russian families. Quite a number did so, and a few married prominent citizens, all of which further enlarged the Anglo-Russian connection.

Charity was an important feature of the community's life. Assistance was organised for the homeless after the 1824 floods, and this continued up until 1917. English women worked with Russians in the hospitals, sewed clothes for wounded soldiers and helped organise relief where needed.

At the beginning of the twentieth century, the British community in St. Petersburg was one of the ten largest ethnic groups in the city. It had its own publications e.g. monthly journal of the English church, the *Nevsky Magazine* and the newspaper *Friendship*, amongst others. These publications charted the life and times of the St. Petersburg British community, their individual lives and fates, and shows the extent to which they had become involved in the daily life of the Russian capital. We can see that many of them had family relationships with Russians, and most of them gave considerably to all aspects of Russian culture. One of the last of the notable Britons who became connected with St. Petersburg and Russia, was Arthur Ransome.

St. Petersburg was a very fashionable city in those far off pre-First World War days, and on a par with the main cities of Europe in every respect. The magnificent buildings, museums, large shops, theatres, concert halls, prestigious hotels and wide boulevards symbolised a lifestyle of culture and elegance. For those who like to be outdoors, there were many beautiful parks and wide open spaces in which to take the air. Hotels on the main streets, particularly the Nevsky Prospect, had large coloured canopies extending out from their entrances across the pavements, with liveried doormen to escort ladies from their carriages and many large and important shops did likewise. Then, as now, the city prided itself on being foremost in culture, arts and entertainment. The world famous Mariinsky Theatre, with 800 artists and patronised by the Tzars, provided the finest in opera and ballet, and with dozens of other theatres and concert halls, the devotee of fine art and entertainment was spoilt for choice.

A Novgorod Monastery which Ransome visited. His planned guide to Novgorod never materialised.

Russian society had a certain social charm, which was the quintessence of much that a society should be and often is not. Ransome was still very much a Bohemian, and therefore, would have appreciated the complete absence of

Above, the visit of the Royal Navy under Admiral Beatty to St Petersburg in 1914. Below, Admiral Beatty during the visit, which Ransome mentions in his *Autobiography*.

snobbishness of any kind and the patriarchal attitude towards servants. In a Russian home, even large ones, a servant was a friend of the family and always treated as such. One facet of Russian life which Ransome may not have appreciated however, was the habit of running the night into day. In practice, the day started at eight or nine in the morning and carried on until the early hours of the next day. This social pattern would be difficult to adjust to if you valued your sleep, and was made all the more tiresome when the 'white nights' occurred and it didn't get dark enough to create the impression of being night.

St. Petersburg was the capital, of course, and at the prosperous end of the whole Russian economy. The upper and middle classes, although relatively small in number, were quite well placed. But for the bulk of the population, however, the situation was quite different. Grinding poverty and starvation were never very far away.

The uprising of 1905 was a landmark event presaging the momentous events to follow. In 1917, the Revolution, both spring and autumn – which was in effect a resurfacing of the 1905 event, shattered this prosperous and peaceful existence. Shootings, searches of property and famine followed. The large foreign community resident in the city very quickly broke down, and those who could do so, fled! They left behind their houses, savings and businesses, which in many cases had belonged to fathers or grandfathers, and where possible, returned to their countries of origin. Those returning to Britain were penniless refugees.

GETTING TO KNOW YOU

Michael Lykiardopoulos (Lyki), was one of Ransome's most important contacts. Being so well connected, Lyki was able to help Ransome enormously by introducing him to Harold Williams, the important and influential correspondent for the *Daily Chronicle*, who knew more about Russia than almost any other living foreign person at that time.

Williams had in 1914, published an authoritative book called *Russia of*

Winter Palace in St Petersburg

Appearance of Tzar Nicholas II on the balcony of the Winter Palace, St Petersburg on 2 August 1914.

the Russians (still a work of reference in the 1990s). He was a New Zealander by birth, but had worked in Russia as a journalist since late 1904, at first for the *Manchester Guardian,* then the *Morning Post,* before moving to the *Daily Chronicle.* A natural linguist, he had a doctorate in languages from Munich and spoke more than forty different languages and dialects. He had a remarkable insight into all things Russian to such an extent that he was sought and consulted by many for his opinions and thorough knowledge, including the British and other Western Embassies in St. Petersburg. He was one of Ambassador Buchannan's most important assets. In 1918, Williams left Russia and returned to England where he began a book on the Revolution. Unfortunately, it was never completed, and he died in 1928. His widow

Right, postcard concerning the Tzar's appearance on the balcony of the Winter Palace from an ordinary Russian citizen:
Lise Rubinsk to Her Highness Milukovskya Alexandra Alekseevna.
20/7/1914
My dear Shura, I've just received your letter and guess that you didn't yet get mine and do not know anything. We now see such days which Europe has never seen before! The total mobilisation, yesterday the war was announced and St. Petersburg now is proclaimed to be in a war state. Such horrid things are happening here, that my heart is going to break. Today there was a church service at the Winter Palace, and I was there in the square in front of the palace when the Tzars family came out on the balcony and the many thousands crossed as one man, knelt, and sang the anthem.....Lise

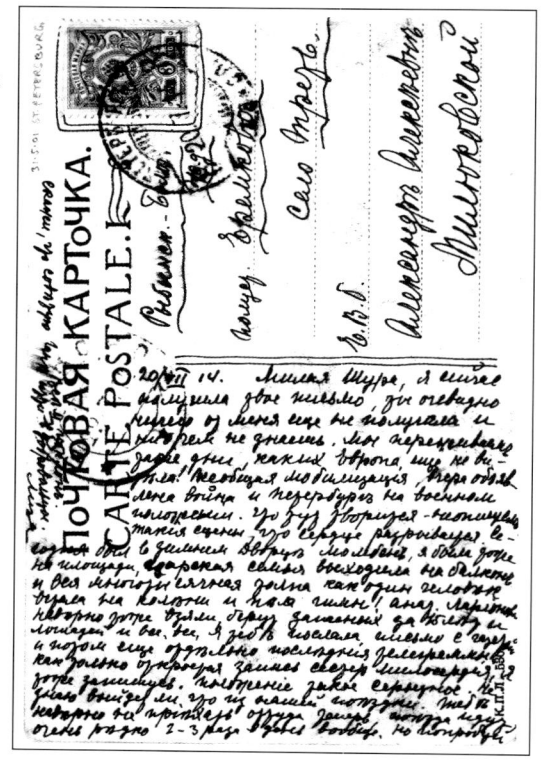

hoped that someone would continue the work and publish Harold's dispatches in a book, but it never materialised. A biography of Harold Williams was published by Ariadna in 1935 titled *Cheerful Giver*.

Arriving in Russia before 1905, Williams had fallen in love with, and married Ariadna Vladimirovna Tyrkova, a fan of Miliukov, the Leader of the Kadet party (Constitutional Democrats). As a member of the central committee, she was able to ensure that her husband was well informed on Russian politics. Williams was introduced to his future wife at the Stuttgart home of leading Russian political exile, Peter Struve. In her student years, Ariadna attended the the same class within the same school as Nadezhda Krupskaya, the girl who would one day become Lenin's wife. Later, Ariadna would spend part of the 1890s incarcerated in Litovski Prison, St. Petersburg for subversive political activities.

HIM Tzar and Tzarina of Russia

Williams was a tall, quiet man, unselfish and extraordinarily kind in every way. He proved the ideal mentor for Ransome, helping him enormously in the early years. Without Williams, it is difficult to see how Ransome would have made all the connections which ultimately made him such an informed person. Their relationship however, due to differences in political perception, did not survive the Revolution.

The Tyrkova family had a large country estate managed by her brother Arkady at Vergezha, a village to the south, south east of St. Petersburg. The Williams family normally lived in a flat on the Starorusskaya in St. Petersburg, but often week ended at the family country estate, to which their friends and acquaintances were sometimes invited. H.G. Wells had been a former guest and Ransome, in the fullness of time, would be a frequent visitor too. The principal value to Ransome however, apart from the helpful advice and the linguistic skills, were the people he in turn was able to introduce; people whom he might never have come across or taken too long to find for himself. Some of these more important persons, such as Sergei Oldenburg of the Academy of Sciences, Rodzianko (who later became President of the Duma) and Gutchkov (who eventually played an important part at the time of the Tzar's abdication) both Octoberist leaders who held power in the third Duma (the lower chamber of the Legislature). Then there was the writer Remizov (later exiled to Vologda along with Stalin and Lenin's sister), and many others. All these were to prove invaluable in providing help and information during the subsequent early upheavals.

Introductions were quite plentiful at this time. One source, which was to have a lasting beneficial effect, was to a group of artists and painters associated with theatre art in St. Petersburg. The painter Konstantine Somoff was a member of this group, and he was introduced to Ransome by Hugh Walpole. Ransome records that he 'drank tea many times with the painter Somoff.' According to Walpole, Somoff was one of the most successful painters in the country, but was a 'sad, charming, ugly man, with beautiful eyes'. Somoff in turn, introduced Ransome to Dimitri Mitrokhin, a brilliant up-and-coming artist who would illustrate *Old Peter's Russian Tales* in 1916. Walpole, on the introduction of Somoff, would also become a useful member of this group. As a result of all these introductions, Ransome started to become well-known and well-connected; all of which would be to his advantage and benefit in the years ahead.

D. Mitrokhin by O Vereisky 1925

The origin of this group of artists and painters is described by the Prima Ballerina Tamara Karsavina in her autobiography:

> I have already mentioned that our director, Teliakovsky, did much towards encouraging national art. Hitherto, the same official painters had done the scenery and costumes year in, year out. Teliakovsky now adopted a policy which required much courage, and meant going against the grain of traditional, self-contained organisation. Painters from outside the small official circle, such as Golovin and Karovin, were appointed to the theatre, and shortly Bakst was to make his debut as a stage painter. These artists, together with Alexandre Benois, Doboujinsky, Soudeikin, Ransevet, Somoff, formed the nucleus of a rebellion against the stale standards of art. By the untiring energy of Diaghileff they were united into a separate group, under the name of Mr. Izkoustva, the 'World of Art', which entirely severed itself from the academic group'.
>
> (*The Street* - 1929)

Benois lived in a large house at the south end of Glinka Street, and was considered the leader of this group. He became a theatre art director and co-founded the Diaghilev Ballet. He died in Paris in 1960. The Russian Museum in St. Petersburg (a huge gallery of Russian art housed in the Michael Palace) has a wing named after him, and his niece Nadia Benois, a contemporary painter and designer for the ballet, was mother of the actor Peter Ustinov. A plaque on the outside of the Glinka Street premises records the Benois family occupation from 1808 to 1958.

In 1908, Mitrokhin moved to St. Petersburg from South Russia, having attended art classes in both Moscow and Paris. He was subsequently invited by Konstantine Somoff and Alexandre Benois to participate in a joint exhibition; thus becoming a part of this group, to which other artists and painters would also become acquainted.

The publication of *Old Peter's Russian Tales* was very important for both English writer and Russian painter. For Ransome it was his first book of fairy tales, and for Mitrokhin, it was his first graphic work in the modern style. From the book *Mitrokhin*, he says, 'Old Peter meant for me the turn to the modern art'.

Ransome much admired Dimitry Mitrokhin's art, and never lost his high regard and respect for his style and quality of work. In letters to Dimitry Mitrokhin from Ulverston dated 1962 (over 46 years after the publication of *Old Peter's Russian Tales*), he says:

Dear Dimitry,
...I was very satisfied and got great pleasure looking at the book (catalogue of 1958 Russian Exhibition) about you and your drawings with a lot of reproductions including Old Peter. How I would like to visit Russia again but it is too late now. I am 78 years old... It might be so nice to have a magic carpet which could take me to the other end of Europe where I could be at a tea party with samovar with my friend who I haven't seen for over 40 years... Now it has passed more than 30 years since I was in Russia and I can still read very fluently in Russian, but I can't write in the language... I am sending you a new book with my drawings just for myself. These drawings were done 20 years ago and now I draw worser, much worser! I think that only rare paintings could keep their artistic impulse for so long and for so high a professional level. You possess all these gifts thanks to your ability to never feel satisfied of what you have done.

It is clear that Ransome had a soft spot for his old Russian friend, and in spite of the cold war they still managed occasionally to correspond. Mitrokhin managed to outlive Ransome, and died in Moscow aged over 90 during November 1973.

Dimitry Isidorovich Mitrokhin married Alice Bruschetti in 1910. She was of Italian lineage although, the family had been in Russia for more than 200 years. She was a sculptress and ceramist in her own right, but unfortunately, she died of hunger during the siege of Leningrad in the Second World War. He married his second wife Lydia Andreena Tchargra in 1948. She had a reputation for having a devilish character, which certainly showed itself during his last years when she made life difficult by stopping most of his friends from visiting him. Sometime around 1989, she emigrated to Holland and settled in the Amsterdam area, taking many of her husband's works with her. In spite of this, however, it is pleasing to note that a large number of folios of Mitrokhin's work remain in the Pushkin Museum in Moscow.

Mitrokhin is almost a legendary figure in the eyes of the modern generation of artists. He is indeed the only contemporary Russian graphic artist whose career started in the days of pre-revolutionary Russia. His career was pursued untiringly, systematically and with rare creative success. His rare gift of poetic contact with fairy-tales; his keen sense of what a book should be, and his individual ornamental style in book decoration allowed Mitrokhin to add a great deal to the achievements of Russian graphic art in the decade before the October Revolution, and to earn himself considerable prestige among the younger members of the 'world of art' group. Mitrokhin is a classic example of someone who would have enjoyed universal recognition in the west, but for Russia's post revolution isolation.

Russian troops during WW1

In 1916, Mitrokhin formally joined the 'World of Art' group and, following the October Revolution, became head of the 'section of prints and drawings' at the huge Russian Museum in St. Petersburg – a post he retained until he moved to Moscow in 1923. His work went on and in addition to *Old Peter*, Mitrokhin produced illustrations for many books, such as: *Sept Médailles* 1920; An edition of *Epicoene* by Ben Jonson 1920; *The Gold Bug* by Edgar Allan Poe 1922; *Les Misérables* by Victor Hugo 1923; and *Merry-go-Round* by Boris Pasternak 1925. In discussing his art one day, Mitrokhin said:

> I do most of my drawing with the lead pencil. Then I like to paint them in with watercolours. Such a method of work must have come out of my long experience

in the field of engraving. The pencil often strokes like an engraving tool, like a dry point. Sometimes I use crayons, but I'm not a painter; the colour in my work plays a secondary role... When I'm asked which of my works I value most of all, I always answer – those that I'll do tomorrow. Because your whole life's work is in preparation for what you'll do tomorrow. When I look at my sketches, those that I like best seem to be the work of somebody else; on the other hand , I perceive the insufficiencies to be my own.

(*Mitrokhin* - Aurora Art Publishers, Leningrad 1977)

Anyone fortunate enough to view the folios of original work in the archive department of the Pushkin Museum, can only conclude that this is an extremely modest self-assessment of his abilities. Mitrokhin's work is of high quality, with a leaning towards traditional art, and would be recognised as such in any period. Good fortune must have been in the stars for Ransome to meet such an artist, and just when he needed him!

August was fast approaching and the storm clouds of war were beginning to appear on the horizon. During his few remaining days in St. Petersburg, Ransome was seeing Williams almost every day, and together they witnessed the appearance of the Tzar Nicholas II on the balcony of the Winter Palace. He had been hidden from view and separated from the populace for many years. On this day also, Nicholas publicly took the same oath that Alexander I had taken at the time of Napoleon's invasion: he swore not to make peace until the last foreign soldier has been expelled from Russian soil. On 2 August Russia declared war on Germany (Britain did not declare until the 4th.) In a letter to his 'aunt' (Mrs Collingwood) dated 12th Ransome reports the growing preparations for war:

> All my hairy Russian friends have shaved their heads and gone into uniform, and wept, and kissed me on both cheeks and gone off to fight Germans and Austrians, and I am simply longing to be with them... The tennis court where I was playing a month ago here is a cavalry camp. The streets are full of soldiers. And, well, I always admired the Russians, but never so much as now. You know how our soldiers go off in

The Tzar visits Russian troops

pomp with flags and music. I have not heard a note of music since the declaration of war. They go off here quite silent in the middle of the night, carrying their little tin kettles, and for all the world like puzzled children going to school for the first time.

This left Ransome feeling that, having wasted enough time already he ought to return home to explore his options. He left on 18 August, got to Hull on the 24th, and reached Hatch on the 27th.

The first objective on arriving home was to try and secure some work. He commenced with a trip around various newspaper offices offering himself for journalistic work in Russia, but not being in the best of health and looking poorly, he did not inspire a lot of confidence, and most newspapers already had their correspondents in place. Such visits were interspersed with writing, fishing and various trips to see his mother in Leeds and the Collingwoods at Lanehead, before ending up again at Hatch to see Ivy and his daughter. In the November, Ransome made a start on *Old Peter's Russian Tales* from some of his previous translations, while in December, *Aladdin and his Wonderful Lamp* was completed and passed to Nisbit & Co publishers. Due to the constraints of war, it did not become available until 1919.

The quest for work was not successful. Francis Ackland, Under Secretary for Foreign Affairs and a friend of the family, suggested that he forget any thoughts about enlisting in the Services, particularly as his poor eyesight would be a handicap, and to concentrate on how best to use his writing skills and knowledge of Russian.

Chapter III

Where East Meets West

With a few vague commissions, and taking the advice of the Foreign Office, Ransome left England for the third time in late December 1914 to return to Russia. Due to the German control of all the Western Baltic, he was obliged to go by train up the Swedish coast to the top of the Gulf of Bothnia, then sledge down a frozen river between the two railway systems, and finally by train down the length of Finland before arriving in Petrograd on 30th (St. Petersburg having changed its name). Visiting friends and fellow journalists, and sizing up his new position took up the first two weeks. Meetings with Harold Williams were frequent, the two men having become staunch friends. Williams mentioned at some point that he hoped his family would be able extend an invitation for Ransome to visit the Vergezha family estate situated in the country.

Moscow Kremlin walls. Ransome fished here.

Meanwhile, a period of two and a half months was spent in Moscow (not the capital city then) on the recommendation of Williams, to gain experience and learn more about Russia from the city that 'faces both east and west'. Ransome's first task on arrival was to visit the Kremlin to see the Great Tzar Bell – the world's biggest bell (a 202 ton cracked monster that never rang). He had learnt about it as a child, promising himself that one day he would visit it. Initially, Ransome put up at the Siberian Hotel, but found it a most unpleasant place when he was attacked by armies of bugs during the night. A complaint was made to the chambermaid who summoned a bug-doctor, complete with a little bag containing magic powders and syringes to deal with the bugs waiting in ambush in the corners, cracks, beds and walls.

Moscow, Kremlin. The Great Bell is mounted on a plinth at the foot of Ivan Veliki Tower. Cast in 1730, it weighs 200 tons - the largest bell in the world. It stands 19 feet high and measures 60 ft around the rim.

The bugs won in the end, so he did not stay there long.

Moscow was a big sprawling city, even in those days, and so it was necessary to find some accommodation away from the city centre that was economical. A room was rented in the home of a widow and her family at 66 Donskaya, to the south of the city. It was close to the Donshoi

The Great Canon was cast in 1586 for Fydor I.

Monastery and necessitated a modest journey to get into town. Some of the Donskaya up to about number 30 survives, but that section where Ransome stayed has either been removed, or renumbered, making it impossible to identify. The widow Viktorov had a number of children to bring up, and fortunately for Ransome, none of the family knew any English, which forced him into areas of the Russian language which he normally would not use. He rented a one room bed-sit and was happy there, especially when in the company of the children.

Lyki had a fashionable flat in a large imposing building in the centre of Moscow, just a short walk from his Arts Theatre. Ransome was a frequent visitor, to both the flat and the Arts Theatre, where he said he was often favoured with tickets to performances which he might not otherwise have seen. Some of these delights appear to have been: three plays of Turgenev, Chekkov's *The Cherry Orchard*, Alexi Tolstoy's *Tzar Fedor*, and Maeterlinck's *The Blue Bird*.

His old friend the novelist Hugh Walpole was also in Russia, having come out the previous September on behalf of the Red Cross to learn something of the country and its language. Unfortunately, he was never able to achieve the Russian linguistic skills of either Ransome or Peters. Early in January 1915, Walpole, now working for the Russian Red Cross, decided on a quick trip to Moscow. He and Ransome had been acquainted from the Owen Mansion days of 1908, and agreed to meet. Amongst their various discussions, they talked about the construction, method and technicalities of writing books – skills which came naturally to Walpole. Ransome was impressed and anxious to learn, but Walpole unfortunately, did not stay long. He disliked the city and after only a short visit, returned and settled in Petrograd, which he much preferred. Six weeks later, Ransome followed, having stayed in Moscow longer than he had originally intended. Back in Petrograd, he was anxious to confer with Walpole as evidenced by diary entries:

March   26 Arrived Petrograd 10 - No letters @ GPO
Saw Walpole. Gellibrands
27 Telegraphed Whishaw - Saw Walpole in the evening.
28 Edward Gellibrand
Walpole about *Elixir*

He was very interested in securing Walpole's writing expertise for an opinion on *The Elixir of Life*, the book Ransome had almost completed while in Moscow. Ransome had mixed feelings about it and didn't want to spend more time on it if it was unlikely to find a publisher. Walpole, who was not feeling well at the time, laughed and indicated that he should complete any revision and send the book off straight away! To return the favour, Ransome introduced Walpole to Harold Williams.

The first three days were spent staying with the Gellibrands, before leaving to visit Norman Whishaw in Tartu to complete the revision of *The Elixir*. With three weeks peace and quiet, the book was finished and he returned to Petrograd to get it typed up. The book was a historical novel for adults set in 1735. The cover of the book describes it thus:

> This is a story of mystery, magic and love. The central figure is one who, having discovered the *Elixir of Life*, has mastered death, and unless he loses his precious phial cannot die. The sinister character of this strange man finds its contrast in the sweetness and beauty of his so-called sister, the heroine of the romance.

It was published by Methuen & Co. London in 1915. With *The Elixir of Life* posted to London, he devoted all the available spare time into a book on Russian folk tales – for which he already had a contract. It also justified one of the original reasons for going to Russia. The book was given the title of *Old Peter's Russian Tales* and the writing of them gave Ransome immense pleasure. Initially, the idea had been to gather fairy tales and translate them straight into English for children to read. He was later to find that direct translation was not the way to convey Russian stories to English children. The difficulty lay in the difference in cultures. When a Russian is telling a tale to other Russians, there is an assumption, which is inherent in

The Moscow building where Michael Lyiardopoulos had his flat. Now offices.

Grandfather tells Russian fairy tales to his grandchildren.
The plate, by M Schegov from the National Library of Russia, is taken from the *Tales in the North of Russia* (Moscow 1914) and was the inspiration for the style which Ransome chose for *Old Peter's Russian Tales*.

their culture, of some implied background knowledge on the part of the listener, irrespective of age. This does not apply to English children. Ransome realised that in order to achieve his aim, the right way was to learn the tale off by heart, and then to re-write it as a complete story without cluttering it up with endless detailed explanation.

It follows, that there were, and still are, a large number of books available on Russian folk tales. Ransome read a huge number of them from a great many sources before deciding on which stories he would use as the basis for ideas. Some of the books he chose included: *Tales from the Caucasus* – Moscow 1905, *Russian Tales* – Moscow 1910, *The Tales of Russian People* – Moscow 1910, and *Russian Tales* (five volumes), Moscow 1914.

All the stories in *Old Peter's Russian Tales* follow a similar pattern, with old Peter telling his orphaned grandchildren Vanya and Maroosia a tale. The inspiration for this idea came from a picture (by M. Scheglov) in *Tales in the North of Russia* – part of the five volume series published in Moscow in 1914. Ransome worked assiduously and accumulated a vast amount of material on Russian tales, such that he could have produced a much larger book or further volumes at some other time, but very little of the remaining material from his research for *Old Peter* was ever used. In a letter to his mother from his Glinka Street flat in July 1916, Ransome quotes:

Oh, once I loved the sewing maids.
And once I loved the cooks,
But now I'll not love anyone
However sweet she looks.

...And this too, was a translation from a Russian folk tale!

The completed book contained over 300 pages, and consisted of an introduction, twenty-one tales, seven coloured illustrations, twenty black and white illustrations, and nine black and white tailpieces. The book was dedicated to Barbara Collingwood – his first love! As a result of severe postal difficulties, the final proofs and all the Mitrokhin illustrations were shipped home courtesy of Ambassador Buchannan in the British Embassy's diplomatic bag. Publication was by T.C. & E.C. Jack of Edinburgh (later, to be absorbed by Nelson).

Sales of the book were slow at first, but gradually they picked up, and in spite of the publisher's negative expectation, the book went on to be a best seller. The various editions, both at home and abroad have sold thousands, and it was still in print up to the middle 1990s. The note in the front of *Old Peter's Russian Tales* is very revealing.

> The stories in this book are those that Russian peasants tell their children and each other. In Russia hardly anybody is too old for fairy stories, and I have even heard soldiers on their way to war talking of very wise and beautiful princesses as they drank their tea by the side of the road. I think there must be more fairy stories told in Russia than anywhere else in the world. ...My book is not for the learned, or indeed for grown-up people at all. No people who like fairy stories ever grow up altogether. This is a book written far away in Russia, for English children who play in deep lanes with wild roses above them in the high hedges... Russian fairyland is quite different. Under my windows the wavelets of the Volkhov (which has its part to play in one of the stories) are

Left, title page from the *Caucasus* 1905. Right, title page from *Russian Tales* (five volumes) Moscow 1905. Both were major inspirational works for Ransome

beating quietly in the dusk. A gold light burns on a timber raft floating down the river. Beyond the river in the blue midsummer twilight are the broad Russian plain and the distant forest. Somewhere in that forest of great trees – a forest so big that the forests of England are little woods beside it – is a hut where old Peter sits at night and tells these stories to his grandchildren.

A truly delightful account! Was Ransome really revealing his inner self within this passage.

Amongst the trials and tribulations of occasionally falling ill, trying to work, and money worries (which he always had), was concern for his small daughter, Tabitha. She was always in his thoughts and he would worry constantly about how she was getting on, what she might be doing and whether Ivy was doing enough for her. This worry was only slightly relieved by writing letters which often carried delightful sketches or drawings in the margin to illustrate his thoughts. Where possible, it was to show what he was doing, especially if it was something simple which she could understand. Then sometimes the letters would carry rhymes or a piece of poetry. Around this time he wrote an entertaining item for her, mentioning the war, which was way beyond her years to understand, but interesting all the same. In the end, he never sent it to Tabitha, but instead later sent it to his mother for her amusement.

> If Europe would stop being a kettle...
> If only she'd go off the boil...
> If only the hubbub would settle,
> So that fairy tale tellers could toil
>
> Your Dordor would tell you a story,
> The charmingest ever was told,
> About witches, and pirates all gory,
> A-counting their gollops of gold,
>
> A-wiping their knives on their breeches,
> And singing fierce songs of the sea,
> And dancing quadrilles with the witches,
> Swilling rum while the witches drink tea.
>
> For the witchiest witches should be there,
> Brewing potions of snakes' heads and eels...
> The things that a Babba should see there
> Would make other babes burst into squeals.

And then there'd be Princes and kittens
Eating cakes and mouse fritters for tea,
And Princesses crocheting mittens
For elderly people like me.

There'd be Vikings a drinking from flagons,
And dwarfs of the recognised type.
There'd be flame-spitting fire-breathing dragons,
Convenient for lighting a pipe.

Oh if Europe would stop boiling over,
If the sediment only would sink,
Why Babba and I'd be in clover...
Tell me, Tabitha, what do you think..?

Shall we tell them to pause in their riot?
Shall we whisper a word to Berlin?
"If you people will only be quiet,
We've a story we want to begin"

Although Ivy and Tabitha never saw this piece, one wonders what Ivy would have made of it as a poem for a six year old?

Ransome the Correspondent

To succour his spirit, Ransome saw to it that some fishing was never very far away, so it was with great pleasure that a new location was discovered just a short train distance out of the city towards the Finnish border. Lachta, with a large lake and short river leading to the gulf, became one of his favourite spots for pike fishing. It was so close to the city, that it was possible to steal the odd afternoon or evening's fishing without neglecting his obligations or appearing to disappear for days at a time.

To make his writing as conducive as possible, the Williams family fulfilled their promise and invited Ransome to the Tyrkov family estate at Vergezha. This necessitated a journey of approximately 140 kilometres, mostly by train, but with the last few miles from the nearest railway station being covered by river steamer. Their large wooden house was situated on a bluff overlooking the Volkov River, and from the balcony, Ransome had uninterrupted views over the surrounding countryside and to the woods in the distance, where Sadko lived (a character in a Russian fairy tale of the same name). Ransome's

The Tyrkov Estate on the banks of the Volkov River at Vergezha c1910.

room was just off the second floor balcony, where he could either sit and write or retire to his room in peace. Evenings were often spent at leisure sitting on the cliff edge with older members of the family, either playing games and smoking his favourite tobacco (to keep the mosquitoes at bay). And if work had gone well he would treat himself to some fishing in the river for pike, bream or perch.

Ransome was to spend a lot of this summer at Vergezha. He truly loved the place, and in the *Autobiography* enthuses about the peace and quiet, the silent forests and the singing of nightingales, all of which contributed to a happy life-long memory of his many visits here. Sadly, this large wooden house caught fire and burnt down many years ago. There were no traces of its' existence in 1996, other than the small separate bathhouse which was situated by the cliff edge away from the main house.

The Bath House is the only surviving part of the Tyrkov Estate.

Possible site for the Tyrkov residence which was burned down in the twenties.

The village is much the same today as it was in Ransome's time, untouched, very rural and in the heart of the Russian countryside. The model for the images of Ransome's *Old Peter's Russian Tales* was Vergezha, as it was for Harold Williams when working on *Russia of the Russians* (Pitman 1914). Accessible by vehicle in summer, but not so in winter, when everywhere becomes covered in snow and frozen up, Vergezha, along with Terioki, were the two places that he loved most; places where he could relax and do what he wanted away from city pressures. Also, for much of this summer, and to dampen his spirits, Ransome was absorbed in trying to live with the increasing pain and agony caused by piles and stomach ulcers. By July of that year, the pain had become unbearable.

Tyrkov Estate. Steps down to the beach used by Ransome.

Doctors Sokolov and Stucke were consulted in Petrograd, both of whom advised an operation. He wrote to his mother immediately to tell her of the situation, and begged her not to tell Ivy for fear that she might decide to use it as an excuse to come and visit him. Ransome entered the hospital overlooking the Fontanka River on 4 August and had his operation on the 9th. It was all a very disagreeable experience; the anaesthetics did not work, he suffered great pain and was deprived of sleep for four days. It is quite amazing what he went through, even fainting when he tried to stand up nine days later. Many friends visited him to help pass this awkward time, but eventually his situation was made much more agreeable by the appointment of two very pleasant English-speaking nurses from the Baltic provinces. The

From this beach Ransome fished and boarded river steamers.

Fontanka Hospital where Ransome had his operation.

hospital building is still there, but it is now used as a sanatorium.

Doctors Sokolov and Stucke are the only ones whose names appear in the *Autobiography*. Initially, there was some difficulty in trying to identify who they were, but eventually, some information was located about one of them. The surgeon who operated on Ransome was the famous Petrograd surgeon L.S. Stucke. The family of Stucke in Russia began with George Thomas Stucke (1791 - 1852), a Scotsman and military officer who married Catherine Pockim (1798 - 1884). They went to Russia at the beginning of the 19th century on military service and stayed. A productive family, they contributed much to Russia through their children and grandchildren, who were architects, doctors, art historians and musicians etc. The descendants of G. T. Stucke still live in St. Petersburg today, and kindly provided the photographs and history of the family. Stucke's surgical skills eventually allowed Ransome to make a full recovery.

Ransome finally left hospital on 25th, going straight into the care of the Williams family at their city flat in Starorusskaya. He described himself as 'fit for nowt'. It was while resting in the flat recuperating after the operation, that Williams came and told him that the *Daily News* correspondent was seriously ill. With Williams too tired to do so himself, Ransome started writing telegrams to the *Daily News* on behalf of their now incapacitated correspondent. These compositions were very informative, reflected a sound background of knowledge and were welcomed by the paper. The editor responded by asking if Ransome

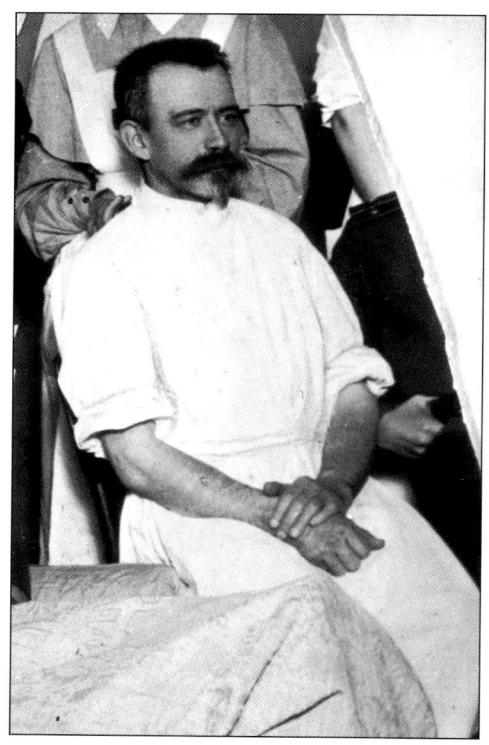

Dr Stuke being prepared to perform an operation 1915/16.

Dr Stuke

would continue sending them telegrams – which he happily did. It was in this rather haphazard way, that Ransome began his career as a journalist.

To what extent the *Daily News* used these early contributions is hard to tell. From the 26 August, which is the first possible date, until the 18 September when Ransome left for England all the articles published were still under the title 'From our Special Correspondent – Frederick Rennet'. To our regret, it has not been possible to establish with any degree of reliability, which were the first articles from Ransome, or when they were published. One is left to conclude that the early contributions were used as supporting evidence for information received from elsewhere. All newspapers of the time were using Reuters, News Exchange and 'free-lance' sources in addition to their own reporters.

Some weeks later, feeling that he was due for a return to England where he could complete his convalescence he sought permission from the *Daily News*, but unfortunately the reply to this request was a telegram ordering him to stay. The Williams family in order to help him over the disappointment, and with some convalescence in mind, took him down to Vergezha for a week, there to sit quietly fishing, while being rowed up and down the river.

In response to orders from his surgeon, Ransome insisted that the *Daily News* grant him a months leave to aid recuperation. He also saw this as an opportunity to try to sort out affairs in England. During most of 1915 and up to his departure for England, Ransome was without a permanent address and was obliged to use the Post Restante for his mail.

Willam's flat at 16 Starorusskaya. Ransome was a frequent visitor here, including convalescence after his operation.

During the month in England, he visited the London offices of the *Daily News*, and received confirmation of his appointment as the official *Daily News* correspondent for Russia. It had become clear that the original correspondent was not going to recover, and this left the *Daily News* free to confirm that

Семейная группа в Лондоне.
Передний ряд: внучка Наташа Борман, мать С. К. Тырковa, А. В. Тыркова-Вильямс, внучка Дина Бочарская, дочь С. Бочарская. Задний ряд: невестка Т.В. Борман, сын А. А. Борман, муж Г. В. Вильямс. Двадцатые годы.

The Tyrkov family. Williams is back right and Ariadna is seated.

Ransome could now have the job. He accepted the post on condition that he be allowed back to England to visit once a year. In addition it was agreed that he could use his discretion as to whether he would stay in Petrograd or go to where any action might be. He also received confirmation that sales of his newly published book *Elixir* were already up to a pleasing 500.

There were visits to Hatch to see Ivy and Tabitha, his mother in Leeds, and the Collingwoods in the Lakes, including fishing whenever it was possible. Hardly any convalescence took place and, still in poor health, he returned to Russia for the fourth time in early November. On arrival in Petrograd, however, Ransome found that he was in an awkward position due to the activities of the secretary of the former correspondent. She telephoned to advise that the man was now much better and was going to resume his post of correspondent. Harold Williams of the *News Chronicle* with whom Ransome was staying, advised that this could not possibly be the case. The embarrassment was only sorted out after Ransome had telegraphed the news editor of the *Daily News* to seek a clarification of his situation. By 13 November, confirmation was received of his position and the telegraph office was instructed to accept his telegrams.

А. В. Тыркова перед войной 1914 г. в России

Ariadna Tyrkova-Williams

Information surfaced later that the secretary had wanted to take over the former correspondent's job herself. It is also interesting to note, that during the six weeks Ransome was away from Petrograd, all the *Daily News* reports from their special correspondent in Russia were still published under the name of their former correspondent – undoubtedly all prepared by the secretary.

His welcome back by the many other correspondents was genuine. They did not treat him as if he was a new boy or an intruder into their circle because he already knew most of them. There was Morgan Philips-Price of the *Manchester Guardian*, Robert Wilton of *The Times*, E.H. Wilcox of the *Daily Telegraph* and Guy Berenger of Reuters amongst others, and they in turn introduced him to many of the skills needed to survive in the job. In some respects, it was almost a case of taking up where he had left off.

During most of 1915 his existence had been somewhat precarious, but with a guaranteed source of income, he was now able to afford accommodation at the Hotel Continental, Basseinaya 28 (in 1918 renamed Ulitsa Nekrasova, the name it bears today). His room was on one of the upper floors and overlooked the adjacent rooftops to the spires of a nearby church (which was destroyed in the 1920s). This hotel was an establishment which hired out rooms for 'long lets' rather than a hotel in the conventional sense, and was nicely placed half way between the centre of Petrograd and the Government offices near the Smolny.

Hotel Continental, 28 Basseinya, Petrograd. Ransome's lodgings from late 1915 until February 1916. Willam Peters who worked for the Russian Ministry of Trade and Industry also lived here.

The hotel was also convenient for visits to Harold Williams, the most important member of this community, who lived just one mile away. Also residing at the hotel was William Peters, an English official who was working for the Russian Ministry of Trade and Industry. Ransome and Peters became good friends, often dining together, and when work permitted, playing the odd game of billiards in the hotel D'Angleterre off St. Isaac's Square. After Harold Williams, Peters was the best linguist amongst the expatriate group at the time. Although not a reporter or into politics, Peters' considerable knowledge of Russian economics was very helpful in giving Ransome an additional perspective to his reporting. Meeting almost daily, they would discuss the current state of affairs, with Peters' putting his economist's point of view to balance the political implications. His prediction of the time when

Sestri River are early 1900s - a favourite Ransome fishing place near the Finnish border.

disturbances might possibly occur for example, was remarkably accurate, as was his forthright assessment of the Russian capabilities. This indirect input was just another source which contributed to Ransome having that 'edge' over his contemporaries. It was Peters' thorough knowledge which seems generally to have been overlooked and underestimated within the overall assessment of the contribution of those who were observers at the time.

Ransome became heavily involved in monitoring the events of the war and the developing political situation in Russia. It was as if he was engaged in one continual round of chasing about the city; visiting officials, attending press briefings and preparing submissions for the censor. He was telegraphing the *Daily News* several times each week with reports, and when possible, trying to finalise work on a batch of old Russian folktales.

THE ANGLO-RUSSIAN BUREAU

The war was not going too well for the Russians at this time, with the result that life was made difficult by the authorities whenever correspondents wanted to visit and make reports from the battle fronts. Obstructions were put in their way and excuses offered to try and prevent anybody from seeing too much. Reporters at the battle fronts were the last thing the authorities wanted. The Russians had for some time been dropping hints that they thought that the English and French were not doing enough on the Western Front to help lessen the pressure in the east.

The Foreign Office got wind of these hints in the autumn of 1915 and set out to try and do

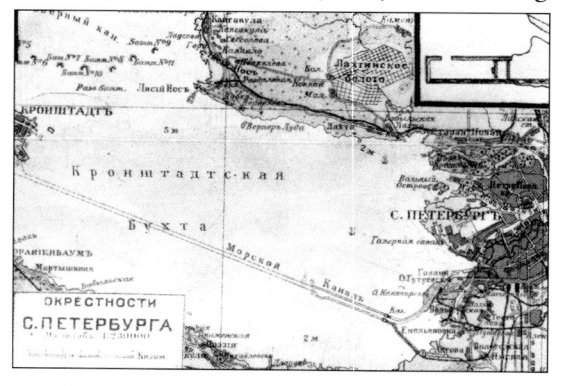

Early C20th St Petersburg map showing Lachta and sea approaches to St Petersburg.

Edward Baker Boulton painting, 'Cattle crossing a Valley'. Certainly one of his finest watercolours and thought to have been given to Edith as a wedding present.

Nicholaeskaya 9, 12, kv23. After Ekateningofsky, the final four weeks were spent here completing the *Guide to St Petersburg*. The building was situated in a side road off the Nevsky Prospect near the Hermitage Hotel. Entrance was through the double brown doors and his flat was the second window above.

Yusupov Palace, Sadovaya Ulitsa, St Petersburg.
The Yusupov's were one of Russia's richest families with palaces of their own.

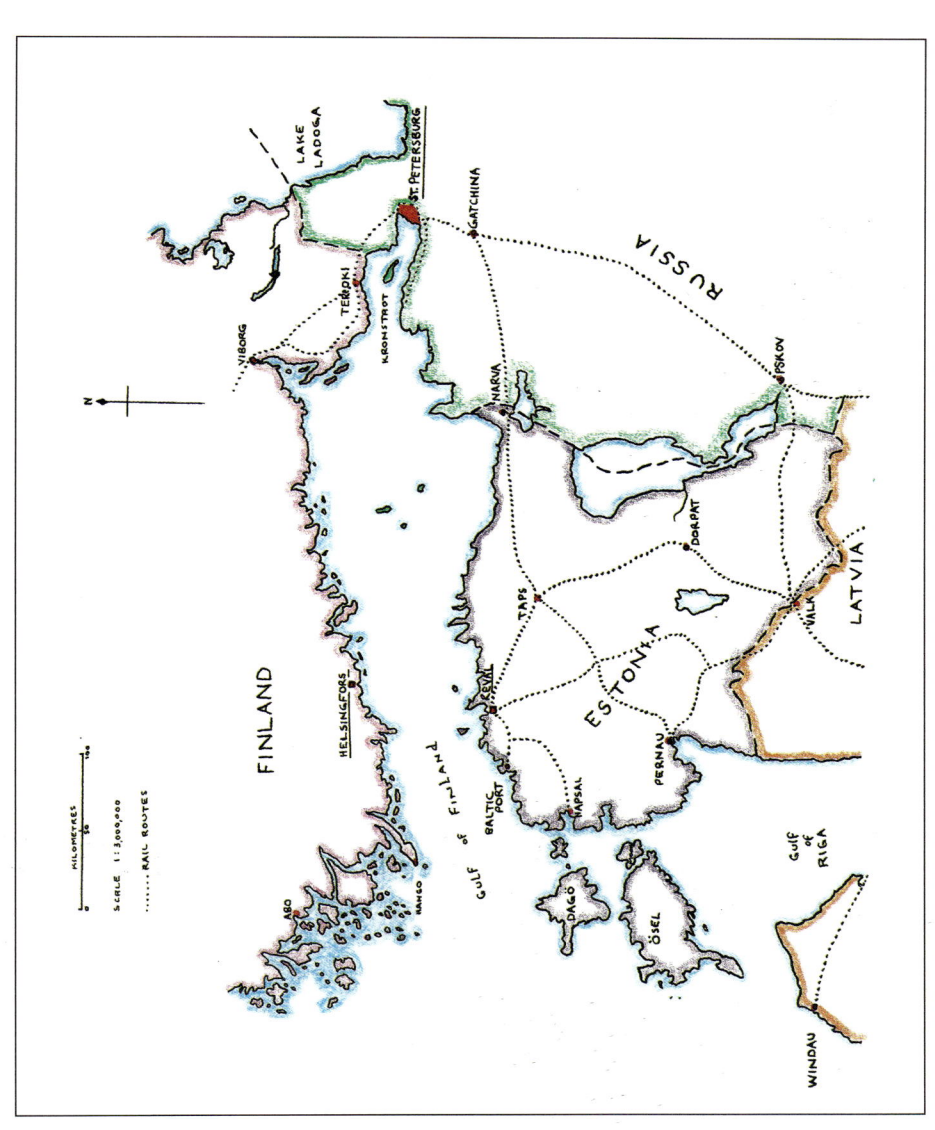

Map of the Baltic States and West Russia showing areas of Ransome's first visit in 1913.

Pushkin Theatre. One of Russia's most important cultural venues.

Part of the 'English Embankment'. Most of the houses shown (and some were palatial) were occupied by British families up to the 1917 revolution.

Russian cartoon dipicting response to the war in 1914.

Ransome's new Glinka Ulitsa flat and Mariinsky Theatre.
His room was on the top floor, 4th or 5th window to the left of the corner.

Tauride Palace in 2000. Home to the Commonwealth of Independent States.

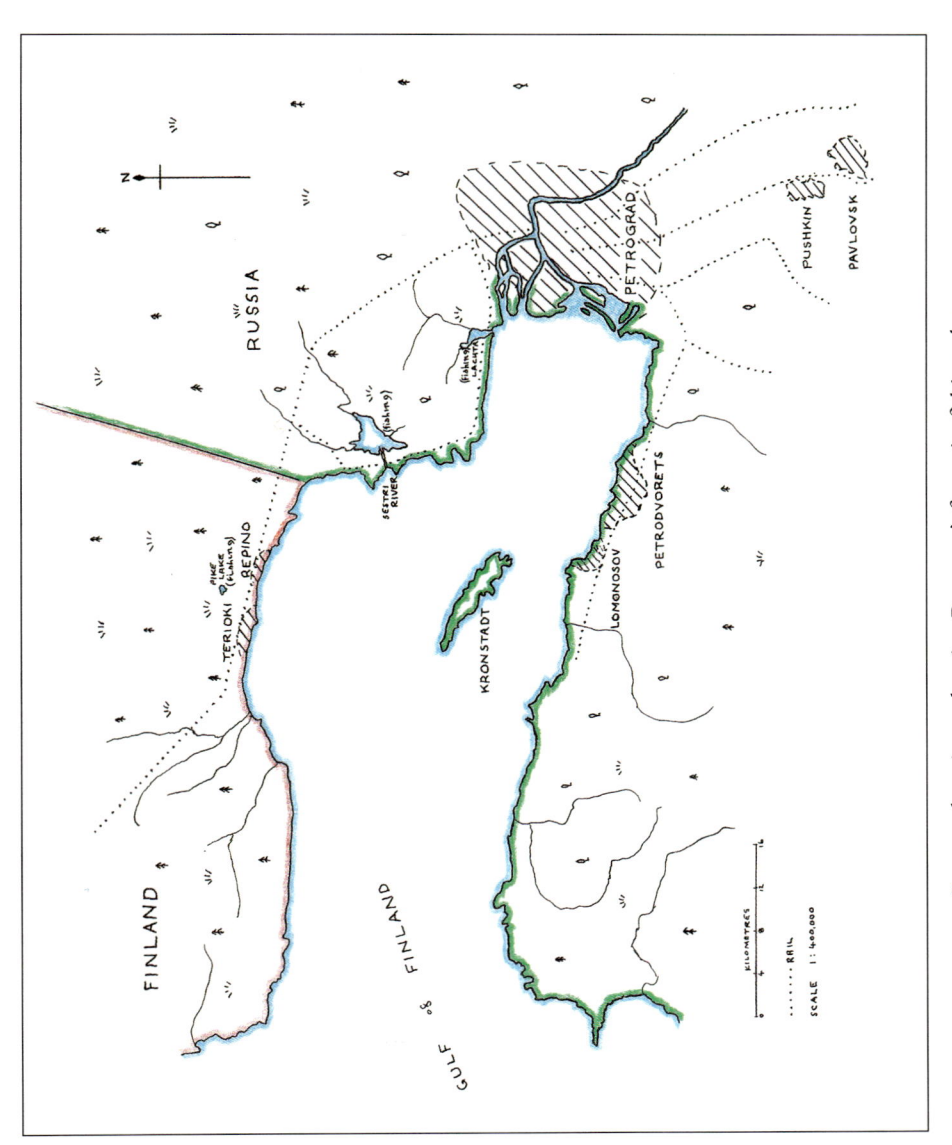

Petrograd environs showing Ransome's favourite fishing places.

Smolny Institute c1900. Built by Quarenghi 1806-08 as a school for girls of the aristocracy. Occupied by politicians in July 1917. Had fame thrust upon it when Lenin and Trotsky directed the October Revolution from the headquarters of the Bolshevik Central Committee and the Petrograd Soviet which had been established there.

Smolny - Hall of Acts middle floor, south wing.

something about it. A number of schemes were considered, but the most practical solutions consisted of:

a) sending a suitably trained army officer to give talks and show some specially prepared films of action in the west at a selection of venues in Russia.

b) printing 10,000 post cards of British soldiers for distribution

c) inviting the top members of the Russian Government to Britain for a conducted tour of certain sites – Portsmouth naval base and Aldershot being two of them.

Donon's Restaurant, 24 Moika Embankment, Petrograd. A favourite with correspondents and diplomats.

All these schemes materialised, but they still didn't fully address the problem of what the ordinary Russian soldier at the front was thinking! Neither Ransome or Bernard Pares, (a professor of Russian and now correspondent of the *Daily Telegraph* in Russia) agreed with the first proposal for a series of lectures with films. It was too selective, too remote and wouldn't reach anything like the number of people who needed to be informed. Apart from which, the officer and upper classes would be too difficult to convince, unless the lecturer chosen fully understood the nature of Russia and was fluent in Russian! A list was drawn up of suitable candidates more-or-less fluent in Russian who could carry off this task. There were only five names on it, one of which was Ransome's. It is with this unique situation in mind, that Ransome came up with his original idea to help alleviate the difficulty.

His idea was that a simple unofficial news agency might do some good by disseminating information to

The building used as the British Embassy in Petrograd before the Revolution. Completed in 1788 by Quarenghi for an ancient family of nobles. In the 1820s it was leased to the Austrian Ambassador before being taken over by the British a few years later.

Russian newspapers about what the West was doing. This would be achieved by the Foreign Office sending out selected newspaper articles which it considered suitable to be translated into Russian by Harold Williams before being distributed to Russian news agencies.

British Embassy staff c1912. Ambassador Buchannan seated centre. Head of Chancery, B Bruce, 2nd from right standing.

With the object of sounding out his views, Ransome made a quick visit to Moscow in January 1916 to visit the Consul-General, Bruce Lockhart. He stayed for a week at 66 Donskaya – the same lodgings as on his previous visit . There were several meetings with the Consul-General, who was in general terms fully in agreement with the proposal. He had been one of those warning for some time at the unease felt in some Russian quarters about what was perceived as inadequate support from Britain. Ransome suggested Lyki as a suitable person to run it – able, home-grown, fluent in Russian and English, and well connected. Williams gave his blessing, before the idea was put before the British Ambassador Sir George Buchannan.

British Embassy staff at work. Ambassador Buchannan seated centre 2nd from left.

Where East Meets West

Sergei Oldenburg the famous historian and ethnographer of the Academy of Sciences.

Alexander Nicholaievitch Benois, the famous Russian painter and stage designer.

Ransome's Friends.
By the end of 1915, Ransome had acquired a number of very influential friends within artistic and academic circles.

Above, Somoff's house at 97 Ekateningofsky, St Petersburg where Walpole stayed. Left, Konstantine Somoff. The famous Russian painter and stage designer. He was a friend to Walpole and one of Ransome's circle of influential contacts.

London had to be consulted for permission and the necessary finance to run the bureau. It was to be called the 'International News Agency' and would operate in Moscow. The main work would be in translating articles from the English press for dissemination. A rough breakdown of costs was submitted, which allowed for one small room, a typist and a messenger, as follows:

Lyki	400R
Typist	150R
Messenger	25R
Rent	90R
Telephone	10R
Incidentals	500R
	1175 Roubles (FO3712824)

With permission and finance granted, the operation came into being, but was renamed by London the Anglo-Russian Bureau. Its main office would be in Petrograd (capital), with only a sub-office at the Consulate in Moscow under Lockhart. The Foreign Office, however, favoured Walpole to manage it (he was recalled for the job), because of his important position as head of the Red Cross Mission and Major Thornhill (An Officer in the Indian Army and assistant Military Attaché, later promoted to Colonel), to be assisted by Harold Williams. At one stage it looked as if there might be difficulties over the choice of Major Thornhill because there was a general agreement between the War Office and the Foreign Office that all Missions would come under the control of General Sir John Hanbury-Williams, Chief of the British Military Mission in Russia. However, a flurry of correspondence between Sir George and the Foreign Office led to the Military Attaché and Thornhill's Mission remaining under the control of the Embassy, to great relief in Petrograd. It is interesting to observe that Sir George Buchannan was a clever and astute Ambassador, and in order to get what he wanted often phrased his requirements and proposals in such a way that the Foreign Office were happy to concur.

Anglo-Russian Bureau. First office in the English Library in the Morskaya, Petrograd c1900.

The Bureau's first office was a room in a large building, thought to have been above the English Bookshop at 38 Morskaya (a fashionable street in those times off the west end of the Nevsky Prospect), but it is an address which has proved impossible to confirm. Because of an unexpected quick build-up of activity, this room soon gave way to a more impressive arrangement on an upper floor of a very large building overlooking the Neva River. With an address of Flat 3, number 6 Admiralty Embankment, the Bureau consolidated itself and became well established. Initially there were very few staff, but with an increasing workload it soon rose to over a dozen. Ransome's original idea was that the operation should remain modest, discreet and as much as possible, 'under cover'. These new offices changed all that to such an extent, that it became more commonly known as the 'British Propaganda Office!' Part of the original concept, therefore, became neutralised.

Anglo-Russian Bureau. Second office at 6 Admiralty Embankment, Petrograd.

In due course, even these offices would not be large enough to cope with the job the Bureau was giving itself: the scale of entertainment and hospitality offered to many Russians would see to that, not to mention the size of the postbag generated by the supply of information. The overall atmosphere soon became more like that of a gentlemen's club. Eventually, a third move was made to offices on the top floor of a building at 15 Fontanka Embankment situated on the north side of the river 250 metres from the Nevsky Prospect.

In a book entitled *The Secret City*, Walpole gives a description of the embankment office.

Anglo-Russian Bureau. Third office at 15 Fontanka Embankment, Petrograd.

I went up in a lift to the Propaganda office and found it a very nice and airy place, clean, smart, with coloured advertisements by Shepperson and others on the walls, pictures of Hampstead and St. Albans and Kew Gardens that looked strangely satisfactory and homely to me, and rather touching and innocent. There were several young women clicking away at typewriters, and maps of the Western front, and a colossal toy map of London Tube, and a nice English library with all the best books from Chaucer to D.H. Lawrence and from the Religio Medici to E.V. Lucas's London.

Everything seemed clean and simple and a little deserted, as though the heart of the Russian public had not, as yet, quite found its way there. I think 'guileless' was the adjective that came to mind, and certainly Burrows, the head of the place – a large, red-faced, smiling man with glasses – seemed to me altogether too cheerful and pleased with life to penetrate the wicked recesses of Russian pessimism.

Ransome was a frequent visitor to the various offices, indeed he often worked and lunched at the Bureau, and in spite of what he says in the *Autobiography*, 'I had never thought of running the thing myself', must nevertheless, have felt 'passed over' when he heard that it was Walpole who had been appointed because of his obvious literary connections. Ransome had published a considerable number of books, articles and contributions over the years, and in this respect was just as qualified as Walpole, and spoke far better Russian than he ever did. There are no records however, indicating that Ransome was ever uncomfortable with the Walpole appointment, and in any event, Walpole may not have known of the Bureau's genesis.

As time went on, the Bureau became large, expensive, and ultimately achieved very little. It was not a success and eventually fizzled out!

Developing as a Correspondent

With all the political developments taking place in Russia and the corresponding demands being made on his time, Ransome felt the necessity to have a more central and suitable address – somewhere he could call his own. To this end, he secured in the middle of February 1916, a large room on the upper floor of a block of flats on the northwest corner of Theatre Square, in Glinka Street. A friend (E.B. Walker) occupying Flat 46 in the same building probably tipped Ransome off that it was available, and to get in quickly as flats in this area were much sought after. The south-facing windows overlooked the Mariinsky Theatre and afforded Ransome (a year later), unrivalled views of the early Revolutionary demonstrations and the fire at the Litovsky Castle – a political prison almost next door on the other side of a canal.

When he needed to send telegrams, the main post office was only a short ten minutes walk away, and the Yusupov Palace, where Rasputin was subsequently murdered was just around the corner from the top of the street on the Moika Canal. After the 1917 Revolution, the main telegraph office that Ransome used (formerly a bank) was on the opposite side of the street to the Ministry of Foreign Affairs in the Morskaya. To get there would have entailed a brisk twenty minute walk.

Ransome was a busy man in 1916. In March, he was given his first limited permission to visit the Russian front as a war correspondent. The visit did not take place until early April when, in company with another correspondent, he managed to get down to Galicia and Kiev. There he met for the first time, General Brusilov, 'the smartest-uniformed and most elegant of all Russian generals', as Ransome records. This was a new experience and one that he much enjoyed. He returned to Petrograd having seen very little, but full of admiration for the Russian troops fighting against an enemy far better equipped and infinitely better supplied.

Glinka Ulitsa view north through Theatre Square. Benois house is on the left corner.

The Russian Army at this time was either in retreat or just holding its ground, and occasionally there were small advances, but overall it was a sort of stalemate which made life politically difficult for the Government. Having to explain away this lack of progress, both to the Allies and the people at large, was a source of embarrassment. However, later in the year, these same troops secured a major victory against the Germans in Galicia, which brought forth congratulatory telegrams from the British Government to both the Russian Government and the Emperor.

It is quite amazing just how industrious Ransome was in his endeavours to fulfil his reporting role. He was continually trying to increase his knowledge of the political scene, was involved with the Anglo-Russian Bureau, and visited the Duma frequently to develop connections with those in prominent positions. This latter exercise may sound a rather tiresome and mundane business, but the political spectrum was very wide at this time, with any number of different political parties vying for position. It was important, therefore, to have a knowledge of who was who in these different factions. This ground work ultimately paid handsome dividends when compiling reports, especially when the first part of the Revolution started in early 1917. It also enabled him to get information from the top so-to-speak, and at the time events took place, particularly when the Bolsheviks came to power in late 1917. By this means, Ransome was ultimately able to establish an unassailable position as a reporter, both in terms of knowledge, and his access to news of events at any time with the Government of the day.

However, when the opportunity arose, there were fishing visits to Lachta, plus a period at Vergezha in June 1916 to complete *Old Peter's Russian Tales*. In 1948, Ransome did a number of broadcasts for the BBC. Most were about fishing, but two were *Russian Tales*, *The Soldier and Death*, and *Stolen Turnips* (from *Old Peter*).

General AA Brusilov. According to Ransome, "the smartest uniformed and most elegant of all Russian generals". They met at Galicia on one of Ransome's trips to the 'front'.

At the end of October Ransome left for a much needed month-long trip to England. Visits to Ivy at Hatch, his mother, but especially to the Collingwoods at Lanehead and Barbara in particular, enabled him to enjoy a few peaceful and very happy days. There were also meetings with officials at the Foreign Office. It was his habit to give a briefing about his experiences and how he saw the war situation from the other side each time he came home. These observations were initially received with polite indifference, but as time went on, particularly during 1917, 1918 and 1919, the indifference turned to outright hostility, as we shall later see.

Where East Meets West

Early December 1916 saw a return to Russia for the fifth time. On the journey home war considerations necessitated a route through Finland and around the top of the Gulf of Bothnia to Bergen. The situation for returning to Petrograd was similar but he went via Stockholm taking the train for the rest.

Journeying on the train through Finland, Ransome, who was walking in the corridor, noticed two people playing chess in a compartment. Always attracted to the game, he opened the door and asked to watch. When the game finished, he introduced himself and asked if he could play the winner! One of the players was a young lady by the name of Lola Kinel. A conversation ensued. She and her older sister were returning home to Russia from the United States, where they had resided for the last six years. Before leaving the train the next day, calling cards were exchanged. They kept in touch and eventually Lola met visiting Ransome at his flat on a number of occasions. She spent quite a lot of time with him and occasionally helped with errands and shopping. There were many visits during 1917 and discussions ranged from politics to poetry, with games of chess in between.

Twenty years later, Lola Kinel published her autobiography, *Under Five Eagles*. In it she gives many details about Ransome covering a period we know so little about; that much of what she tells us is here reproduced in full.

One day in the fall of 1916 my twin sister and I were in a train going through Finland to Petrograd...through the open door I noticed an odd-looking man walking up and down the corridor and throwing occasional surreptitious glances in our direction. He was tall, dressed in a Russian military coat, though without any insignia, and a fur cap. He had long red moustaches, completely concealing his mouth, and humourous, twinkling eyes. I lost the first game (she was playing chess with another traveller) and decided to pay more attention to the second. I was winning the second game when the tall man entered the compartment and said in the most delightful, broken Russian, "May I watch?"...

We immediately made him welcome and proceeded with the game. I won and felt that silly elation one always has on winning at chess. The odd looking man then asked whether I would sometime play a game with him. This time, to my amazement, he spoke English, a kind of English I had never heard before. It was nicer than American English, yet it was the first time I had heard the Oxford accent....imperceptibly too, we got acquainted. The funny looking man was pleasant, I thought. Aside from that accent there was nothing foreign or ostentatious about him; he might have been a Russian, a nice Russian. His eyes twinkled and he laughed readily. He asked about America, which he did not seem to like, and to my own surprise I found myself defending America stoutly (she and her sister were on the last lap of their journey back home from the States).

"...And what are you going to do in Petrograd?" asked the Englishman,

"Oh, I'm going to work. I am going to find a job" I said. He smiled at that too.

The next day, at a little station about an hour away from Petrograd the girls were met by their father. They introduced their foreign friend to him and the men exchanged the large visiting cards, fashionable in Russia at the time. On the Englishman's card was printed in Russian "Artur Kirrilovich Ransom, Correspondent *Daily News.*"

Lola was a remarkable girl from a well-to-do bourgeois family. The twins had had a good education, partly in Dresden, and Lola at any rate spoke five languages. Chess and books were the interest Ransome and Lola had in common, so they kept in contact. 'Our first calls were very formal', she writes. 'We were invited to tea and had invariably strawberry tarts and tea from a huge samovar, which didn't draw any too well'. She found that Ransome, like all foreigners, enjoyed using a samovar and the Russian way of making tea. Her twin sister was soon bored with these visits as she did not care much for books and did not play chess, so Lola began to call alone.

Ransome offered her a job scanning the press every day, and extracting news that would be interesting to British readers, but Lola soon realised she did not know what was of interest, 'Good Lord, aren't you at all interested in politics?' Ransome asked. She explained that she had been away too long and didn't really understand what was happening.

Lola became a frequent visitor to Ransome's Glinka Street flat, and has recorded an amusing description of his room.

> Ransome was a Bohemian. He lived in a huge room in an old boarding house overlooking St. Isaac's Square with the famous Cathedral*. It was the first bachelor room I had ever seen; it had a desk and typewriter in one corner, in another a bed, night table, and dresser all behind a screen; then a sort of social arrangement, consisting of an old sofa and a round table with some chairs around it, in the centre.
>
> And books. They were everywhere heaped on the sofa and even on the floor. Among these books I found occasionally torn soiled socks. I used to pick them up gingerly with my gloved hand, and wrap them up in a piece of newspaper...
>
> "Doesn't anyone ever mend your socks for you?" I asked one day.
>
> "No. Don't bother picking them up. I wear them and throw them away when they get torn. The maid forgot to take them away".
>
> "But then you must buy an awful lot of socks".
>
> "I do. These Russian prachki (laundresses) never bother to mend things. I live like a wild rabbit".

Note: The reference to St. Isaac's Square and Cathedral, is a case of misnamed identity. Ransome's flat throughout the period February 1916 to January 1919, was in the large corner block at the northern end of Theatre Square adjacent to Glinka Street, overlooking the Mariinsky Theatre and the Conservatoire.

"And look at your desk – look at all this dust. Doesn't the maid ever dust here?"

"I would wring her neck if she did. She daren't touch my desk", he said with the air of a fanatic threatened with some danger...

I thought him extremely amusing. This was two or three months after our return to Petrograd, when we had become friends. We all had nicknames by then, Ransome being A.K. after the initials of his Russian style name, my sister was the "Big Twin", and I the "Small Twin".

Early in the relationship, Ransome would occasionally call at her parent's home, but these calls stopped rather suddenly, 'I think he found our people too "bourgeois" though he was not quite rude enough to say so.' Lola continues:

His own Bohemianism was not a pose, but seemed real. He had, I remember, a thorough contempt for men who dressed well, or the least conventionally. He forgave women if they were pretty, but he preferred most Russian women, who do not pose and are simple, to English girls. (A prophetic remark!) For England he seemed to have a queer mixture of contempt, dislike, and love. He was clever, yet childish, very sincere and kind and romantic, and on the whole, far more interesting than his books...

One day I asked him how old he was.

"Thirty-four," he replied.

Quite old, I thought, and, being off guard, replied instantly to his query about my own age:

"Eighteen."

"No, Twin! You are spoofing."

I felt a little thrill.

"Do you mean I look older?"

"You don't look it, but you are so intelligent, so sure... Good Lord, in England you would be still in a nursery – you are a child."

The compliment about my intelligence didn't flatter me in the least. I had heard that before. What I wanted to know was just how old he thought I was.

"Very well, then, how old did you think I was? No lying."

"Oh - twenty-three - twenty-five."

"Oh, A.K! Really?"

For the first few months after Lola's return to Petrograd, there were hardly any signs of Revolution, mostly an atmosphere of disenchantment and food shortages. It was March 1917 before the first Revolution occurred. At the time there were many disturbances in the streets between the different factions, but this unrest did not appear to upset Lola.

On a gorgeous sunny day, with the snow soft and crunchy underfoot, Lola set off to walk from Vasilevski Island (north of the river) to the centre of the city but, after some time, decided to go and visit A.K. instead. He was just on the point of going out to see what was going on when she arrived; so asked her to join him. She records:

> We went towards the river and soon noticed a large detachment of soldiers walking to one of the bridges. With a correspondent's 'nose for news,' A.K. decided to follow them. We had to walk rapidly to keep up with their steady fast march. Just as we were approaching the bridge, right behind the soldiers, we saw a detachment on the other side approaching the same bridge.
>
> A.K. was excited. The soldiers in front of us walked a little slower in a more compact group; the others came straight on. When they were about two hundred feet from us they halted. Our soldiers halted too. The soldiers in the front rank of the other detachment began to kneel down. Almost simultaneously they opened fire. The bullets began to whistle with the characteristic swishing sound, the crack of the rapport coming a bit later. A.K. and I watched intensely. It was like a show, only more vivid. The bullets came faster – one going right between our heads. Holding my hand, A.K. watched with shining eyes. All of a sudden he shouted.
>
> "Christ, Twin, I forgot you were here!" and pulling me by the hand, he began to back, still watching the fight.
>
> "I don't want to go, I want to watch," I said stubbornly. But he pulled harder and began to run, dragging me along.
>
> "Oh, A.K., I want to watch some more", I begged, hanging back. Instead of arguing, he raised me in his arms, and began to run. Only when we had left the bridge and turned the corner where we were free from the bullets did he let me down.

Perhaps Lola, like many before, felt she was immune from bullets. Ransome was fired by the uprising but, was disappointed that Lola showed no excitement or enthusiasm for the Revolution. He urged her to side with the revolutionaries but, she remained aloof in his presence for a long time. However, one day she went to hear Lenin, and kept quiet about it, out of sheer contrariness.

> A.K. was very enthusiastic about the Bolsheviks and I did not want to give him any satisfaction on this point. My neutral attitude both puzzled and irritated him.
>
> "All the young people I know are working for the revolution. How can you be so indifferent and stand aside?" he would say.
>
> "I don't know whether the Bolsheviks are right A.K." I would reply.
>
> "You are very romantic. You are just carried away. You don't know anything about Socialism or economics."
>
> He would grow almost furious at this – as far as was possible with his kindly and childlike nature.

"Then you are against them?"

"I don't know. I want to know first all about them. Perhaps they are fools or dreamers. I am just standing aside and looking on."

"Exactly, when you should be working furiously for one side or the other. The Revolution needs people like you, young, intelligent people. You could easily get a job in the Smolny. They are bound to need secretaries who know English."

"No thanks A.K. I don't want to go to the Smolny," I would say politely and obstinately, and our political discussion would end in a discord...

Her apparent indifference shocked Ransome and he was disappointed that she remained uninterested when it came to politics. "You are only interested in yourself, Twin, you are utterly selfish." To this direct remark, Lola was 'cut to the quick'.

It is quite odd to note, that another one and a half years later, Ransome would feel very different about Russian politics. In November 1918, he wrote to his mother:

It's no good; the Russian Revolution has failed utterly in altering me personally. And once I get a little peace and quiet and get my sketch of the development of the revolution written, I shall write FINIS and fetch politics a good boost with a boot in the latter parts, and return with no regrets whatever to pen, ink, tobacco, fishing and the lake country.

Chapter IV
Year of the Revolution

In this period there were regular visits to the Duma (the lower chamber of the legislature), and meetings with persons such as Oldenburg, Gutchkov (a Royalist), and Miliukov (Cadet Party). Despatches for the *Daily News*, were frequent, and assembling them from the many meetings he attended, took up much of the time.

By 1917, Ransome had become fluent enough in Russian to be able to hold a conversation. He always said that he had no political affiliations to any party whether at home or in Russia. Indeed, Ransome was non-political, but if he has to have a label, it could only be 'Liberal'. He was never a communist, or even a socialist, nor did he ever idolise any of the Russian leaders. Perhaps some commentators would find it hard to believe, but he maintained that it was this non-party approach which had endeared him to the prominent Russian politicians at the time. Moreover, they thought they would get fair and unbiased reporting; a factor which was considered when he applied (not without some difficulty), for a press pass to attend the meetings of the Duma. The Government also wanted control over random photography, particularly where correspondents and foreigners were concerned. Ransome applied for a permit, which was granted at the end of February 1917.

The 'Soviet' of Workers' and 'Soldiers' Deputies' asked if he would show the British Embassy the statement of the War Industry Committee. This he did, and was anonymously rewarded with an envelope addressed the correspondent of the *Daily News*. In it he found a ticket admitting him to the Soviet 'with the right to speak but not to vote'. Ransome made full use of the ticket. This position allowed a better understanding of what was going on and who was influencing events. In the *Autobiography*, the position, as he saw it, is succinctly put:

> Chance had brought me into the Soviet of Soldiers' and Workers' Deputies long before other correspondents had thought that body worth observing. From the first day they met it was obvious that the Soviets held what power there was, and that the Duma was an impotent survival. The story of 1917 is the story of the demonstration of that all-important fact.

Throughout the period 1916-1924, Ransome always reported what he saw in a sharp, clear and concise manner, although, being in a privileged position with regard to inside information and what was developing, such reports did not always find favour in Government circles at home where the full extent of what was happening was not, in those early days, fully appreciated. Looking through those Foreign Office records which survive, it is clear that there was a considerable gulf between what Ransome was reporting on for his paper, and the expectation of British Government officials. It is that gulf which ultimately brought Ransome into conflict with those at home. Copies of his reports and letters show, that Ransome's determination to report events 'as seen' or 'as they are', never changed. As a result, his exposition of the Russian situation created endless hostility, and gave the Foreign Office and the Intelligence Services a permanent headache throughout the entire period he spent in Eastern Europe.

The dominant feature underlining Ransome's relations with the British Government, was the annoyance they felt for the way his reports, which appeared to be of mostly pro-Russian content, were being published by the *Daily News*, and later, by the *Manchester Guardian*. It seems to us of utmost importance, that ALL events relating to Ransome need to be considered in this light, including the Government's response in trying to deal with him.

On 2 March the *Daily News* telegraphed Ransome to cut down his telegrams to vital matters and to keep messages short! Two weeks later they would regret sending such a missive!

Around the middle of March, Lenin arrived in Petrograd. On 13th March there were serious disturbances in the city, including the battle for the Litovski prison almost next door to Ransome's flat. This battle he was able to witness from his top floor front window. A descriptive account of this battle in Ransome's handwriting is on file. He wrote:

> The Commisariat was immediately across Glinka Street... There were machine gun posts (established by the police) commanding the road between the conservatoire and the Mari Theatre. The [Theatre] Square was under fire from the prison, I saw people running across it shielding their heads from the bullets as if from a molten shower, while others pushed farm carts and abandoned motor cars and anything else to serve as cover, while from captured machine guns and rifles they fired at the prison and at a machine gun post in the attic over my room. The policeman there was killed early, so I was told by the doorkeeper when I came in from the street, and though the walls were pockmarked above all our windows by the bullets, by some miracle not a single pane of glass was cracked.

A similar but more lengthy report appeared in the *Daily News*. In his despatch to his readers at the time, however, he pointed out that on this occasion, 'the battle has come to me!' The previous day, Ransome had gone to

Litovsky Castle c1900. Prison for criminals and political enemies. No longer in existence.

Litovsky Castle on fire during the 1917 Spring uprising. Specifically commissioned by Ransome from Mitrokhin as the cover picture for his proposed book on the revolution. It was assumed destroyed after police raided his Glinka Street flat in 1919, but amazingly was re-discovered by Tatiana Verizhnikova in the UA Rysakov's collection.

the Astoria Hotel in St. Issac's Square in search of news. This building was the city's largest and its most prestigious hotel (built in 1912) which had been taken over by military authorities at the beginning of the war. It was crammed full of officers, some were on leave, some convalescing, as well as families of high ranking officers and a large group of Allied officers. Ransome had gone there, hoping to witness a meeting between the revolutionaries and the officers, but nothing happened while he was there. At some late hour he left for his flat walking along the Moika Canal and recorded what happened to him.

Meanwhile, the revolutionary left wing had swept forward towards the river passing my house, which now lies in revolutionary territory. But isolated bodies of police on the roofs of houses were keeping up desultory fire. I had a narrow shave from a hand-grenade which was dropped from a roof and exploded in front of me. Twice I was stopped by revolutionary patrols. I found heavy firing going on up and down my street.

By leaving when he did, Ransome missed the sacking of the hotel, as well as a possible threat to his life!

The officers in the Astoria had given an assurance that there would be no attacking people in the street from the hotel, if the revolutionaries would leave the building alone. It is not clear what sparked off the sacking, but it is thought that an agent, hidden somewhere on the top floor of the hotel, turned a machine-gun on the soldiers and persons in the street below. The precise origin of the gun fire could not be established, but appeared to come from above a suite of rooms occupied by the family of General Prince Tumanov, commander of a Cavalry Division at the front. In response to this provocation, the revolutionary forces brought up two motor vehicles with machine-guns and blasted away at the hotel wrecking the rooms occupied by the Tumanov family and the suites on either side. Considerable damage was done by the street hordes, who then stormed the ground floor smashing all the plate glass windows, and wrecking the interior.

The English officers present did not attempt to join in the fighting. Their main concern was for the women and children, whom they collected together in order to protect them. They did, however, inform the crowds in the hotel that they would not interfere with their agenda provided that their women and children were not attacked, otherwise they would defend them. This brought forth cheers and a promise from the revolutionaries, which they scrupulously kept.

The following day, Ransome attended the Duma to be brought up-to-date on the night's disturbances. More and more troops were being brought from the front to try and quell the revolutionary activities, but as soon as they arrived in Petrograd, they were met by large crowds who invariably persuaded them to come over to their side. The overall situation was volatile, with approximately 215,000 factory workers and some 150,000 mutinous troops being stirred up by the revolutionaries. Such were the difficulties experienced

Navy Barracks (left) and Regional Military Soviet on the right c1927. The church of the Annunciation of the Virgin in the distance no longer exists.

by the Government in trying to maintain some order that they only held on to power by the skin of their teeth. Indeed the Government just bumped along for the next few months, barely able to offer any direction or positive

Petrograd Central Post Office. Both post office and telegraph services were here up to the revolution. Still in use today.

rule at all. Other political parties, notably the Bolsheviks, were able to use this situation to great effect and enhance their position in anticipation of taking power.

This was a busy couple of weeks for Ransome: he was often telegraphing two or three times a day with the rapidly changing news, and on one day actually sent eight! Never again did the *Daily News* criticise Ransome's reportage! Running about for days and nights at a time to get information for the despatches meant going without sleep, and as Ransome was never in the best of health, was enough to leave the poor man exhausted. "I am tired cOMPletely OUT", he complained in a letter to his mother dated 1st May.

On the personal level Ransome recorded on the 15th, the great difficulty of getting food, and the stupid and dangerous act of lowering all prices! The Tzar abdicated at this time. It created little fuss. Nicholas II could not, or would not, make the necessary changes to ensure the survival of the Romanov

Tauride Palace. Built in 1783-89 for Catherine the Great's lover Potyomkin. Between 1905 and 1917 the State Duma, the provisional government and Petrograd Soviet, all met here. Ransome was a frequent visitor to the Chamber of Deputies.

dynasty, in spite of the advice of many well-intentioned people including Buchannan, the British ambassador. As a result the Kerensky Government was instituted to run the country.

It is interesting to observe that there is very little in Ransome's writings or reports regarding the position of the Tzar and his family. He hardly appears to notice them or to comment on their existence. The Tzar had become weak through poor advice and indecisive ministers. This showed by a falling off of support at all levels, although such lingering support as there was, seemed to be from the aristocracy and middle classes, and only a little with those lower down the social scale. The Empress Alix, of course, was German, and was generally disliked by a large part of the population because they believed she had a foot in both camps. Her behaviour was sometimes erratic and meddlesome, and they saw her as someone wielding far too much control from behind the scenes.

Nor is there anything much in Ransome's writing about Rasputin – the mad monk from Siberia. For a period during the early part of the war, Rasputin had considerable influence over the Court, largely due to his hypnotic powers in appearing to cure the Tzarevich of his haemophilia. A period was then spent away in Siberia, but on Rasputin's return to the Petrograd area, the Court again came under his influence. This was especially noticeable during those periods when the Tzar was away at the front and the Empress sought Rasputin's advice. Through his mystical and magnetic charms, he improved his hold over the Court by advising the Empress that her son would die without his help. When not at Court, Rasputin led a debauched life, often frequenting Petrograd bathhouses looking for pleasures of the flesh. Such behaviour in one so close to the Court was totally unacceptable. The secret police began to take an interest and had him watched.

Rasputin was an important figure in the run-up to the Revolution. When the Tzar was away, he was, in effect, deputising for him and, being supremely confident in his acquired position, changed four Prime Ministers, appointed a number of other Government ministers and generally tried to influence the affairs of state. None of the people he appointed, however, turned out to be much good. Rasputin was quite ignorant of state affairs, became far too powerful, was corrupt and ended up splitting the nation. His presence and influence at Court was detested by many,

Tauride Palace. Chamber of Deputies.

and he began to realise that he had many enemies in the Government and the military. Never a person to be bothered by what others thought about him, he boldly informed the Empress that, should anything happen to him, the Tzar would fall and his family would not live beyond two years. It turned out to be a most remarkable prophesy.

Felix Yusopov was a member of Russia's richest family with royal and state connections. Along with a few other like-minded souls, he hatched a plot to remove Rasputin from the public scene. The idea being, to tempt him to the Yusopov Palace on the pretext of meeting a very attractive woman — the Princess Irina. Once there, he would be given wine and cakes laced with poison. When Rasputin arrived, he was shown to a room below ground level [now a museum] and provided with the appropriate refreshment. The wine and cakes appeared to have little effect. Yusopov, thinking that perhaps Rasputin was surviving by divine power, left the room to get a revolver. In spite of being shot, Rasputin still managed to crawl up a back staircase leading from the basement to a room above, and out into the garden. He just would not die! The conspirators, alarmed at the situation they had created, carted his body away and dumped it nearby in the Neva River. His body was subsequently recovered, where it was found that the water in the lungs showed that he could not have been completely dead when entering the river.

Perhaps Ransome didn't see these matters as being of sufficient importance? But it does seem a bit odd, especially when the Yusopov Palace, where Rasputin met his end, was only a couple of minutes walk away from his flat at the end of Glinka Street.

These events of spring 1917, which lasted for about two weeks, constituted the first part of the Revolution. The contents of his dispatches for the *Daily News* must have impressed because, he received a telegram from J.L.Garvin, editor of the *Observer* – a Conservative newspaper, asking him if he would become their correspondent. He was delighted. This appointment opened different doors, although complementary ones to those of the *Daily News*, and life was much easier.

Following this first uprising, life settled down to some sort of artificial normality, but still there was a lingering expectation in the air. The country had been shaken to its roots, but the job was not complete. The Government behaved as if it was all over, and tried to continue as if nothing had happened, but the people knew that the business was unfinished.

Ransome's regular visits to the Duma continued during the following months, and was just part of the never-ending task of constantly having to assess the political temperature in order to keep his readership at home well informed. Meeting other correspondents at this time was an integral part of daily life, as was seeing friends, and fishing at Lachta, whenever he could escape from the city for a couple of hours.

As the spring wore on, it was clear the Bolsheviks already had considerable influence in the Petrograd area. An uprising in July, partly spontaneous, but partly contrived, failed to secure them power. As a result, Lenin went into hiding and Trotsky, was arrested. Trotsky was not held in detention for long. The Kerensky Government, however, was weak from both diplomatic and military failures. It will be remembered that most ordinary Russians wanted an end to the war – an end which could only be brought about by the warring nations having a conference in Stockholm.

This failure to instigate a conference and work towards peace, together with a conspicuous lack of military success at the front, gave the Bolsheviks the added strength and impetus needed to establish a position where they could take power. It became clear to Ransome, it was only a matter of time before something happened and they became the Government. His reported views on the Bolsheviks were dynamite! And were totally opposed by the Government in England. The Foreign Office were very unhappy, and thought his reports, which were contrary to the accepted view, would give the wrong impression. J.L.Garvin of the *Observer* sent Ransome a despatch explaining the Allied policy. But Ransome was unrepentant, as the following extract from a letter to his mother on 6 June shows:

> I am in the throes of trouble with Garvin, who sent me a long and most excited telegram about Allied policy because I had to telegraph that the Russian socialists were by no means satisfied with the same. That is of course unfortunate for us, but I can't alter it by telling lies about it, and pretending that all is for the best in this best of all possible worlds, so I think it quite possible I shall have to stop being correspondent for the *Observer*. I shall be very sorry if so, because though he may easily get a less well-informed correspondent to write him more cheerful telegrams from his point of view, the result will only be that he himself will get a false notion of what to expect. I do my level best to give an accurate idea of things here, but, bless my soul, only God who knows all things could really give an accurate view. I think I give a more accurate view than anybody else, judging from the way in which the Russian papers almost exclusively quote from the *News* as the only paper which gets near understanding the position.

British officialdom and Ransome were poles apart! But what an odd world this is, when the Liberal *Daily News* sends him a congratulatory telegram for his efforts and a cheque for £50 to underline their pleasure!

History shows that Ransome was right in these matters. At the time Britain, as one of the most important and powerful countries in the world, did not want to believe what was being reported, because it did not accord with what they hoped would be the outcome of both the war and Russia's position.

Their great fear was, that if the Bolsheviks came to power, they would take Russia out of the war leaving the Western Allies to fight on alone. So it is possible to understand and sympathise with the British Government's point of view.

The summer drifted on, with Ransome in quite good spirits and enjoying himself, as a letter in August to his mother shows:

> My spirits are slightly better, principally because I did actually get out of Petrograd a week ago for three days of which I spent two and a half and two nights in the train, going to and from Headquarters, where I got through the business I was there for without any difficulty, and had half an hour free, which I used in getting a dirty boy in a dirty boat to row me up the river above the town drains, and hold the boat while I bathed. Well that was jolly, and though the water was like pea soup, the evening light was all the better on account of its opacity, and I splashed about in it with great joy and some humiliation at finding how weak a swimmer I have become... Further I've had satisfactory news from the D.N. [*Daily News*] about an allowance to help in meeting the gigantic expenses incident on living here. So the barometer stands momentarily set fair.

With the general situation giving the impression of being in limbo, and thinking that there would be enough time to make a quick visit to England before there were any more dramatic events, Ransome left Russia on 9 October and arrived in Edinburgh via Aberdeen on the 17th. The British authorities were now conscripting into the military all males who did not have an exempted occupation. In returning from abroad, Ransome was concerned in case he was forced to join up on arrival at a UK port. To avert this possibility, however, he was provided with a dispensation document by the Petrograd Embassy. A measure, perhaps, of his importance to them. The last thing they needed at this time was, for Ransome to be press-ganged into the army.

A quick round of visits followed; seeing his mother, snatching some fishing at Fonthill (near Hatch) and making a trip to the Collingwoods at Lanehead. He also had the good fortune to meet and lay the foundations for two important new friendships in Molly Hamilton and Francis Hirst. Mary Agnes Hamilton worked with Hirst, but later would become the Labour M.P. for Blackburn, while Hirst was then editor of the *Economist*.

With events exploding in Russia in his absence, Ransome was anxious to return there as soon as possible, but this would prove to be more difficult than usual. Due to the enormous political upheavals, and the Bolsheviks seizing power and forming the new Government, Ransome found he could not complete his visa documentation for the journey. Consultations with the

> British Embassy,
> Petrograd,
> September 18th 1917.
>
> To The Competent Military Authority.
>
> I hereby certify that the bearer Mr ARTHUR M. RANSOME has been employed for the past three years on important work in connection with the Embassy and is at present so employed. His visit to England is of a temporary nature and he is required to return to continue his duties in Petrograd.
>
> *George W. Buchanan*
> His Majesty's Ambassador.

Ransome's dispensation from Military Service.

Foreign Office in London proved helpful, and enabled him to set off for Stockholm via Bergen and Christiana, carrying a diplomatic bag to give to the Legation there. Two weeks of constant battle with the Swedish Bolshevik representative Vorovsky, finally produced a rubber stamp in his passport enabling him to proceed. This rubber stamp did not guarantee entry into Russia so it was with some trepidation that the long railway journey up the Gulf of Bothnia and round into Finland close to the Arctic Circle was undertaken. Leaving on 21 December, he finally arrived in Petrograd late on Christmas Day without mishap.

The year drew to a close with daily visits to the Smolny Institute the new seat of Government, the girls high school having been closed in the preceding summer (see picture in colour section). Occasionally he would see Trotsky or other Bolshevik leaders. To round off the year there were a few social meetings, dinners and parties. Convention has it that one person who came into focus at this time was Trotsky's secretary Evgenia Petrovna Shelepina. He began seeing her almost every day if only to collect notices being handed out.

Ransome in Russia

Above, Smolny - Government Offices 2000
Below, Smolny Hall of Acts . In this hall the All-Russian Congress of Soviets conferred power on a Bolshevik government led by Lenin which controlled the country from here until March 1918. After the revolution, Ransome visited almost every day to collect 'handouts' from Trotsky's secretary.

In these last few days of the year, Ransome had occasion to visit the Commissariat of Foreign Affairs (huge circular buildings fronting Palace Square), to seek a censor's stamp in order to send a telegram. While wandering through the corridors of this building, he records in the *Autobiography*, how, hearing the sound of voices he opened a door to find a few people in a room, including Evgenia and her sister Iraida. Evgenia offered to guide him through the building until they found a censor to stamp the telegram. Both girls were actually working for different Government ministries at the time, but had probably met prior to journeying to their flat together. It is possible that he may have known of her existence before this time, but if this was the case, it is unlikely that it would have been any more than someone he had seen on visiting a ministry.

Ransome and Evgenia had much in common following the October Revolution. He, believing that the Bolsheviks were the only group able to run Russia and with an interest in reporting them, and she, because of being a Bolshevik member and her party forming the Government. This change of

84

Government however, brought about a change in her employment. Their shared belief in the Revolution outcome and its progress, probably formed an integral part of their growing relationship; indeed without some form of common understanding it is doubtful whether their relationship would have begun in the first place. Ransome tells us very little about her, except to mention that she was 'the tall jolly girl whom later on I was to marry and to whom I owe the happiest years of my life.' In a letter to Tabitha, dated May 1918, she is described as: 'a big girl as big as Dor Dor who carries a revolver and a sword and is a fierce revolutionary.' Dramatic stuff! Maybe a little licence here for the benefit of his daughter? She wasn't quite that dramatic, although she was a tall girl and did carry a revolver [see *Chapter VIII : Evgenia Shelepina and the October Revolution*] while she was secretary to the minister for Foreign Affairs. Within a year of the Bolshevik takeover however, her sympathies for them began to wane, and not long after she was happy to be thinking about a life elsewhere. In later years, it is doubtful whether she would have wanted to be thought of as having been associated with them.

Petrograd Ministry of Foreign Affairs access door in Ransome's day. Not now in use.

It is indisputable that Ransome believed in the Revolution because, it became clear as time went on that there was no alternative. In this matter he was joined by all of the western correspondents, irrespective of political affiliation and the great mass of the

Telegraph Office used by Ransome after the Revolution and still in use today.

Lenin and Stalin - Enemies?

Russian people. He had been there in Russia throughout and had revelled in it from the beginning. This great support for a revolution was all very well. What it did not take account of was in the results that might flow from it. Most Russians wanted a revolution – a change in the way the country was governed, but what they did not want was the Bolsheviks that they got, although in the early stages, most people were prepared to give them the benefit of the doubt rather than have another upheaval or see a return to the old order.

The Bolsheviks were the largest single party, but in a minority against all the other political groups combined. They managed to seize power by sheer bluff and cunning due to their superior foresight, planning and organisation. The open society that they planned with free voting, did not last long. In the first round of voting, the Bolsheviks lost. No free voting occurred again. Ransome got to know all the Bolshevik leaders as events progressed, including Lenin and Trotsky and was influenced and charmed by Karl Radek, an intellectual who controlled the Press Bureau at the Commisariat for Foreign Affairs. Radek became one of Ransome's closest contacts in the new Government, assisting with information on Bolshevik plans and helping with access to ministers, as well as offering occasionally, invitations for a quiet game of chess.

Ransome first came into contact with Radek when a messenger came to his Glinka Street flat asking him to call at the Foreign Commissariat. A few weeks previously, on the journey from Sweden to Russia, Ransome had left a collection of books and possessions with Vorovsky in Stockholm for forwarding. These items had arrived in Petrograd, and Radek, without any scruples had opened the parcel to find in it a Shakespeare, a chess board, a mixed collection of books on subjects as wide as navigation, fishing, chess and folklore. This variety of books intrigued Radek, who wanted to see what type of person could have such interests. Good fortune again for Ransome, as Radek became his closest and most helpful Bolshevik friend.

Radek was quite well educated – universities of Cracow and Berne. He had spent a year in prison during the 1905 revolution and then worked on a number of illegal newspapers. At the beginning of the war he was in Germany, but escaped to Switzerland, where he joined up with Lenin. In March 1917 he was in the party with Lenin and about 30 other revolutionaries that went in a sealed carriage from Switzerland, through Germany to Stockholm, to await the Bolshevik Revolution. Writing later, Radek confessed that the carriage was not sealed at all, they were simply obliged not to leave it and had two German officers sat inside watching them.

After seizing power, Radek, along with all the other Bolshevik leaders lived in the newly requisitioned Astoria Hotel. His wife was called Rosa and they had a small child. Along with Trotsky, he was an important negotiator for the Russians at the 1918 Brest-Litovsk Peace Conference. By 1927 he, like Trotsky, was out of favour and was exiled – the original ideas of the Bolsheviks having been overturned by a new regime under Stalin.

Ransome's passes to the Smolny and Kremlin

Petrograd - Demonstration outside the Angleterre Hotel 1917. Ransome frequently played billiards in this hotel.

Workers demonstrating near the Moika Canal/Litovsky Castle, Petrograd, November 1917.

Petrograd - Nicholas/Moscow Railway Station c1910. Ransome used this station for trains to Moscow and Vologda.

Year of the Revolution

Petrograd - Nevsky Prospect near St Catherine's Roman Catholic Church c1900.

Petrograd - St Isaac's Square.
Before the Astoria Hotel was built c1910.

Astoria Hotel built 1912. Ransome stayed here on his his return from Stockholm with Vorovsky in 1919.

Above, LB Kamenev. Occasional spokesman for the Bolshevik movement.

Left, Karl Radek. In charge of the Press Bureau at the Commissariat of Foreign Affairs. He was Ransome's closest friend/contact in the Bolshevik government.

SMOLNY

In February 1997 we were able to gain access to the Smolny, (which nowadays is the home of the city Government), and were accorded a privileged view of some of those parts of the building that were used, or had a place in the events at the time of the Revolution. Privileged, because the Smolny is a working Government office and not open to the public – Russians or otherwise! Once inside, our empty bags were x-rayed, but had to be given up just the same. The two cameras that we had held no interest for the armed guards, so we kept them with us. A minder lady appeared, relieved us of a small fee and off we went.

An important part of this building is the Hall of Acts, which is a huge auditorium in the south wing on the second floor. This was where Lenin, Trotsky and other Bolshevik leaders made speeches to their comrades following the uprising. Our minder lady took us in and switched on the lights, the auditorium normally being left in darkness to save costs. With eyes adjusted, we could see just how big it was with the numerous rows of seating extending the full length of the hall. The interior is still the same as it was when the Bolsheviks left for Moscow with banners and hangings on the walls. Lighting is by rows of huge chandeliers, while on the floor there are attractive carpets laid in the aisles. The only change from 1917 being in the provision of more modern seating with fitted translation facilities, as the auditorium is still occasionally used. We found it quite awe inspiring, to stand for a few moments gazing around, taking in the atmosphere, feeling the presence of so much history from the past.

Almost next door to this hall was a large room used as an official museum for some of the central players in the Revolution and for some of the former leaders of the Communist Party. Pictures of famous people lined the walls, while glass-topped cabinets display small books, letters, notes and artefacts etc.

A trek along, what seemed like miles of carpeted corridors and up some back stairs brought us to a small side corridor at the south end of the top floor. Our minder lady inserted a 'prison-sized' key into a large eight foot high white door, and announced without any warning,

"This is room 67, Trotsky's office and that of his secretary!"

We were dumb struck! It was so unexpected, as we had no idea that these offices were still in existence. To add to the drama, our minder, did not know where our interest lay or what we were looking for.

Our entire assessment of Evgenia, as it relates to her job with the Bolshevik Government, changed in a flash, when we saw the lay-out of the office where she and Trotsky had worked. She has traditionally been referred to as Trotsky's secretary, but the common perception of a secretary being in a front office or in a side room down the corridor does not apply here. A more reasonable assumption is that Evgenia's position was that of a personal assistant. She had her desk in the same room as Trotsky, separated only by a partition which extended across just part of the room and in the early days, had actually shared a desk with him. Many of the decisions affecting Russia during that momentous period were taken in this room, and consequently she must have known an awful lot of what went on throughout that period. When Trotsky was out, she ran the place – it's as simple as that! Evgenia set out in some notes for Ransome her early experiences of being a Bolshevik, and how she became employed as Trotsky's secretary. These notes form a separate chapter and are reproduced at the end of the book.

Behind the partition and a screen, was a small area used by Trotsky as night quarters when the pressure of work was too great and he could not get home. The night quarters, like Lenin's, were furnished with a simple iron-framed bed, the usual chamber pot, wooden card table for a bedside table, and a wooden chair etc. Oh, and a small bedside rug on the bare floor! All very very basic. Evgenia's section had a desk with her typewriter and a table lamp, a hat stand, some simple wooden upright chairs along the partition behind her desk and some large wooden pigeon boxes constructed along the wall opposite her desk to act as a filing cabinet. The two offices had been 'mothballed', nothing having changed or been altered since the Government vacated in March 1918 and moved to Moscow.

We were given an opportunity to spend a few moments alone in these offices, just to soak up the atmosphere. To sit at Evgenia's desk and suddenly feel that you are trespassing on somebody else's privacy was quite humbling, especially as for a moment one got the feeling that she might just pop back into the office at any time! It was a moving and thrilling experience, just to stand there and appreciate the significance of this large office, where so much history was made in 1917.

To say that the Smolny is huge, is an understatement. The central corridors alone down each of the three floors are big enough to take a double-decker bus! These corridors are also so long, that pictures hanging at each end cannot be distinguished when viewed from the other end! Nor can the offices on either side be seen from the corridor, but are entered through large 'church-type' doors every 15 metres or so, to ensure privacy. To emphasise the scale of the building, Trotsky mentions in his memoirs that Lenin had said, 'although we are in the same building, we are so far apart that we need bicycles.' It is quite surprising in spite of being a frequent visitor, Ransome never mentions or comments on the Smolny in his diaries or letters home. The Smolny was originally built in 1806-1808 by Quarenghi as a boarding school for girls of the aristocracy – some school!

In the early part of 1918, meetings with Trotsky, or other officials at the Smolny were occurring daily. Ransome would visit Evgenia there to collect whatever notices were being doled out, and on occasions, to meet her after work for a walk or the odd 9km tram ride home. Ransome describes in the *Autobiography*, how they were both boarding a tram after her work one day, when it started moving before Evgenia was properly on, dragging her along the trackway. Because she was strong enough to hold on, she escaped the certain disaster which would have befallen her had she let go.

Chapter V
Dissatisfaction at Home

Ransome's despatches following the Revolution for the *Daily News*, and from 1919 for the *Manchester Guardian*, reflected his considerable knowledge and understanding of why the political system was the way it was. The Foreign Office by this time was becoming seriously concerned with what appeared to be his pro-Russian reports and tried on a number of occasions to silence him – even persuading Scott, the editor of the *Manchester Guardian*, to promise that nothing of Ransome's would be published that was prejudicial to the Government. Adding fuel to the fire were similar complaints from Embassies in other European Capitals. The Foreign Office even wrote to Sir George Buchannan at the Petrograd Embassy asking if he could do anything to restrain Ransome (FO371 3086). But nothing changed! Few officials in those days were prepared to stick their necks out and support Ransome in his predicament, with the exception, perhaps, of Sir Basil Thomson, Head of Special Branch.

The 'low', to which Ransome had sunk in the eyes of the Foreign Office is reflected in various comments in their files: 'Out and out Bolshevik, 'Openly recognised Bolshevik agent' and 'Undoubtedly capable dangerous agent' (FO 371 3086/3106). There cannot be any doubt that many of the officials at the Foreign Office were convinced that Ransome was an agent, so set were they in their views – so set, in fact, that they couldn't see that there might just be another point of view.

One official who wrote on Embassy embossed paper from Helsinki states that he has known Ransome for several years, ...'and I consider him to be in that most unsatisfactory of all categories: a literary dishonest character. As for the lady in question, she is of course notorious!' But, it was 'the lady in question' (along with others), who helped with support and influence, and thereby became a key asset to Ransome's efficient and knowledgeable reporting as time went on.

Ransome however, stuck at it and never wavered in his view that there was an element of justice in the overthrow of the old order. He was quite definite in his opinion, that the British Government's view of the situation was misguided. Ransome was convinced that the only workable policy was for the British Government to back the Bolsheviks and prevent Russia from falling under the war machine of the Germans; a situation to which they eventually succumbed. Up to the time of the first uprising most correspondents held similar, if sometimes diluted views, as Ransome, but as 1917 wore on he was alone with, perhaps, the exception of Philips-Price and Lockhart, who had recently returned to Russia. Ransome always maintained that his main objective was to report what the situation was and to offer the best explanation for it. The British Government was not in a receptive mode for this style of down-to-earth reporting and consequently the result was great mistrust. We can see in this attitude a clear example of the way in which both the French and British Governments harboured an unbalanced view in the war against Germany – a view that interfered with their ability to see what was happening in Russia.

Vologda - Railway Station. Still the same as when Ransome visited.

This position gave rise to a stubborn conviction by the Allies that the problems in Russia in the latter half of 1916 was the result of German influence at the Russian Court. The blindness displayed by the Allies in looking at Russia's growing problems is illustrated by an Allied diplomatic conference held in Petrograd in January 1917 – just a month before the first uprising. The purpose was to try and push Russia towards better efforts on the Eastern Front and to organise events in harmony with Western war objectives. Lord Milner and Sir Henry Wilson represented Great Britain, while Gaston Doumergue, the Minister for their colonies, represented the French.

This diplomatic conference presented a superb opportunity for the Western statesmen to see for themselves just how serious the Russian situation was. They did not look too closely, nor were they even concerned. Had they done so, they would have seen the problem of their policy towards Russia. There was a complete failure in the ability of the delegates to realise that first Kerensky, and later, Lenin's rise to power was founded on a guarantee that peace would be the objective. The trouble was

Vologda - Kirillovsky Street in Ransome's time.

Russia had become involved in a major internal political crisis, and as a result had lost almost all her ability to wage war. The situation was so grave that the Russian Government could not work or apply the efforts necessary to solving the country's problems without terminating the war. The country and the army had had enough. Most people wanted the war ended. In trying to drive the Russians to further conflict the Allies were only providing support for the agitators, dissidents and minority groups. As Ransome saw and understood from the middle of 1916 onwards, the demands of the Russian political situation were at odds with the demands of the Allied war.

Vologda - Main Square. Now a wide open space with only the Golden Anchor Hotel in the background remaining.

It must be pure speculation, just how different the European situation might have been had the British Government listened to the advice it was getting from Ransome and Philips Price, and not a little from some influential persons at home whose views were prominently reported in the main press.

DIPLOMATIC MISSIONS TO VOLOGDA

In early March Ransome went by train with Raymond Robins (head of the American Red Cross Mission in Russia) to Vologda – a small, but strategically important town some 350 miles to the east of Petrograd. Life for the Missions and Embassies was becoming precarious in the early part of 1918, or so it was thought. Lockhart (formally Consul-General) prevailed on Ransome to journey to Vologda with a view to finding, and securing for the British, a building suitable from which to operate a base for keeping in touch with the Russians. This brief was outside his job as a correspondent, which meant the *Daily News* would not cover the expenses. Lockhart wired the Foreign Office for permission to provide financial assistance as necessary. The message was:

> Very urgent! from Lockhart. Ransome *Daily News* correspondent is remaining in Russia and will probably go with my party and Americans. He will not be attached to my mission, but his help and co-operation will be very useful (and) as he will not be able to obtain money from his paper, may I finance him according to my discretion. (FO 371 3321)

Vologda - Golden Anchor Hotel where Radek and Ransome gorged themselves.

A Foreign Office minute supports the proposal on a basis of the value and co-operation that he will be able to give, but notes; 'Mr Ransome is very much in sympathy with the Bolsheviks and would certainly be useful to Mr Lockhart. As it turned out, the journey was a total waste of time, and four days later all the people involved bumped back in the Red Cross carriage to Petrograd. The pilot-flag Ransome carried to stake his claim was never used, but retained, and flown on his own boat many years later. Ransome describes Vologda as :

> ...a little, simple country town, white with snow. There was hardly a brick building in the place, but little log-houses of one or two storey's, broad untidy squares and street markets, with churches in every open space, white churches against the blue winter sky, churches capped with towers of every kind of intricate design, showing the great bronze bells hanging in their airy belfries beside domes of gold or green, of plain grey lead and of violet deep blue, thickly sown with golden stars. (AB 240)

Vologda is much the same today (1997), but there are many more brick/stone constructed buildings forming the main town, than when Ransome visited. It is a beautiful, isolated city and has an attractive river meandering through the centre with many gold-domed churches lining its banks, just as Ransome describes. It is a very Russian place, as different from St. Petersburg as St. Petersburg is from Newcastle! Shortly after the revolution of 1917, Vologda was closed to visitors, particularly those from the West as it

Vologda - Church of St Nicholas. Vologda is full of similar churches

Dissatisfaction at Home

became an exile area. In time, Lenin's sister, Stalin and Remizov, to name but three, would spend time in detention here.

Four months later, Ransome again made the journey to Vologda, but this time on official business with Radek from Moscow to act as an interpreter. The reasons for this exercise were similar to that undertaken for the earlier visit. Some Western Missions and Embassies looking for a safe haven had left Petrograd in favour of Vologda, which the new Bolshevik Government didn't like. It wanted them to return as they were thought to be 'at risk' and could not be guarded properly there. In fact, no such risks existed: it was all a ruse to get such Missions as there were back to Petrograd, where the Bolsheviks could keep an eye on them, and to prevent any Missions with ideas of leaving Petrograd to change their minds.

Because the railway line from Moscow to Vologda had been blown up, they were obliged to undertake the 800 mile journey round via Petrograd. They arrived in poor shape and very hungry. Accommodation was

Vologda - The building which was the American Embassy in Ransome's day.

provided at the Golden Anchor Hotel where both Ransome and Radek gorged themselves on 15 eggs apiece. So much for food rationing! As with the former visit, nothing came of it, and it all proved a waste of time. So they journeyed back to Moscow a few days later.

CORRESPONDENT IN MOSCOW

In March 1918, the entire Bolshevik Government vacated the Smolny Institute in Petrograd and moved down the line to Moscow. It initially installed itself in the Metropole Hotel for a period of three months, before taking up residence in the Kremlin. Evgenia joined Ransome at the Elite Hotel some time later. Ransome would remain mostly in Moscow until, with the approaching landings by the Allies at Archangel, his position and that of other British Subjects, would become unsafe.

Shortly after establishing himself in Moscow, Ransome made a flying visit back to his Glinka Street flat in Petrograd to collect some things. The flat was retained throughout this period. He contacted Lola.

> "Twin, will you do some shopping for me? I have got to catch the night train back to Moscow to-night; I promised to attend to this and don't know how I can manage it – I have so many other errands to do."
> "Why, certainly, A.K. I shall be glad to do it for you." I said, thinking that anything was good that would break the monotony a little.
> "Very well. Here is the list. It's books, so I know you will enjoy it. Just take a cab and go from shop to shop." And, handing me a closely written long list of books and some money, he departed.

Lola took a cab and went on a round of the bookshops. She spent an entire day finding books, getting two thirds of those on the list, which included *The Mexican Rebellion*, *Partisan War*, *Guerrilla Warfare and Tactics*. These titles puzzled her, although she had no time to look through them or think what they might be for. Ransome greeted her enthusiastically at the end of her mission.

> "Oh, how jolly, Twin!" he exclaimed. "Where did you find so many?
> By Jove, you have done well! Trotsky will be so pleased!"
> "What!" said I. "Trotsky? What do you mean?"
> "The books are for Trotsky. He couldn't get anything in Moscow; the best book-stores are all up here, you know, so I promised someone I would look around. Trotsky is building a Red army, you know, and, not being a soldier, he doesn't know much about it. So he is trying to learn all about it from books.
> And he is clever enough to do it, too."
> "Oh, great Scott, A.K! You are a pig, asking me to help your silly Trotsky with his army. Oh, A.K! I will never forgive you this." But A.K. roared and chuckled and went away, highly pleased with himself and his little trick and leaving me all disgruntled.

And that, as far as we know, was the beginning of the famous Red army.

That 'someone' mentioned in the foregoing piece almost certainly refers to Evgenia, as she was known to Trotsky, although she was still at the Ministry of Foreign Affairs at the time. As the months went by, Lola became more interested in the Bolsheviks and considered how she might join them. She was sure Ransome would know, and he had already sent her a note informing her of an intended trip up from Moscow. So when he arrived, she was surprised to hear that he had a proposal which would change all her plans.

> "Look, Twin," he said almost immediately, "you speak German, don't you?"
> "We do."

Dissatisfaction at Home

"And does Babushka know German too?"

"Oh, grandmother speaks beautiful German. And beautiful French. But why?"

"Now listen. If you and your babushka can pretend you are German, I think you can get out of Russia; you could all three get to Poland."

"But how?"

The new German Ambassador in Moscow was arranging for the transfer of all prisoners of war back to Germany. Ransome knew this, and that some of the trains would pass through Petrograd. His proposal was that they should leave the country and he would arrange passports for them. Within a few weeks it was all arranged; Lola, her twin and the grandmother left the country, and slipped out of Ransome's life forever. (No positive reference to Lola, her sister, or any of her family has been found in any of Ransome's letters, papers or diaries).

As the spring turned to summer in 1919, life for British subjects in Russia became increasingly difficult due to the deterioration in relations between the Bolsheviks and the White Russians. This situation became even worse with the impending Allied intervention to help the Whites. Ransome was aware of the situation, and in anticipation of problems should the White Russians get to Moscow, arranged for Evgenia to be put on his British passport. She would have been seriously at risk as a Government employee had they done so, but as luck would have it, the situation did not arise. In fact, she never used any passport or documents other than her own Russian ones and retained her maiden name up to the time she and Arthur married. By July the White Russians were making territorial gains. Those British subjects who had not left Russia were exposed to the possibility of internment should the Allied landings take place. In their separate ways, both Ransome and Evgenia were at risk, and this difficulty had increased by late July to the point where it became impossible for them to stay in Russia.

Evgenia's view of the political situation was changing and she had a pressing desire to move away from the centre of political activity. Her high profile job had left her feeling vulnerable and she was looking for some quiet form of employment. In late July, Vorovsky came to the rescue once again. He was looking for secretaries to staff the Russian Legation in Stockholm and offered to take Evgenia with him. On July 27 she left for Sweden by way of Berlin. In the meantime, the Lockhart Mission was ordered out of the Elite Hotel in Moscow and Ransome, unable to keep his lines of communication open, decided to go to Sweden also. As an exit point Finland was closed, due to the civil war raging there, but also because the British Government had asked the Finns not to let Ransome through. Radek, however, offered to help, by providing Ransome with papers as a Russian courier. He must have found this situation hilarious, having a Lettish interpreter with him to translate his Russian into English! The understanding being, that if the Germans stopped him, the Russians would stop a German in return until he was let through. He finally managed the journey via Petrograd and then took passage on a ship across the Baltic.

In early August the Allies landed at Archangel. It was an attempt to control German forces in order to prevent Allied supplies falling into their hands. It was also intended, once the first objective had been achieved, to do something about toppling the Bolshevik Government. Irrespective of how you look at it, the Allies did not possess sufficient resources to achieve the desired objectives, and in a way, displayed amazing ignorance of Russian conditions. The whole episode had been half-hearted and futile. A lasting legacy of the 'Intervention Policy', was the creation in the Russian Government of a suspicion of Western motives, which to some extent, is still with us today.

At the same time as the 'intervention' began, Ransome was on a ship which briefly stopped at Helsinfors for clearance. Although Evgenia had left Russia before him, he found on arrival in Stockholm that she was still in transit somewhere and he had arrived first! She eventually turned up a month later having spent most of the time in Berlin. A note to the Foreign Office from the Stockholm Embassy records: 'Mr Ransome has just arrived from Moscow travelling as a Bolshevik Courier on one of the Swedish ships from Petrograd. He has a Swedish visa permitting him to remain here for a month and proposes to keep in close touch with Bolshevik Legation. Ransome states that when he left Moscow on August 2 all British Subjects were well.' An immediate second note to the Foreign Office observes: 'Mr Ransome is working entirely on the side of the Bolsheviks and has a Russian mistress who was Trotsky's private secretary'. (FO371 3997) By 8 August, Ransome had applied to the British Embassy for permission to live in the Russian compound, but this was refused on the grounds that it would not be appropriate and could cause problems. As Evgenia could not live in the British compound, Arthur and Evgenia set up their first home together in rooms near the sea-approaches to the city. It was a pleasant little house which offered unlimited fishing close by – always a major consideration with Ransome. This address has proved impossible to locate and remains a mystery.

Evgenia's problems increased, when shortly after her arrival, Sweden (under pressure from Britain) decided to break off diplomatic relations with Russia, and to expel the Russian Legation where she was working. In the autumn the war suddenly came to an end, but the intervention by the Allies in Russia continued. Lenin's belief that the British, French and Germans would ultimately combine against the Bolsheviks, proved correct!

Attached to the Stockholm Embassy was a Major Scale. His business was Intelligence. He and Ransome knew each other from the time in 1917 when they were both attached to the Petrograd Embassy. During the autumn of 1918, some understanding between Major Scale and Ransome was reached including the sending of his newspaper reports back through the Secret Intelligence Service. The SIS suggested this subtle arrangement ostensibly with a view to making life easier, but more than likely because of a desire to exercise some (editorial?) control. In practice however, the arrangement with SIS was temporary, and did not amount to much. It is difficult not to conclude that in an association with the Secret Intelligence Services, Ransome saw such arrangements as one sided – much more as a benefit to him than it was for them.

Ransome and Evgenia remained in their rooms until late January 1919 before being expelled from Sweden. This proved to be a major crisis for Ransome. Having been out of Russia for nearly six months, he was a little out of touch as to what was going on in that country but he still had unrivalled contacts in the Soviet Government. So rather than return to England and lose everything, he and Evgenia took a calculated risk, and returned to Russia. Although Ransome had limited permission to bring Evgenia to the United Kingdom, his decision was almost certainly influenced, besides other considerations, by information that she was an undesirable and was not really welcome. Initially, the Bolsheviks had declined to allow him back, believing he was working for the Capitalist side, but a letter from Litvinov to the authorities in Moscow changed that. He reminded the Kremlin that Ransome was a journalist who could be useful in counteracting the interventionists, and it worked. Litvinov was in Stockholm at the time waiting for a passage to Russia. He had been interned in a British gaol and was exchanged for Lockhart, who had been in a Moscow gaol.

They left Stockholm on 30 January 1919 as part of Vorovsky's expelled Diplomatic Mission. Also included in the departing party were three other newspaper correspondents – two Norwegians and a Swede. Altogether, there were about 25 people in the departing party, including children. A Foreign Office memo to the Swedish Embassy dated the day after the Russian Legation left, wanted to know whether Arthur Ransome was remaining in Stockholm and if he was at present helping the Bolsheviks. The reply included, 'I understand that Ransome is working for our Secret Service but that he is not to be trusted.' (FO371 3997) The sea crossing to the Finnish port of Abo was prolonged due to ice, but on arrival the entire party was escorted to a train and guarded for the remainder of the journey to the Russian frontier.

In Petrograd, they found things very different. Gone was the fighting, the armed men and soldiers in the streets and the noise and general hubbub of Revolution. Instead, the city was quiet and almost deserted – the contrast was immediately noticeable. All accommodation, clothes and food were now rationed and controlled by the state. An application for a room (you were not allowed two) produced one in the Astoria Hotel, a place that Ransome knew well. There was no food and no heating – just hot water to make tea, and it was the middle of winter!

Litvinov, who had been in the party from Stockholm, wanted to visit the Petrograd Soviet, now established at the Smolny. Ransome decided to join him, and as the two men got on well, walked the two miles there together. They remained for the rest of day, with an invitation to stay to dinner by the Petrograd Commissars. No doubt Ransome was hungry by this time, but what was on offer was only soup with shreds of horse flesh in it! Later that evening, half the party decided to continue to Moscow on the night train, and Ransome, thinking it would be a good idea, decided to join them. Evgenia was with him all the time.

On arrival in Moscow, Evgenia went home to live with her mother and sister. She had no difficulty in getting employment with the city Department of Education – it was only her fifth job since leaving college.

A Guest at Scotland Yard

On arrival in Moscow, Ransome set about trying to get a room. Litvinov had assisted by providing a covering letter to Karakhan of the Commissariat of Foreign Affairs. Karakhan was described by Ransome as 'a handsome Armenian, elegantly bearded and moustached,' and by Radek, irreverently as 'a donkey of classical beauty'.

The new rules for accommodation required all foreign visitors to be housed in the Kremlin. Ransome was somewhat unhappy at this and asked Karakhan, who was able to obtain the necessary authorisation, if it was possible to have a room in a hotel in the ordinary way. Most hotels were full, but eventually one was found for him in the renamed Red Fleet. Conditions were poor, as Ransome records in *Six Weeks in Russia*: 'That night my room was so cold that I went to bed in a sheepskin coat under rugs and all possible bedclothes with a mattress on the top'. He slept very badly and next day went in search of a better room at the 'National'.

The 'National' didn't have a spare room, but Ransome learned that someone was leaving the next day, and the following morning successfully laid

Dissatisfaction at Home

claim to the room. It turned out to be a very pleasant one, next door to the kitchens and therefore not so cold. The two hotels were only a few hundred yards apart, so moving should have been a simple operation, but it was exceedingly cold and Ransome seems to have spent the rest of that day moving his things from one to the other.

All food was rationed. When paying for his room at the beginning of the week, he was given a card with the days of the week printed along its edge. This card gave the holder the right to buy one dinner a day, and when it was bought, that day of the week was snipped off the card so that you could not buy another. The meal consisted of a plate of very good soup, together with a second course consisting of a scrap of fish or meat. The price of the meal varied between five and seven roubles and the quality according to the cook!

The meal could be obtained at any time between two and seven o'clock. Living hungrily through the morning; at two o'clock Ransome used to experience relief knowing that at anytime he could have his meal. Feeling in this way less hungry, he would then postpone it hour by hour, and in the end actually dine around five or six. (Shades of his Chelsea days here!) Although all food was controlled, some could still be had at exorbitant prices through speculators on the black market. These prices were so prohibitive that they were beyond what Ransome felt he could pay. There was general starvation throughout Russia at this time, more through lack of transport, than through lack of food. The years of war and the later Allied blockade, had reduced the transport infrastructure to a fraction of its former capability.

Similarly, other conditions were extremely poor. Ransome records that even in the Kremlin, the ministers and their officials had no heating, but kept working by wearing their outside coats and from time to time, getting up to flex their fingers and wave their arms about in order to stop their hands from freezing. In the short term, however, the present complicated Russian situation required quite a lot of explaining, certainly more than could be crammed into a few newspaper articles. In order to overcome this hurdle, Ransome proposed to explain the situation more fully by producing a small book. Unfortunately, it was to be delayed until he returned to England, but *Six Weeks in Russia 1919* did come!

A total of one and a half months were spent in Moscow, devoted entirely to studying the new Government and its workings. Many meetings occurred with ministers and officials, which was an agreeable task, as he knew them all. These meetings produced a considerable collection of notes, which he hoped one day to use towards a book on the history of the revolutionary period.

So in spite of the physical hardship of being in Russia during this period, it is unlikely that Ransome was contemplating a return to the UK, partly because of the decision made in Stockholm to return to Russia, partly because of the perceived difficulty of obtaining permission to cross the Finnish border, partly because of the book requirements and partly due to the unique position that he now held in his relationship with all the leading Bolshevik figures.

Ransome had a list of the names of all Government Ministers, with their various ministries and telephone numbers, which he carried in his pocket. He also carried a covering letter signed by Lenin. This letter was an instruction that Ransome was to have free access to all the ministries. This was TRUST with a big T. So we can see what a unique position Ransome had – a position not enjoyed by anybody else! As a consequence, it is not an exaggeration to state that Ransome was by far the best connected and most informed Western correspondent in Russia by this time.

A journey to the UK came about because he was approached by two Americans, William Bullitt (later Ambassador to Moscow), and Lincoln Steffens (a left wing journalist) with a suggestion that London might find his knowledge of the Bolsheviks and their Government useful, particularly as there was a hint that there might soon be an end to 'Intervention'. Before he left he had his last interview with Lenin. Lenin's vision of a socialist Europe seems to have been centre stage, but Ransome listened and made notes. Before the two men parted Lenin asked Ransome if he intended to return, to which he replied, 'I should be very sorry to think that this was my last visit to the country which I love only second to my own'. Lenin laughed, and paid him the compliment of telling him that, 'although English you have more or less succeeded in understanding what we are about and I would be pleased to see you again.'

The three men travelled through Finland to Stockholm, then via Bergen and Newcastle to London. On arrival at King's Cross Station, Ransome was met by a man in a dark suit and bowler hat! He approached and said,

> 'Mr Ransome?'
> 'Yes'.
> 'You are required to come with me to Scotland Yard at once'. The head of the Yard wants to see you!

When they got there, he was shown into Sir Basil Thomson's office. The interrogation started:

> Thomson: (with serious intent) 'Now I want to know what your politics are'.
> Ransome: 'Fishing'.
> Thomson: (He stared) 'Just what do you mean by that?'
> Ransome told him the truth, that in England he had never had any political views whatsoever, that in Russia he believed that this very fact had let him get a

clearer view of the revolution than he could otherwise have got, that he now had one clear political opinion, which was that Intervention was a disastrous mistake, and that he hoped it would come to an end and release him to return to other interests. After a further hour of questioning the following morning, Thomson relented and eventually came round to accepting Ransome's viewpoint. Thus ended his arrest. (AB 267)

Ransome would not have known what Thomson reported to the Foreign Office. His report marked CONFIDENTIAL was dated 25 March 1919 and sent the same day. The following extract from his report makes it clear that Ransome was largely successful in conveying his feelings:

> ...It is quite true that he thinks that the Bolshevik Government ought to be recognized by the Allies, but says that that is quite consistant with refusing to allow their propaganda to enter this country. I am satisfied that he is not a Bolshevik in the sense that Price is; in fact, he spoke pretty strongly about Price. But he thinks that if something is not done soon, Russia will slip into a state of anarchy which will be far worse than the present situation. He appears to have been very closely in touch with all the Bolshevik Leaders, and is perfectly frank about what they told him. I think myself that we shall be able to restrain him from bursting into print. He wants to go to the country for six months to write a book.
>
> All he wants to be allowed to put in print for the moment is a description of the ceremony of the Internationale, which must have been very funny. He declares that he himself is absolutely anti-Bolshevik. He is seeing Boyce at M.I.1.C. [Military Intelligence] this afternoon, so I have not written out all he told me.
>
> He says that the great need of Russia is transport, and that he was earnestly asked by the Bolsheviks whether he thought that English engineers and locomotives could be supplied.
>
> (signed) Thomson (FO 371 3959)

The Foreign Office, however, took a completely different view. They interviewed Ransome at some length the day after the Scotland Yard visit, and an official recorded in their minutes:

> After 4 hours conversation with Ransome I believe he can do more harm in this country than even Price. Lenin would not waste two hours with him unless he thought he could be most useful to him here. What Lenin wants in England just now are people who will take up his policy and at the same time declare they are anti-Bolshevik. Ransome will do this to perfection, if not by writing, at any rate by talking to people.   (FO 371 3959)

No meeting of minds there. Although the substance of what Ransome said at these interviews was to prove correct, the Foreign Office, however, was aware of the numerous articles that he had published in the past, such as the one in which he criticised the British Government's internal policy and another forecasting that it would fall. Articles of this kind, especially when written from outside the country, did him no favours and antagonised many of the establishment. It is quite understandable to see why some officials of the Foreign Office, who had been offended with some of these early outpourings, particularly where they lacked credibility, mistrusted what Ransome had to say.

Other articles criticised aspects of the Government's foreign policy, which showed Britain generally in a bad light. There were calls to have him arrested and tried under the Defence of the Realm Act. One official thought a wire ordering 'British Subject Ransome to come Home' should be considered. But in the end, wiser council prevailed, and nothing happened. As another official later noted, 'this is politics and he hasn't actually done anything for which he could be successfully prosecuted.' It was also noted that, 'Price is much worse, and we haven't got any grounds to prosecute him'.

Another cause for concern was the Soviet style uprisings in Germany, Bavaria, Latvia and Hungary in the spring of 1919. Three of the uprisings were in January and the others in March and April. All these were eventually crushed, but not before causing a lot of worry and making the Government jittery. Perhaps this explains why the Foreign Office, who were interviewing Ransome in the aftermath of these earlier events, took the line they did in the comments quoted above.

So eight days after leaving Moscow, Ransome was interrogated like a criminal! The two gentlemen who had come with him were somewhat astonished! The gulf between what Ransome had spent years trying to achieve by reporting the facts on the ground, and what the British Government wanted to accept, was as wide as ever. He was incensed with his treatment by the Government in ordering Special Branch to arrest and interview him, but had, to some extent, become inured to the continual hostility of the Government to the new Russian order and their inability to see what was staring them in the face.

Ransome the Spy?

In Ransome's dealings with Russia from 1916 to 1923, particularly in publications and in the press, he has been accused of being a Bolshevik, a Red, a Communist, and a traitor to Britain. Included with these accusations is another that he has been a spy at different times for both sides. To some, he

Dissatisfaction at Home

was a Bolshevik sympathiser spying on Britain for the Russians. To others he was an agent of the British, reporting to one of the Secret Service agencies or the Foreign Office.

A spy is a person secretly collecting and reporting information. Was Ransome in this category? He openly talked to the Governments and Security Services of both sides, and was in the habit of mixing with diplomats, agents of many sorts, correspondents and military men of all nationalities. It is no secret that he was known to all the principal Bolshevik leaders and was trusted (up to a point) by them. It is also no secret that he was a convenient conduit for conveying what they were about and their ideas to the British Government. Nor is it a secret that, in spite of loathing all that Ransome appeared to stand for, the Government still found this trouble-maker, who spoke the Russian language and who had absolutely unrivalled access to the leaders of the Bolshevik Government, a convenient source of information, and carrier for their messages to the Russians. So did Ransome have any secret knowledge which he used to the advantage of one side or the other?

Between 1918 and 1923, a number of meetings occurred between Ransome and Lenin. All required appointments and all were carried out in a business-like manner. The preferred language for conversation was English, although a sprinkling of Russian crept in from time to time. In most cases, questions for which Ransome sought answers were usually submitted in advance. After the main business of the meeting was out of the way, and if there was still time, their conversation would range in a general way over the politics and subjects of mutual interest, but the meetings were formal although cordial, and were always conducted in an atmosphere of trust.

Rumour has it that Ransome and Lenin once played a game of chess, but this has been found impossible to substantiate, and is unlikely to have ever taken place. Even during his earlier days in Switzerland, anybody who wanted to meet Lenin required an appointment. Lenin's time was totally committed to the cause, there being little time for relaxation or jollity of any kind. Ransome also had some interviews with Trotsky on much the same basis. There does not appear to have been much, if any, informality at either the Lenin or Trotsky meetings.

Added to these meetings, were the hundreds of other appointments and interviews conducted with various Soviet ministers in the Kremlin. These were spread over a six year period, and may not have been conducted with as much formality as with Lenin and Trotsky. Not at any time was there any conceivable possibility that Ransome was acting other than in the utmost good faith. The mutual trust he had created between himself and the various persons that he dealt with depended on it. Perhaps if there is anything to be read into these interviews, and we may never know of course, it was that Ransome may have communicated in such a manner or used such a tone of voice, that he conveyed a level of importance higher than he actually had.

The all-important point for us in this, is to realize that Ransome carried out all his duties, whether for his newspaper, or for one government or the other, with COMPLETE OPENESS. Each side was well aware of what was going on – nothing was ever carried out in an under-hand manner or in secret. Ransome is unlikely to have had any secrets to offer the Russians other than those he was required to pass on – such were the constraints on his relationship with the British Government. Similarly, Russia had few secrets in those days, so he was unlikely to have had any. Ransome had access to every Government minister, all of whom were at pains to give him information if it would help their situation being explained to the West. There were times, when information Ransome brought to the British was considered important or of great interest, but it was never stolen or obtained by surreptitious means. Ransome could, more-or-less, only pass on the information he was given. We are talking of a period when the Russian system was in its infancy, and far from being the sophisticated administrative machine that it eventually became under Stalin.

So we can see that information passed to the British Embassy came with the full knowledge of the Russians, and vice-versa, and each was free to put whatever interpretation they wished, on it. Of course, it follows that occasionally what Ransome said may have been misinterpreted, particularly where news was not convenient or to the recipient's liking. We know that the British Government experienced difficulty because, their agenda was in conflict with the information that Ransome and others were giving them.

Ransome committed himself to reporting on Russia as he saw it and not necessarily in a way that governments, others, or his readers wanted to see it. It was this commitment which finally lost him the position of Special Correspondent with the *Observer*. He was passionate that Russia should get a fair hearing, and did everything possible to ensure that this position was not jeopardized. Not at any time did Ransome stray from this line. Those who would assume from some isolated action or temporary involvement with the Security Services of either side that it was otherwise, seem to us, to be misunderstanding Ransome's character, motive and objective.

Time and again in looking at the overall picture, Ransome had reported that the Bolsheviks were the only organisation with the necessary talent, energy, enthusiasm and organisational skills that were likely solve Russia's dreadful problems, and whether we liked it or not, they had come to stay. It is in this light that one should view Ransome's mode of reporting, and not

Dissatisfaction at Home

look at it as if it was just 'blind faith'. His many years of studying the political spectrum and being close to the decision makers had brought him to this view. It is difficult to believe though, that during their first few years in power, Ransome did not know something of the notoriety the Chekka had acquired in liquidating vast numbers of citizens who did not suit the Bolsheviks purpose. Surprisingly however, Ransome is somewhat silent on this aspect, which suggests that he may not have known the full position or decided to keep quiet about it. The Chekka in those early days, by the way, was only concerned with dealing with dissidents of the Revolution, and did not operate a spy network, which later became the hallmark of its successor organisation.

After the Autumn Revolution, Ransome had conveyed to the Foreign Office that the Bolsheviks were unlikely to be shifted from power. And so it turned out to be. The reasons why this would be so have been given, but it still took seven years for British recognition to take place – a vindication of his long battle, if ever there was one – and then, it was only after Stalin had come to power – the most brutal leader of them all!

Ransome didn't gloat, but all his prophesies ultimately came true. It is clear that some of the officials in the British Government, and particularly those in the higher ranks of the Foreign Office, were breathtaking in their arrogance. If only they had listened and understood it is likely that the whole relationship between Russia and the West might have been on a far better basis, and without the seventy years of mistrust. It is interesting to note, that in the letters sections of the serious press of the time, there was considerable support expressed about Russia for the very views that Ransome was reporting. There were also views expressed supporting the British Government.

There were the occasional very short periods when Ransome was on the pay-role of the Foreign Office, or Military Intelligence, which technically meant that he was their agent for the duration. In reality, however, this was always to cover expenses for those occasions when the task was outside that for which his newspaper employers could reasonably be expected to cover his costs. At no time did Ransome consider himself as an agent, in the literal sense, and if you had asked him if he was, it is almost certain he would have laughed in sheer amazement.

The truth about Ransome is contained in the words of the real British agent who worked with him and knew him well. In *Memoirs of a British Agent* [Putnam] page 266, Robert Bruce Lockhart wrote:

> Ransome was a Don Quixote with a walrus moustache, a sentimentalist, who could always be relied upon to champion the under-dog, and a visionary whose imagination had been fired by the revolution. He was on excellent terms with the

Bolsheviks and frequently brought us information of the greatest value. An incorrigible romanticist, who could spin a fairy tale out of nothing, he was an amusing and good-natured companion. As an ardent fisherman who had written some charming sketches on angling, he made a warm appeal to my sympathy, and I championed him resolutely against the secret service idiots who later tried to denounce him as a Bolshevik agent.

Perhaps the last word on this matter should be left to Ransome himself. In a letter from Stockholm to his mother in December 1918, the subject is covered at some length:

> Your letters are the greatest delight to me, especially when you harangue me about politics, and tell me the truth that I am not fitted to have anything to do with them*. I agree most heartily. I am no good at them and I hate them, and as you know it's only accident that I've had to take an interest in them. But there was no question about the compulsion. I should have been the worst kind of rotter if, having been sent to Russia to supply accurate information, I had given false information because it would have been more welcome. I've been through all my *Daily News* dispatches, and, modest though I am by nature!!!, I must say I was astonished at their accuracy, seeing that they were always written in great haste, and in circumstances which made it very difficult to get at the truth. Everything I have said about the actual nature of your loathed Bolsheviks, has been confirmed over and over again since. So I cannot find it in me to regret having told what I knew was as near the truth as I could get. As for me myself mixing in politics, I hope I never will. (Beg your pardon... Macaulay would have written 'shall'**). Quite apart from the fact that it's impossible, I rather gather from what friends from England tell me, that I have earned an unpopularity as colossal as it is undeserved. Malevolent devils seem to be inventing all kinds of lies about me. That, however, can't be helped, and lies however flourishing for a time in the long run defeat their own ends. I should be more worried about them if I were a politician, and not a mere writer who wants nothing more than to be quit of war and politics alike, and free to write fairy stories...
>
> Your affectionate son

Anyone writing a book such as this would almost certainly like to be able to report the unearthing of a spy, and we are no different. It would add a bit of spice, give the book that something extra and enhance sales enormously, but unfortunately we have to disappoint. Nowhere have we found anything positive, not even in Ransome's behaviour or circumstance which would genuinely qualify him as a legitimate spy.

---

*Ransome's father had been a Conservative activist.
**Ransome had been reading some articles by Macaulay (English historian and essayist).

To add to the woes of the British Government, a second front was opened up in the quest to deliver to British readers the truth about the Revolution and Intervention. The correspondent of the *Manchester Guardian,* Philips Price, towards the end of 1918, published a pamphlet called *The Truth about the Intervention of the Allies in Russia*. A white A5 sized document with large red lettering on the front and printed in Bern, set out the facts for all to see. This publication reported in quite a pointed way, all that Ransome had been saying for years, and more. The Foreign Office were not happy and wanted Price arrested, but could not find a suitable pretext on which to do it. Bruce Lockhart in a letter to the Foreign Office noted:

'Mr Price – undoubtedly clever and much more sincere in his Bolshevik sympathies than a journalist like Mr Ransome.' (FO 371 3988)

To add to the general difficulties, unhappiness with the contents of Ransome's reporting surfaced from another quarter. The censor in Washington complained that his reports were being published in the *New York Times* verbatim, and were damaging. The implication being that the British should do something about it, but as the Foreign Office reluctantly pointed out, these reports were only political and could not be censored however unpalatable they might appear to be. Ransome's reports covered many columns, were very full, and contained reasoned arguments. The official complaints died, while the reports continued.

Chapter VI
Ransome as Diplomatic Emissary

During 1919, Mrs. Ransome was staying at a house in Malling, Kent, and with a large amount of material and copious notes that he had brought with him, Ransome joined her there for a rest. He set about producing simultaneously, a report for the Foreign Office and a book, *Six Weeks in Russia 1919*. The book was published by Unwin and sold in large numbers. It set out what the political situation was really all about and aimed to show that support for the war between the White Russians and the Bolsheviks could not be justified.

Ransome had left Russia believing that the days were numbered for the policy of Intervention. Now he heard that, far from ending, it was to be expanded to include finance and equipment to enable the Whites to fight a major war. He also found out that he was barred from leaving England. With the news coming in every day of the advances being made by the Whites, he became fearful for Evgenia in Moscow lest the city should be taken, although he did record that he thought that such a situation was unlikely. Her chances of survival however, should such an event occur, he thought to be very poor.

Ransome applied to the Foreign Office for a document to enable Evgenia to enter Britain. He was genuinely concerned for her safety, and hoped that such a document would assist in getting her out of Russia, as well as facilitating what visas might be necessary depending upon the exit route taken. The application was banded about between various officials, but none were in favour of granting such a blanket approval, believing that Evgenia's presence in the UK was undesirable. They did concede, however, that if she presented herself at the Helsinfors (Helsinki) Embassy with her Russian passport, a conditional visa to enter Britain would be granted. Ransome was not happy about this, having devoted a considerable amount of energy and pressure to get what he wanted, but there was little he could do about it. The Foreign Office were not going to help.

The news he was hearing about Russia was depressing! Ransome was beside himself on hearing the information; that the Baltic Republics were now a base for White forces, Gen. Judenitch was moving his army towards Petrograd, Siberia was lost, the Ukraine had been taken, and Gen. Denikin was gaining ground in the south towards Moscow. The big problem for Ransome was how to get to Russia and get Evgenia out with all the UK Government departments ranged against him. He tried to kill time and console himself with lots of fishing. He dashed about the country trying various places from the Meon to the Medway, and from Norfolk to the Lakes. Games of chess and visits to friends also helped to keep him sane for awhile. Then a surprise call came from C.P. Scott, editor of the *Manchester Guardian*. He had read the recently published booklet, *Six Weeks in Russia in 1919* and asked him to make a visit. His reporting had clearly impressed the editor, who promptly offered Ransome the job of special correspondent covering Russia, Finland and the Baltic States; Price having gone off to edit other publications in Eastern Europe. He mentions the new appointment in a letter to his mother from Hampstead, dated 13 June 1919:

> The *Manchester Guardian* of yesterday had a two-column article on my book, in evident effort to outdo the *Daily News*, and today I have a letter from Scott, repeating his offer that I shall become their correspondent in Russia...

So desperate had Ransome become to get his papers back and get out of the country, that having discovered there were no sources in Russia able to provide up-to-date reports, he wrote to Ernest Boyce of the Secret Intelligence Service offering his services as the most suitable person for the task. 'It seems to me to be blazing madness for us to have no one in Russia capable of getting firsthand news at the top...' He went on to state how he was able to keep in touch with affairs, and his friendly position with the leaders of all the different political groups. Ransome clearly, was hoping that SIS might bring some pressure to bear on the Foreign Office to let him go. Unfortunately, the Foreign Office did not listen to this request and nothing came of it. How desperate Ransome had become was amply demonstrated by the trip he made (against all advice) a few weeks later to Moscow across the civil war lines.

Many weeks were to pass before, with the help of Lloyd George, the *Manchester Guardian* and Sir Basil Thomson (Scotland Yard), he was able to leave with papers for Norway and Sweden. Even then, the journey was not straightforward. The only available transport to Newcastle was by coasting steamer. He boarded the steamer in London with a pier-head jump, clutching typewriter, just as it was casting off. Further aggravation came on arrival at Newcastle, when the ship he was due to depart on could not get its coal bunkers on board because of a dock strike! But in spite of all the trials and tribulations, and with little fuel, the ship finally managed to get to Bergen on time for Ransome to catch a train for Oslo and Stockholm. Good fortune took the shape of a dirty little Estonian steamer called the *Kalevipoeg*, that was about to leave for Reval (Tallin) in Estonia. Ransome records in the *Autobiography*: 'Most of the woodwork in her had been torn out. She was in sore need of paint. She had no heating. Her decks leaked. But she moved, and brought me at last into the harbour of Reval, with the old castle on its rock, looking out over the bay.'

The way forward was still blocked. The problem confronting him was how to get to Moscow with a civil war raging? Any route would have to cross both the White Russian and Bolshevik military lines, and all crossing points were closed.

The political situation in Estonia was very unstable. It had become a newly independent state on the collapse of Germany, but felt undermined by the presence of a White Russian army still in the country near Reval. With this situation, their security was far from guaranteed. The Russians generally despised the Estonians and were against any form of independence for them. Judenitch's army were determined, once the Bolsheviks had been defeated, to return and deal with the 'potato republic' in a suitable manner! While the protective presence of the Royal Navy was welcomed, some Allied forces were also threatening a withdrawal of support if any diplomatic advances were made to the Soviets.

Ants Piip - Assistant to the Minister of Foreign Affairs. Later, State President.

The Estonians, it can be seen, were in a precarious position and therefore, forced to consider whatever alternatives there were for survival, irrespective of outside influences. The time for appeasing one side or the other had come to an end. It was time to do something and the first objective was to look for ways to stop the war with Bolshevik Russia. It so happened, quite independently, the Bolsheviks were also looking for a way to end the conflict, just as they had in the conflict with Germany. They had already intimated that they were willing to recognize Estonian independence, but it was conditional upon Estonians ending all support for Judenitch. This obviously put the Estonian Government in an awkward position.

Little of this was known to Ransome as his little ship sailed into Reval. He had been out of Eastern Europe for more than six months and was not abreast with the latest Estonian politics. It is at this point in the crisis then, that Ransome enters the story. He went to see Mr Piip, assistant to the Estonian

Minister for Foreign Affairs, and told him that he wanted to go to Moscow, and why. In reply Mr Piip indicated that the Estonians could fight no longer and wanted to make peace with the Bolsheviks. The objectives could be achieved at once if Ransome could get to Moscow – delivering a message for the Estonians, and getting Evgenia out of Russia. For practical reasons, this situation could not be made public, as it would convey the wrong impression with resident forces hostile to the fledgling state (see map in colour section).

Ransome agreed to take a note to Litvinov on behalf of Estonia, if a crossing point could be agreed between the two sides. Mr Piip agreed to send out a wireless message and asked Ransome to return for a further meeting after he had consulted with Otto Strandman, the Estonian Prime Minister. At their next meeting, Mr Piip and Ransome discussed the situation in detail. The Estonians concluded that very little could be done having received a refusal from Moscow to the proposal. Ransome however, was determined to get to Moscow by some means or other, whatever the cost, and nothing was going to put him off. Deciding that the refusal was not an adequate reply, Ransome scribbled on a piece of paper: RANSOME ALREADY LEFT FOR MOSCOW, then handed it to Mr Piip. 'Give me two days start and then send this', Ransome said. Piip was doubtful, but thought Ransome would be able to get through the Estonian lines.

Otto Strandman,
President of Estonia in October 1919.

A very sketchy account of the trip is provided by the *Autobiography*. Ransome says early on in this account, how twelve hours later he crossed out of Estonian territory into that controlled by the Bolsheviks, and was promptly arrested! Asked where he was going, he replied 'English correspondent, going to Moscow'. The local officer commanding informed him that he would be shot! Ransome replied 'it would be a mistake to do that', suggesting that if they made a mistake, they would not be able to put him back together again, but if not, they could always carry out the sentence later. This logic seemed to make sense, particularly when he mentioned that he was on his way to see Lenin. The soldiers did not believe him, but nevertheless, thought they would err on the side of caution and take him to battalion headquarters. With that, the affair became a tea-party – the officer becoming a charming host, even apologising for the quality of the tea.

At battalion headquarters, the commander was annoyed at Ransome being brought in instead of being shot, but the same logic worked here. His position was to be referred to a higher authority. Eventually it was decided to send him to Moscow under arrest, the last part of the journey being in a springless cart in charge of a young commissar. Long before they reached Moscow, they were on good terms with each other and talking freely. On the way to the War Commissariat, where he was due to be delivered, he stopped off at the Commissariat for Foreign Affairs to find Litvinov in his office reading the delayed telegram that Piip had sent on his behalf. Litvinov rang up the Commissariat for War and Ransome's difficulties were over.

Ransome went off to find Evgenia so as to advise her to prepare for the return journey. That evening they dined on a 'feast of potato-cakes eked out with a bottle of Horlick's Malted Milk Tablets', which they treated as sweets eating one after another. Visits to a number of officials followed, together with a visit to Professor Pokrovsky, head of the Commissariat for Education, to let him know that he was about to lose Evgenia, one of his most able assistants.

Before leaving, there was a meeting with Lenin, who informed Ransome that, initially he had not approved of *Six Weeks in Russia*, but after he had heard from Radek, changed his mind. Radek, currently in a Berlin prison, had praised it for the personalities and for showing the Bolsheviks in a new light as human beings – publicity which would do their cause no harm.

Ransome was anxious to get started on the return journey to Reval for his own and Evgenia's safety, and to let Mr. Piip know how his message had been received. They were provided with papers and assured that there would be no difficulty until they had left the Russian lines. Arriving near where the front was thought to be, Ransome hired a horse, cart and a boy, piled on their luggage and set off escorted by a single Russian soldier also with horse and cart.

The first night was spent in the semi-ruined house of a country doctor camped amid ferns and flowers. The following morning they continued with the occasional sound of firing from time to time. Coming to a small collection of farm people in the road they asked where the front was. The group stared at them and pointed in the direction from which they had come. With that the soldier and his cart turned round and drove off at high speed for home.

This group of people viewed them with suspicion, particularly having arrived with a Red soldier. Ransome said, 'We are on our way to Marienhausen; how far is it? And, can you let us have some boiling water to make tea?' The woman led the way into the nearby farmhouse, and while the water was boiling, Ransome set about burning every scrap of paper that might be misunderstood. The menfolk stood watching and began to talk amongst themselves, perhaps a little fearful of what they were witnessing. Then Evgenia came to the rescue! They were travelling with their own small tea-kettle and she noticed that the woman was 'eyeing' it. She said, 'We are going to England and will not need this. Would you like us to leave it with you?' A friendly smile spread over the woman's face. The men were still somewhat hostile as they finished their tea and got up to leave. Some of the men thought they should keep them as hostages, but were dissuaded by the woman. Once out in the road, Ransome turned to the boy and told him that they were now on the White side of the front, and would he prefer to go back? After a moment's thought, the boy said, 'I have brothers on both sides. It is all the same to me.'

Evgenia sat on top of the loaded cart, while the two men walked alongside. They must have made a pretty sight as they continued on their journey. At some point they were stopped by a soldier on horseback who questioned them on their destination, but nothing specific. A little later, galloping horses could be heard coming up from their rear. They kept moving. As the leading horseman caught them up, Ransome turned round and roared at him,

'Have you got an officer with you?'
They stopped and said they had not.
'Are you going to Marienhausen?'
'Exactly so, Excellency.'
'On with you and tell them I am coming.'

They saluted and continued on their way. On approaching the village they found a collection of irregular troops under the command of a non-commissioned officer. And once in the village met, 'an extraordinary collection of Lettish irregulars, Robinson Crusoes, some with fowling-pieces, a few with rifles, and some with pitchforks.' The lot being lined up as if on parade. All the people presented arms, pitchforks and all. The corporal, with a purposeful salute, stood before Ransome awaiting orders.

'Have you arranged lodgings for the night?'
'At once. At once, your Honour.'

The corporal went off towards some houses and secured a room for the night for them in the home of a Jewish family. Ransome asked for their luggage to be brought in, and for the horse and cart to be ready outside to leave at six-thirty next morning. Some apprehension surrounded these orders in case they were not met, but as it turned out, and to his amazement, they were. Also, of course, having burned all their papers, they had nothing to show that they had any right to be where they were. At six-thirty in the morning the cart, the horse and boy were all ready. Their luggage was piled in, and with Evgenia on top, set off on their way again. This latest success being due to a loud voice, and a certain amount of audacity. This sort of luck, as Ransome recognized, only worked with certain types of irregular troops.

They marched on and on, enjoying the morning sunshine, when at last they saw approaching a long column of cavalry. Fearing that this was perhaps where the luck ran out, they continued slowly, with Ransome smoking his pipe. The young officer in command stared at Ransome, and suddenly shot forward, pulled up his horse, and exclaimed, 'What luck! Now we can have that other game of chess! We were on the point of stopping anyhow.'

Ransome had last met this officer at Tarnopol in Galicia, when the memorable game of chess they were playing was rudely interrupted just as the officer was winning. He halted his men, field kitchens were set up, and while soup was being prepared Ransome and the officer had their game of chess. The officer won. Ransome mentioned that they were on their way to Reval. 'I'll give you a chit to our General,' he said, and told them where to find the staff. The rest of the journey was almost an embarrassment. The general was found in a railway siding and immediately put his carriage at their disposal for the journey to Reval with apologies for the cockroaches in it. So ends this amazing story.

These details, such as they are for this incredible journey, come from Ransome's published *Autobiography* – a principal source. There is, however, much that is missing, particularly when one considers that the distance from Reval to Moscow is close on 900 kilometres. It must be said, that with the Russian winter fast approaching, this sort of journey could hardly have been done by just some walking and the odd donkey ride or two! Perhaps he has just recorded the salient features for us, or the story has been slimmed down for convenience? Then there is also the question of the arrangements for the initial meeting with Ants Piip. How did he come to meet him?

Ransome left an assortment of notes and stories about this trip, some typed, while others are hand-written, and some are different versions of the same section of the journey. There is an additional account in a draft autobiography, and then there is the serialised version which was published in the *Manchester Guardian* during the spring of 1920, to consider. No one item or source, however, covers the whole journey in detail. This leaves the researcher faced with having to study the various contributions in order to come up with something approaching what could actually have happened.

Looking, therefore, at what has been left to us as a whole, we arrive at an account which differs somewhat, both in detail and circumstance from the one reported above from the *Autobiography*.

The journey to Russia via Reval was forced on Ransome merely because, Finland would not grant a transit visa. It seems, however, that Ransome could be 'at home', so-to-speak, with foreign politicians wherever he was. Mr Piip was, in all probability, a 'heaven sent' choice in whom to investigate a passage to Moscow. He was a former Assistant Professor at the Petrograd University prior to the October Revolution, and after it, a member of the Estonian Foreign Mission in the same city. It seems logical to assume, that Ransome must have known of him from that period. Ants Piip was present at the Dorpat peace-treaty meeting, which was attended by Ransome; he also enjoyed a rising career becoming Prime Minister, and later Head of State. He subsequently held various official positions but died in a prison camp in 1941.

After leaving Mr Piip on October 15, Ransome consulted with a colonel at Estonian Military Headquarters. He then left Reval on the night train for Valka. The train was unheated, which didn't make for a comfortable journey. Being so cold, he didn't get any sleep either and was irritable. On arrival next day, he went to the local army headquarters where he was able to have a wash and shave in the billet of one of the staff officers. General Peter was the officer commanding the unit and he made Ransome, as apparently he did with all visitors, inspect the barracks and sample the food that was given to the soldiers. Then there was dinner, with generous amounts of vodka and raw cognac. The General was a heavy drinker and very hospitable, but in trying to keep up with him Ransome developed a bad headache and became sick.

Later that same day, the journey east was continued by narrow gauge railway to Marienburg, (Aluksne on modern maps) and thence Maliup, to spend the night with an Estonian Captain and his wife (see map in colour section). At around half-past five the next morning, he set off for Seydenitz (Liepna) in a two horse-driven black chariot borrowed from a nearby estate. It was planned that Ransome would cross the border between the White and Red armies a few kilometres to the east of Seydenitz. When he arrived at the village, he found that fighting had broken out making the crossing impossible. The only alternative was to hope that a crossing could be made somewhere further to the south on Lettish territory where there was less activity.

By nightfall, the thirty kilometres south to Balovsk (Balvi – see map in colour section) had been covered, and sanctuary was sought in a large house. This building had been requisitioned by the Estonian Army, was pleasantly situated more-or-less between two large lakes, and provided agreeable accommodation for the officers who were most hospitable and insisted on revelling far into the night.

Early the next morning (day four, note!), Ransome was in a hurry to start, but there were no soldiers or carts in sight as the officers were still sleeping off their late-night revelry. This small town was in Lettish territory, so the population were reluctant to help the Estonians. Eventually at around half-past nine, three four-wheeled carts were procured together with some horses, and they got off. Each cart had a bale of hay in it for a seat, and some soldiers with carbines riding shotgun. The journey continued in silence for many miles, nobody wanted to talk. It was very cold and the men were very nervous. There was fear of the outlaws and partisan gangs thought to be roaming the area, and talking would distract their attention from keeping a good lookout for them. For the first few miles out of Balovsk they drove on an open road, through open country, although the road worsened when it passed into the forest. These roads were, in effect, no more than wide dirt tracks, and prone to numerous potholes filled with water, covered in branches or small logs.

Just after midday, the carts slowly approached two farms. As they passed one of the houses, the driver of Ransome's cart jumped down and ran over to a shed arrangement at the side of a house and grabbed an armful of dried peastalks with leaves and pods. He crammed them in between Ransome's legs and vaulted back up on the cart. An old woman, who must have seen the theft ran out into the open from a doorway, and stood there cursing and waving a clenched fist above her head. Ransome thought the stuff had been taken as fodder for the horses, but instead, the driver took a pod and split it, dropping the dried peas into his mouth – so hungry was he. Ransome by this time was also very hungry, but found the peas inedible and had to spit them out.

By early afternoon they were in an area where the state of the road was very bad and progress had become slow. It was also an area where spasmodic firing could be heard due to the proximity of the border, which was masked by woodlands and a swamp. Ransome and a couple of the soldiers got down off their carts and started walking on in front. The carts were quite some way behind when a figure appeared hurrying forward to meet them. He was a commander of Lettish irregulars with perhaps fifty soldiers under him. He explained that they were not on good terms with the Reds, but would do their best to help with crossing the border. Ransome and the commander set off for the Lettish staff office; the carts did not come any further as they were already within sight of the enemy, who held positions on a rise of ground on the far side of the swamp. The staff office was a peasants cottage with one big room, and housed a few children, one old man, three or four women and about a dozen young men.

A discussion of sorts ensued as to the best way forward. Little was achieved until someone mentioned Ignagtovsky, the old man who had a farm nearby in no-mans-land. With the old man in the room volunteering to take a message, the commander hastily scribbled a formal letter to the Reds. Addressed to the

Ransome as Diplomatic Emissary

Commander of the Red Company holding the post by the windmill, it described Ransome and said that he had all the necessary documents. It also contained a proposal that three Reds should advance to a ridge in the middle of the neutral ground between the fronts, and that three Whites should accompany Ransome to the same spot with nobody carrying arms. With the old man safely on his way with the note stuffed down between his skin and shirt, a gentle smoking haze settled on the room as everybody relaxed into general talk. After a while, the old man returned

'The letter has been delivered', he said 'Ignagtovsky sent it onto the Reds at once by one of the women.'

'And the answer?'

There is no answer. How could there be. I gave the note to Ignagtovsky, who sent it on. I came back'

Confusion seemed to reign. The Letts were not willing to leave the farmhouse and set off across the marsh in broad daylight without agreement from the other side, and the old man was not prepared to run any more risks. This left Ransome with a problem as it was now getting on for the middle of the afternoon and a crossing had to be made before dark. So desperate was he to proceed, that he was prepared to take a chance if he could reach the next farm. Further discussion persuaded the assembled people that he would try and get Ignagtovsky to take him to his farm in the neutral area if they could get him to the adjacent farm in between.

The commander was somewhat relieved that he and his men were being absolved of any further obligation to see their charge to the crossing point, so it was agreed! After a general handshaking all round and wishing of good luck, everybody stepped out of the peasant's cottage. The dozen irregulars left and carefully followed a circuitous route, so as not to be seen, to a position where they could cover the windmill area in the event of firing breaking out. The Commander left with Ransome on the short walk to the next farm with two soldiers following behind carrying the bags and typewriter. They continued along a wide track which was really a continuation of the same road, but due to the prolonged war, was looking disused. A few minutes walk over a rise and then into a little hollow brought them to the farm where Ignagtovsky was in the process of harnessing a four-wheeled cart.

Dressed in rags with long hair and an immensely long beard, Ignagtovsky was immediately identifiable by both sides in this conflict. He agreed to the proposition of the Lett Commander, that he would take Ransome to his farm in the middle of No Man's Land, and eventually, to the border. The Commander and his soldiers returned to the cottage having satisfied themselves that they would receive a report in due course that Ransome had crossed safely. Ignagtovsky placed a bale of straw on the cart for seats. The luggage was piled on, and they drove off out of the yard and along the track towards the Red trenches. Ignagtovsky was silent for a time, but made numerous side-glances at his passenger as he steered the cart along the track, perhaps wondering where Ransome's sympathies lay in this conflict.

Ransome asked, 'How do the Reds treat you?'

Ignatovsky hesitated a moment and said diplomatically, 'I have nothing against them'.

'And the White's'.

'I have nothing against them either. Some of my sons are on each side. No, I have nothing against either. If only they would stop fighting'.

He carried on criticising the war when Ransome asked, 'Are you Russian'

'No,' he replied, 'I'm Roman Catholic'. It seems likely that had Ransome asked him his nationality, he would have replied, 'from hereabouts' – so worried were the local population about being seen as favouring one side or the other.

Coming to his solid, log-built farmhouse, they were met by another old man who had come out to meet them. The interior consisted of a single large room, the logs roughly trimmed on the inner surface and left bare. A huge stove at one end had a large cubby hole behind it, from which two children inspected Ransome like inquisitive mice inspecting a prowling cat. A woman, who was raking the stove, turned and invited everyone to sit. She apologised for having no tea, which did not matter as the men preferred to smoke. After talking about the merits of different types of tobacco for awhile, the old man piped up, 'The letter has been taken to the Reds,' and Ignatovsky nodded.

Some discussion ensued about how these people survive in such a place with all the bullets and shells flying about. The old lady said, 'We can always get out of the way of the bullets, but the shells can land anywhere,' as if they were immune from one but not the other. 'We want the war to come to an end so that we can lead normal lives again!'

Then the woman, who had delivered the letter and Ransome's business card to the Reds came back. She was a short stumpy woman with yellow hair, and appeared somewhat younger than the woman of the house.

'The Reds will meet you as asked,' she said. Ransome, anxious to move, got up, but noticed that both the old men stayed put. They had changed their minds, were very reluctant to go any further and made excuses about their age and physical health etc.. The two women scolded them and thought their actions feeble. They would walk to the border alone. With the luggage split between the two women and Ransome, they set out from the farm with the two old men and the children watching them.

As soon as they were away from the house, the women turned the conversation back to the only thing that mattered to them. 'Are you going to make them make peace?' the younger woman asked.

'I wish I could,' said Ransome, and tried to explain. The old woman went on about how the English can do anything, and ought to make both sides stop the fighting because they don't really want to fight. Ransome tried his best, but it was clear that neither woman was able to understand irrespective of how detailed an explanation that he gave. When they were screened by some trees, Ransome gave each of the women some Tzarist roubles, which they seemed pleased to have, although, the younger woman at first refused, saying that she was pleased to do anything if it would help us give them peace. No doubt, her hopes and confidence were shaken a bit when Ransome pressed home the gift.

'There they are,' said the older woman. A hundred yards ahead and just below the windmill, there appeared some half-covered trenches with the odd head protruding above. The track along which they were walking was crossed by barbed wire with a closed gate, and then wound up over the rise towards some small buildings, the roofs only just visible behind the slope. As they got nearer, a man came out of the trench and was quickly followed by two more. Soon there was a group of men beside the windmill, clear against the evening sky, so clear indeed, that Ransome was worried in case they should prove a tempting object for any Lettish partisans behind wanting to settle a few old scores. Fortunately, nothing happened. Presently, three young soldiers separated from the rest, walked down the slope, opened the gate at the wire fence and joined the approaching group.

Ransome stepped forward with greetings, and showed them his passport and such papers as he had, as well as explaining his desire to get to Moscow as soon as possible. A short consultation ensued between the Red soldiers, after which they indicated that Ransome could come in, but would have to wait with the unit until further orders had been received. (Ransome's command of Russian was crucial throughout this episode, and without this ability, it is doubtful whether he would have succeeded)

The Red soldiers were surprised that there were no White soldiers with them. Ransome explained that he felt it unnecessary to bring them as the women could carry his bags and take back the message that he had been well received. Nevertheless, they were disappointed at not having a ceremony with parliamentaries on both sides, white flags, and all the pomp of a temporary armistice. The arrival of an Englishman accompanied by just two peasant women carrying bags was an altogether less exciting affair than they had expected.

With the bags and luggage divided up between some soldiers, the party made its way over the rise to the hut the unit was living in – a similar large, one-roomed peasant's cottage as the ones on the other side of the border. 'Are you hungry?' they asked. Ransome explained that he had had nothing all day apart from some dried peas.

'We can do better than that,' they said, 'though we cannot do much.' A samovar was soon boiling and they sat down to drink cherryleaf tea with slices of black bread. The Commissary was much more interested in Ransome's papers, particularly the letter giving him freedom to ask questions about the workings of Government departments, signed by Lenin. He stuck a candle on the corner of a table, and then went through the papers one by one.

It was getting dark outside, when a horse and cart turned up to take Ransome to battalion headquarters, where he would spend the night. A soldier was sent with Ransome to explain the situation to the battalion commander, but no other guard accompanied them, and even he was only going because of another errand. Those remaining at the post shook hands with those leaving, with a message to Ransome, not to forget a greeting from the front to Moscow, when he got there. The soldier vaulted up on to the cart and they set off. Ransome had only been there an hour.

The three kilometre journey was along a continuation of the same road, weaving in and out of small hillocks, and up and over small rises. It was quite dark and so he was unable to see the extent of the landscape as they came to a steep hill. The driver and soldier got off to relieve the strain on the horses. Ransome was asked to remain where he was, probably out of good manners, but he decided to join the others walking. Thinking it would be in his interest to know to what extent he was held as a guest or a prisoner, he stopped to light his pipe, and the cart quickly drew ahead up the slope leaving him on his own. Nothing happened. Nobody was bothered and he had quite a job catching them up. In a note, Ransome says, 'It was the oddest, most pleasurable feeling to be alone on that hillside in the dark already within the lines of the Russian Soviet Republic.'

They came at last to a village and drew up in front of a large one-storey house. Many people were in the warmish room as they entered from the road, and Ransome's glasses steamed up temporarily blinding him. Continuing through to an inner room, Ransome found a hive of activity as the battalion commander and another officer were busily making preparations for the garrison to be relieved during the night. It was agreed that Ransome would spend the night here and go on to regimental headquarters early the next morning. With that, a bench was found, and he stretched out falling instantly asleep after such a long day. An hour and a half later he woke up, caused by the pain of his metal compass in the hip pocket digging into his back. When he opened his eyes, the Commissary was standing looking down at him. 'I was

Moscow, Kremlin. Offices where Evgenia worked.

Maliup (Malupe). Ransome spent the night here and borrowed a two-horse black chariot next morning from a nearby estate for the next stage to Seydenitz (Liepna).

Balovsk (Balvi). Ransome spent the night in this building which
was used as a barracks in the civil war. Now a school.

Dirt road (2001) from Baltinovo to Marienhousen showing forested areas, little changed since
Ransome's time when he and Evgenia passed this way with their carts. The war front between
opposing sides was in this area.

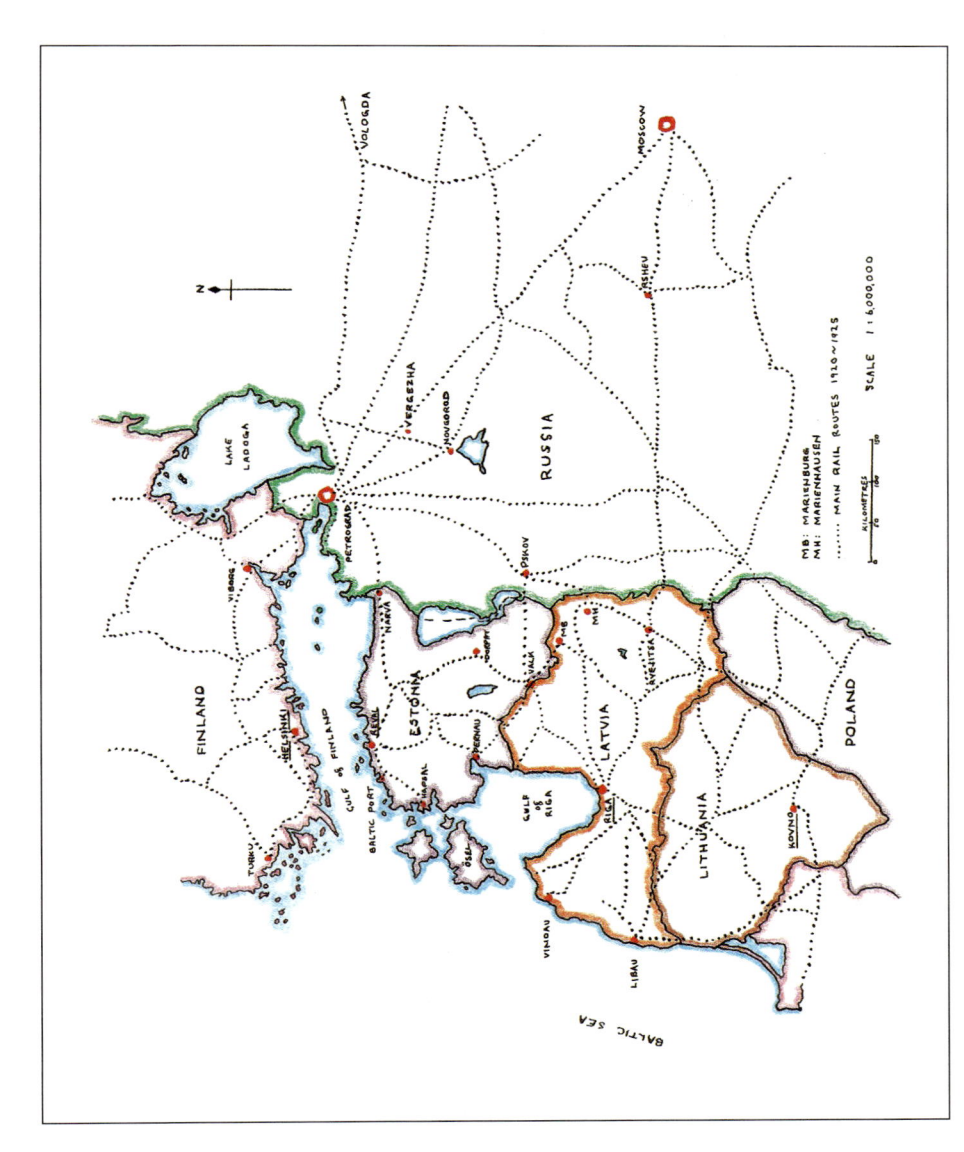

Map of Western Russia and the Baltic covering Ransome's 1919 route from Reval to Moscow.

Baltinovo (Baltinava) to Marienhousen (Vilaka) dirt road showing open country areas. The road is wider and better maintained than in 1919.

Smolny. Trotsky's office had the last two windows to the right of the large window under the roof.

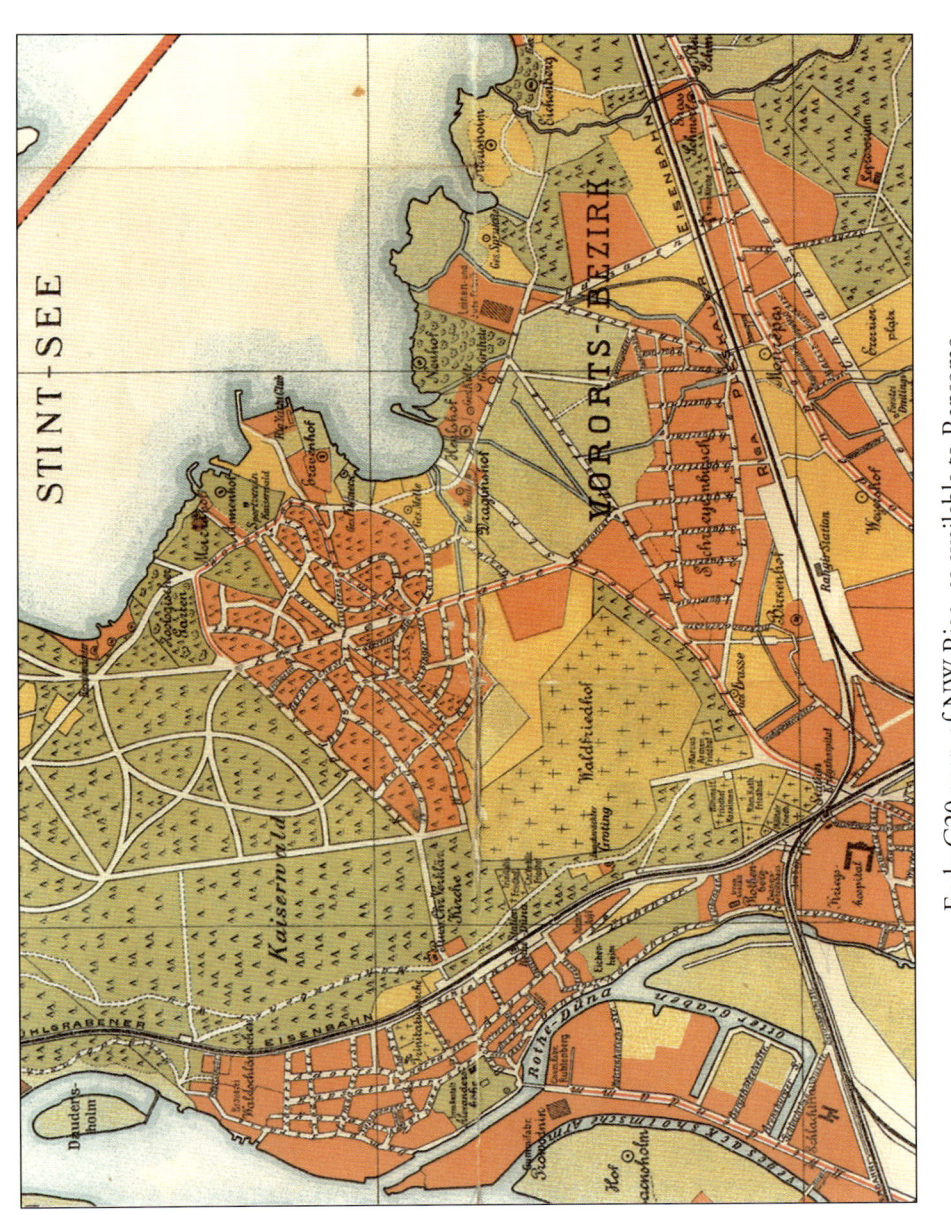

Early C20 map of NW Riga, as available to Ransome.

No 25 Stralsunder Strasse. The house next door and similar to the one Ransome lived in the Kaiserwald area of Riga.

Alexandro-Nevski Lavra. Trinity Cathedral.

This page, Trotsky's office in the Smolny.
Overpage, Evgenia's office as she left it in 1918.

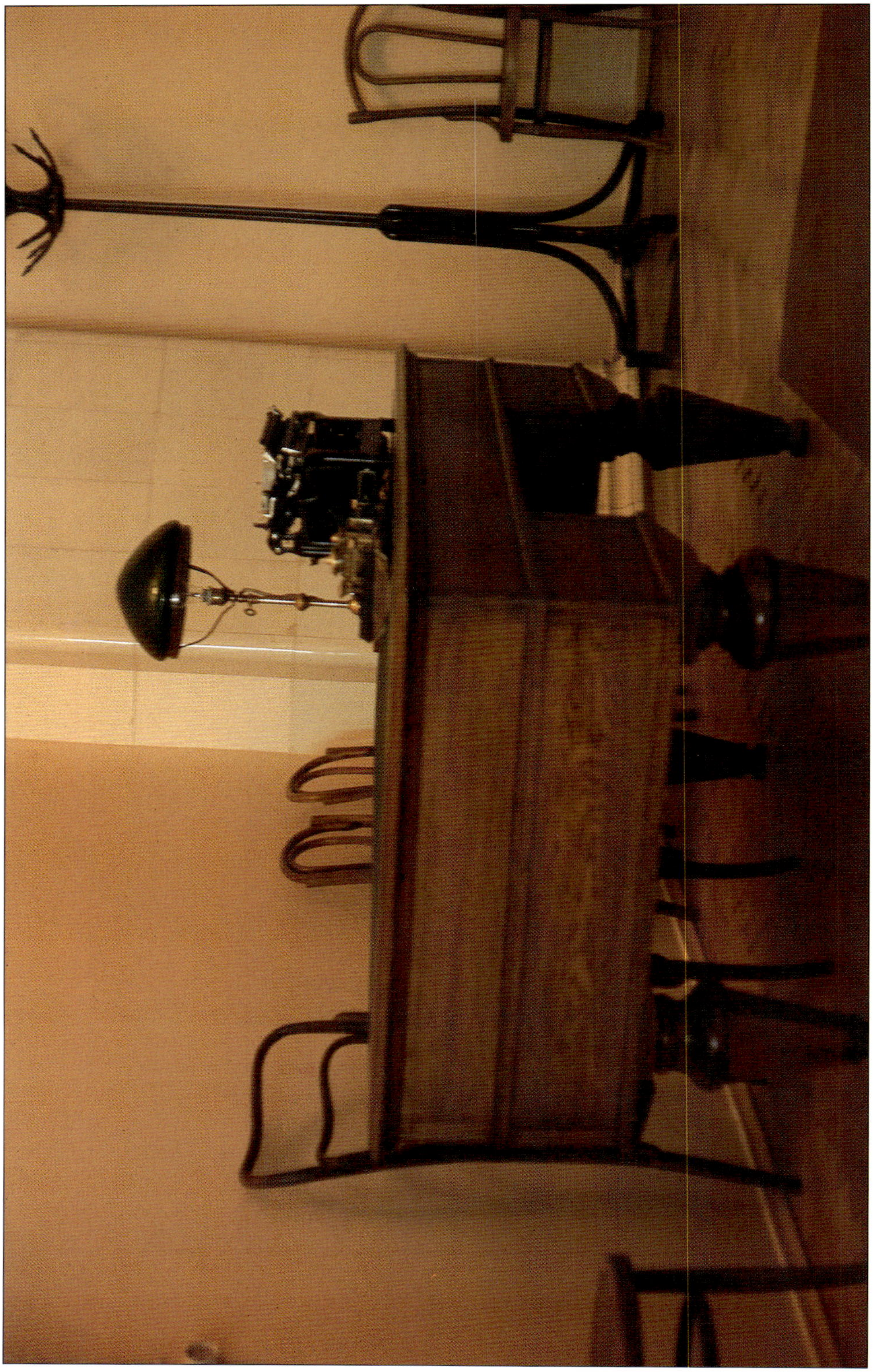

wondering if you were asleep,' he said, 'or if you would like some tea. The master of the house has a samovar boiling in the next room.' Ransome rolled off the bench and joined the Commissary and the local commander in an adjacent parlour with the owner of the house, for tea.

It snowed during the night, and was still snowing the next morning when Ransome woke at half past six. He found a man with a cart waiting to take him to the regimental staff headquarters – it was day five. It was very cold as they set off. The road was much better than the last two days and lay in almost a straight line over slightly undulating countryside, with patches of forest here and there. They approached the regimental staff unit, but found it was in the process of moving, and were redirected on to Bukovoe for further orders. The Lettish driver, reluctant to go any further, said he didn't know the way. He was hoping to get out of it, but detailed directions were given, enabling them to set off at a slow pace in the snow and slush on the eight kilometres journey to Brigade headquarters.

The road was very wet and deep in melting snow and mud. Sometimes they had to walk when the cart wheels slipped into deep ditches at the side of the road or when they came to hills. Progress was very slow, and both men were suffering from extreme cold. The forest sheltered them for some of the time, but usually they were in open countryside and faced the full force of the weather. Six hours of travelling had made them very tired and they longed for a rest, when, to great relief, an assortment of white buildings came into view on a rise away from the road. This was Brigade Headquarters, situated on a low hill above a river. In one of the buildings there was a large room walled with maps, orderlies hurrying in and out and a soldier banging away on a typewriter with two fingers!

A tall officer in the uniform of the old army turned from his table and asked Ransome what he could do for him. Ransome replied that most of all he wanted something to eat, and to be allowed to continue the journey as soon as possible thereafter. 'As for something to eat,' the officer said, 'I am shortly going over to my own quarters where there will be some sort of dinner ready in an hour. As for the other part of your business, it depends not on me but on the Political Commissary, who will be joining us for dinner. Perhaps you will make your way across the river and make yourself at home in my quarters.' Ransome did this and presently, the officer came in and took off his boots, inviting Ransome to do the same. Over dinner a long discussion ensued between Ransome and the officer over aspects of the war and the likely outcome.

The Commissary appeared from time to time, but didn't stay long as there were operations in progress at the front. This activity prevented Ransome from getting the next stage of the journey arranged. Until this could be done, it seemed a good opportunity to make some notes on the trip so far, but having had very little sleep during the previous few days, he soon found he was too tired to work. Going outside, he found to his surprise, a soldier set by the door as a guard. Ransome was somewhat annoyed at this, but attributed this precaution to the Commissary. Back in the room, a bed was close by which had a programme of the Communist Party on the pillow. He laid down on what must have been the Commissars bed, and hardly had time to wonder what the Communist Party Programme was all about before falling soundly asleep.

It was already quite dark when Ransome was woken by someone flashing a candle in his face. A boy of about eighteen, in a uniform much too big for him said, 'Are you the Englishman? They have telephoned that you are to go to Korsovka [Karsava] to the Staff of Division, and I am to go with you.'

Ransome was up in a minute, but there were considerable difficulties in getting a horse, and it was not until half an hour later that they were on the road to Manchero. The boy and Ransome sat side-by-side on a bundle of hay in a cart, the boy clutching a large loaf of bread, and Ransome trying to spare his typewriter from the jolting. They chatted idly about the war, the boy being particularly interested in Ransome's travels and his visits to Moscow.

They got on well and Ransome warmed to him. The Revolution, the boy said, had interrupted his studies. He had intended to read history at university. 'Now I suppose I shall never be anything but a soldier: but perhaps I am nearer to events than ever I should have been in the university library.' He was the typical idealistic young man, having been brought up in a Bolshevik family, and genuinely hoped his side would win the war.

Korsovka (Karsava) railway station. Ransome passed through on his way to Moscow and on returning with Evgenia, arranged horse and carts here for the dangerous journey through the civil war lines.

At Manchero Station they obtained two glasses of tea. Ransome offered his driver some of his saccharine as there was no sugar anywhere, and sweeteners were new to him. He was very reluctant to take this strange stuff, but with difficulty was persuaded. Yet when he took some, he drank his tea like nectar!

Two seats were obtained in a little box in the front wagon attached to the 'Letutchka', a train of cattle trucks operating near the front for carrying away the wounded. There were seven people in the box huddled together which helped to keep them warm. At Korsovka they drove from the station about two kilometres along a fairly good road to the Staff of Division. It was about one o'clock in the morning when the two travellers arrived at this large house on the road leading into the village. An officer of the Staff was on duty – an officer of the old army, very smart, wearing the insignia of the Red Army. The Bolshevik boy handed Ransome over, so-to-speak, and having done so, sat down on a seat next to the stove, and instantly fell asleep like a tired child.

The young officer apologised for the delay caused at Bukovoe, and sent a soldier to wake the Commissar, who presently arrived, sleepy and inclined to be cross, but forgot his annoyance in the interests of talking to someone from the other side of the front. He advised Ransome that another train of cattle trucks might be going to Rejitsa (Rezekne) in the early morning and that there was just a chance of catching the connecting train to Moscow. He also added, that although they did not want him to think that he was a suspect, they would have to send a soldier with him to Moscow. Ransome records that he was very glad about this, as he would be assured of a trouble-free trip. Papers were accordingly made out for a certain Dragunevitch (the soldier) and Ransome.

Presently Dragunevitch turned up, and though rubbing the sleep from his eyes, gave the impression of being an efficient companion, for he carried a bag complete with bread and rations for the day. 'Apples,' he added, 'We can buy in Rejitsa.'

Such little touches appealed to Ransome. Dragunevitch was an orderly, and probably typical of the class of Russians whose education had been cut off by the war. He explained that he had volunteered while under age, but was now not fit for anything except to continue as an orderly having the instincts of a gentleman. As for education, he was able to read and write, but had forgotten almost everything else other than the names of a few European capitals. Ransome found him a talkative companion, capable of silence, but with a great sense of humour, and a love of self importance (Ransome heard him in conversation with some fellow passengers on the train telling them how he had accompanied him from England, after which to avoid difficult questions, he withdrew, looking anxiously at Ransome to see if he had detected his silly game). All the same, he was an excellent companion.

At Korsovka station it appeared that Dragunevitch was on the best of terms with the Commandant, who let them wait and drink cherry leaf tea in his room until about six o'clock, when another train arrived with cattle trucks of wounded from the front. They climbed into a wagon and sat uncomfortably on their luggage for the horrible journey. At every stopping place they could hear the groaning of the wounded fellows in the next wagon, but while the train moved, these sounds were drowned out by the bumping or clanging and squeaking of the wagons.

The Moscow train had left by the time they got to Rejitsa. The next train was not due for another eighteen to twenty hours or so. Leaving their luggage at the station, they walked into town and sought a room in a hotel somewhere.

Rejitsa was a muddy little town, reasonably well organised to all appearances, but suffering seriously from the prolonged war. There was nothing in the shop windows except old rubbish. Ransome wanted to buy a couple of glasses for drinking tea, but was unable to discover any source. The market, on the other hand, was crowded. There was plenty of earthenware for sale, some material and goods at big prices. Salt fish, some brown bread and apples were available at twenty-two roubles a pound.

Rejitsa (Rezekne) railway station. Ransome killed time here with a game of chess while delayed on his return from Moscow.

The town being within the military zone was very strictly organised. Thus they could not get a room in a hotel without an order from the Commandant, which however, Dragunevitch was able to obtain on showing their papers. To add to their difficulties, the town, having the first large railway station behind the front, had been turned into some kind of trap for deserters and spies. After getting a little room in the Hotel Continental (which in 2001 no longer exists) or the promise of it once it had been cleaned up, they went across the road to a restaurant kept by a Jew advertising 'good dinners' on a dirty piece of cardboard in his window.

Two dinners were obtained, soup and meat, dirty but otherwise not bad for nearly two hundred roubles. Time was passed drinking weak tea and listening to the Jewish wife, who was sitting in a corner of the room and complaining to a friend of the gross familiarities practiced by her husband with some young woman of the neighbourhood. Suddenly an officer, accompanied by a soldier marched into the room and demanded their papers. Having expressed himself satisfied with the papers, he turned to the woman asking if she had anyone else in the house. She said not, but the officer insisted on inspecting the premises just the same. After dinner they went for a short walk and returning to the hotel, found their little room cleaned and ready for them.

The hotel was a small one-storey wooden house beside a stream, which ran under the road. In the passage to his room, Ransome bumped into a little pig trotting up and down. Finding Ransome's door ajar, he pushed in as they arrived, investigated the room noisily and thoroughly, and quite undismayed by their presence, took his time, and then trotted out into the passage to try another door.

Both men were tired and decided on some rest, but later got up, washed and shaved. While Dragenevitch went off to find out what time the train would leave for Moscow, Ransome explored the back of the premises and found the housewife in the kitchen. She was preparing potatoes and cutlets for supper – a share of which was requested. There was a pretty daughter too, who took a hand in the potato peeling. She said that she only knew a few words of English, but would not divulge what they were. Both mother and daughter were very friendly, and seemed to have no resentment towards the English although, like everyone else, they wanted to know when the British were going to get peace for them.

In the evening they had an excellent supper, for approximately the same price as the dinner. A prior arrangement had been made with a cab to take them to the Moscow station, but it

Rejitsa. Ransome rode in a cart along this cobbled road from the station into town.

turned up at 8 o'clock, some two hours before it was required. As a permit was needed to drive a cab after nine in the evening, they decided to leave straight away, saying goodbye to the housewife, her daughter and the little pig.

Dragunevitch, spurred by his own goodwill and quite unjustified sense of importance, had flourished his papers from the Divisional Staff to such good purpose that they succeeded, when the Moscow train arrived, in getting a couple of top berths in a cleanish carriage. It is a long established tradition in

Russia that he who obtains a top berth and spreads himself upon it remains in undisputed possession. The occupants of the seats below cannot lie at full-length without disturbing their fellow passengers. In the compartment, meant for four persons, there were, in fact, ten. Four sat on each side below while Ransome and Dragunevitch lay out on the boards above. The passengers on the seats below kept up an almost continuous chatter which made sleep difficult, but in between listening, getting some sleep and making tea, they very pleasantly arrived in Moscow the following day, the 22 October

It had taken approximately one week to make the journey from Reval to Moscow, which was much longer than it is reasonable to suppose, he thought it would take. Once clear of his guard, Ransome checked into the National Hotel, which had been more than likely arranged by one of his contacts in the Kremlin.

Return to the West

A round of visits to important Ministers, as outlined in the earlier *Autobiography* account, took place over the next few days. On 27 October, for some unaccountable reason, Ransome was prematurely ordered to leave the National Hotel. No explanation for this has been found. There is a possibility, however, that there was some disagreement between Ransome and Litvinov over this, or something. Bucharin tried to intervene and smooth things over, but again, no details have been found. A disagreement between Ransome and Russian officials was unheard of! When Ransome and Evgenia visited Litvinov for the last time, he gave them a peace offering of six apples and two cigars! So there was something, but whatever it was, remains a mystery! On that evening, the last tea was had with Evgenia's mother before departing the next day for Estonia and the UK.

When planning the return journey, the Russian Government, on behalf of Ransome, sent radio telegrams to the Estonian Government with a view to arranging a crossing point. On 23 October, an intercepted message from Petrograd to Mr Piip, went as follows:

> Arthur Ransome and his wife are leaving on Sunday and are returning by the route by which he came. He requests that arrangements should be made for him and his wife to pass through.

Whether this message was acted upon or not is unclear because, on 29 October another wireless message was sent to the Estonian Government requesting facilities for Ransome and his 'wife' to pass through the front. To confuse the issue even further, Litvinov, in a message to Ransome, asked him to wait once he got into Estonia! A Foreign Office official at the time, was moved to observe on seeing transcripts of these messages: 'It is rather amusing to find this woman called Ransome's wife in a wireless message! I do hope the real Mrs Ransome does not mind. Ransome has evidently got into and has also nearly got out of Russia'. And while all this was going on, British Military Intelligence was advising the Foreign Office to tell Mr Piip not to allow the Ransomes to pass through the Russian front into Estonia. Mr. Piip, however, would not have been listening to any of this advice, knowing full well the mission that Ransome had carried out on behalf of the Estonian Government.

Ransome and Evgenia left Moscow by train on Tuesday 28 October for the 640 kilometre journey to Rejitsa. It was uneventful and they arrived at 4 am the following day. Unable to get into the town at that early hour, their enforced stay at the station afforded Ransome an opportunity to have a quiet game of chess. The man on duty with whom he played the game, later locked up their luggage at the station while they went into town and got a room at the same Hotel Continental. There was no sign of the little pig this time round! The day was spent resting and preparing for the next stage of their journey.

They were up early the next morning and were on Rejitsa station long before dawn. It was very cold, with the temperature way below freezing as they waited for a train to Korsovka. A small train of cattle trucks on its way to the front pulled in and stopped. Some space was found on the floor of a truck and by laying out their luggage, there was somewhere to sit. It was an uncomfortable forty kilometre journey, with body and soul kept together only by lighting a small fire on the floor of the wagon.

At Korsovka they lunched with a Commissar, who apologised for having nothing to offer but soup, saying that food cost so much and that apart from money having so little value, only dishonest men had any to spare.

'In the old days we judged men by how much they had in their pockets. Now anyone who has much in his pocket is ashamed of it, for he cannot have come by it honestly.'

After reading their papers he arranged for a militiaman to accompany them to Marienhausen (Vilaka - see photograph in colour section), where a regimental staff officer would see to the details and formalities necessary for crossing the front. Everything was to be done in a most ceremonious manner, and he signed and stamped instructions which they were to hand to the Regimental Commissar. As it turned out, they never met him. Their actual crossing of the front became accidental owing to the line between the

Ransome and Evgenia, Moscow.

Thought to be the photographs used when Lockhart illegally issued them both with passport documentation during the summer of 1918.

Ransome as Diplomatic Emissary

opposing sides continuously moving back and forth. Telephone communications to the front did not exist and nobody was able to advise precisely where the front was.

Some idea of this situation reached the Commissar just before they left. He came hurrying red-faced from the staff office with the news that there had been fighting at Marienhausen that day! He was uncertain whether to let them proceed, but said 'Well if you do run into the thick of it, you had better sit tight in the first cottage you see, and wait there until the Whites capture you.' Ransome agreed, but the Commissar was clearly unhappy about it, and the last they saw of him he was standing in the road watching them in obvious gloom.

Ransome and Evgenia set out then from Korsovka into the unknown. They had two little wooden springless carts. In one was a Lett driver with a militiaman carrying a rifle and half the baggage. In the other, driven by a small boy, was Evgenia and the rest of their bags. Outside Korsovka, the carts turned off the main road to replenish their hay for the journey, and knowing that they would overtake him, Ransome went on alone on foot, walking hard and stamping on the frozen ground in an effort to get warm. There was bright sunshine with no heat in it, a hard frost, and a wind that chilled to the bone. The country was hilly. At least it would have been thought so in Russia. There were dips and rises, never very steep. There was always forest in sight and only now and again a glimpse of a distant horizon (see photograph in colour section).

It was already dusk when they came to Batinovo (Baltinava), the village where Ransome thought they would spend the night. There was no one about. Many cottages were passed, all of them empty. There were no lights anywhere. The front cart with the militiaman stopped. He got out and came back to consult, and Ransome got a sudden glimpse of the vagueness of this kind of warfare. 'Something has happened' he said. 'Perhaps the Whites are in the village.'

So Ransome's cart went ahead with the other close behind it, as Ransome would probably be able to be better than he at explaining things should the Whites be in possession. They drove on into a deserted village, and stopped by a biggish cottage. A flag was flying at the door, but it was too dark to see its colour. Both drivers were in a state of nervous panic, and Ransome dared not leave them for fear they would bolt for it, baggage and all. So they collected in a group by the front door of this cottage and, leaving Evgenia with the carts to shout if there should be any problem, started banging on the door. The place resounded with the peculiar echo of an empty house. Suddenly a voice close by in the darkness asked 'What is it?' Ransome explained, as it were, into space. Someone pushed by to the door, unlocked it, walked in and asked Ransome to follow.

The man felt his way about inside, found a candle, lit it, and held it while they all looked at each other. He was a stout, jolly fellow, a leader of guerrillas or partisans. 'Lucky you did not come yesterday' he said. 'The Whites came in ten days ago and we only cleared them out this morning.' Ransome asked if there was anywhere where they could get something to eat. The man said there was, and presently they were all walking away in the dark over ditches and holes in the road followed by Evgenia controlling the two carts and their much relieved driver. He took them to the home of a feldsher (partially qualified doctor) who had remained throughout the White invasion. Practically everyone else in the village had fled.

The feldsher lived with his wife, three children, five dogs and an enormous collection of palms, ferns and other plants in pots in a largish one storey wooden house. He could not go away, he explained, because of his plants, otherwise he would have left when the Whites came in. They asked if they had treated him badly? 'Not at all.' On the other hand they had made much of him as the sole representative of the population. But he had had to feed a lot of them. He and his wife fed Ransome's party also and were surprised when they insisted in paying them. Some beds were made by placing planks of wood across the seats of chairs in the room with the palms, cactuses and huge ferns. The dogs prowled in the undergrowth and some kittens lost themselves noisily behind a great barricade of flower pots.

In the morning the two little carts were ready in the yard. It was very cold with a hard frost, but bright sunshine and less wind than the day before. Travelling was pleasant, and they went forward at a good pace on a road in very decent condition. They had travelled about six miles through country like southern Wiltshire, before they were stopped by a patrol – a very unhappy officer with a dozen men, who let them pass. A little further on they were stopped again. The officer who examined their papers was obviously surprised when he saw that the party was headed for Marienhausen. But he ironically wished them luck, and let them pass. That was the last they saw of Red troops. They drove on enjoying themselves mightily in the bright sunshine. Shooting was heard to the left, and rather unexpectedly to the right, as well. It was very cold. Now and then they walked while the little carts climbed a hill, now and then holding their luggage, while they rattled down the other side. They had driven twenty versts (old Russian measure of about two-thirds of an English mile). Nothing of particular interest happened until only they had another eight versts to go, when they came to a group of people outside a farmhouse at the side of the road.

Ransome thought it was a good chance to get warm, so he jumped off the cart and spoke to the oldest man. He learned that the Reds had left

Marienhausen, that the Whites might be there at any minute, and that they had left the last Red outposts far behind – probably the half company who had stopped them at the side of the road some miles back. All the luggage was transferred to the one cart and, Ransome gave the militiaman a paper to show that he had done his duty by them. Worried about his position, the militiaman immediately turned round and headed back the way they had come. They were shortly joined by a Jew driving a cart, who willingly took some of the baggage, possibly as some sort of passport for himself.

The old Kulak, (original driver) whispered a warning to Ransome not to trust the Jew. 'I know him and I do not like him', he said.

They had driven on a few versts when a military horseman riding out of the forest came at a fast pace along the road, carbine slung across his back. They had no idea whether he was Red or White. But as he came close up, the blue uniform signified that he was Estonian.

'Where are you going to?'

'London', Ransome replied.

He laughed, and Ransome explained they were on their way to Marienhausen, and asked him who they might find there.

'Go ahead', he said finally.

The Jew explained that he was carrying luggage for the group, and was allowed to pass.

Further on other scouts passed going in the opposite direction. They stopped them, and the Jew told them they were going to Riga, apparently the only place he could think of. Then they rode forward, and Ransome gave them the same answer as he gave to the earlier soldiers, but they seemed dissatisfied, so a high tone was taken, and they were then asked if they would be good enough if they were riding on to Marienhausen, to confirm to their staff office that the group was coming so that some sort of lodging might be ready for when they arrived. This piece of impertinence did what was necessary, and they very courteously promised to do their best for them, saluted and rode on at a gallop.

At dusk they came into Marienhausen. The cavalry had already gone and there was no one of any authority except more Lettish partisans, who did their best for them, did not ask for any papers, (which was lucky because they did not have any) and gave them a soldier to requisition a room for them.

This soldier asked, 'How are things with the Reds?'

'Hungry and cold.' Ransome replied.

The soldier replied, 'They are humans just like us. I am sorry for them. England helps us with guns and uniforms and things. I do not know why we are not at peace with them. Couldn't England make us all at peace?' The soldier looked into a building, but came out with a dissatisfied look on his face. 'Very dirty in there' he said, 'It will be better next door!'

Next door he found for them a fine room, in the house of a Jew. The room was quite empty, having been the secretariat of the Reds who had evacuated the place three days before.

At this point, there are no further sources to carry the research forward beyond that covered in the *Autobiography*. It is certain that, after the group left Marienhausen the next day, they went to Balovsk before striking westwards (it is believed) towards the railway line which led to Marienburg, Valga and Reval. The route from Korsovka to Balovsk was very roundabout; rather like going from London to Liverpool via Newcastle, but it was almost certainly dictated by the changing position of the front, possible crossing points and the vagaries of the war. The Ransomes (as they were referred to) both arrived safely in Reval on Wednesday 5 November, the journey having taken them just over a week. (The dirt roads in this part of Latvia are much the same as they were all those years ago except, that today (9/2001) they are wider and better kept to take motor transport. From time to time, the occasional four-wheeled springless horse-drawn cart can still be seen taking goods to market).

The Foreign Office, not noted for being favourably disposed towards Ransome, did record in some minutes of a meeting, their admiration of his journey to Moscow and back across both the White and Red Russian lines on hearing of these exploits. Ransome, of course, would never have known of these sentiments.

In Reval Ransome saw Mr. Piip and all went as planned. An armistice was agreed between the two sides, and a few weeks later Ransome attended a meeting in Dorpat where both Estonians and Russians sat down to conclude a peace-treaty. This was the first sign of the end of the Interventionist wars, which gave Estonia twenty years of independence lasting up to the Second World War.

Nearly eighty years after Ransome completed this epic two-way journey across the Russian civil war lines, a document surfaced in the Library of Congress, Washington archives showing that, on the return journey from Moscow Evgenia couriered out of the country a small hoard of valuable items. This document, 265 NKVD, from *Revelations From The Russian Archives*, edited by D.P. Koenker and R.D. Bachman, records 32 diamonds and 3 strings of pearls being collected in Moscow for delivery outside Russia. Finance from the sale of these items was to be used to support foreign Communist activities.

At the time, this could have been a laudable exercise as the Russian Communists were hoping for similar parties or organisations in neighbouring countries to rise up in Revolution, but it could also have been a 'cover-up', for someone to use the situation for personal gain, knowing that she was leaving the country. To entrust a twenty-five year old female with valuables worth over one million roubles, and who is about to set off on a very risky trip across an active war front on foot, does stretch the imagination somewhat...

The dates given in the document fit in with the event, but the assertion that Evgenia was Ransome's wife, and that she was taking these valuables to England, are both mistakes. Evgenia in this period was persona non grata in England, although if the situation demanded it, the Consul in Helsingfors was instructed by the Foreign Office that he could issue a visa.

The question is: did Evgenia smuggle valuables to the West?

It is entirely possible although improbable, but without further supporting information difficult to prove one way or the other.

Chapter VII
Correspondent in The Baltic States

Mr. Piip met Ransome in the street a few years later and told him that he had been going through the 1919-1920 archives and he had a very honourable place in Estonian history. Ransome recorded that it was the only time anybody had thanked him for his amateur meddling in somebody else's affairs.

Having got to Reval, with Evgenia safely on the same side of the front as himself, he collapsed with a return of the usual stomach troubles and a sharp attack of brain-fever. They took a room at the Hotel "Kuld Lõvi" (Golden Lion) and, with the aid of a good doctor and nursing from Evgenia, he pulled through. The room they were in was a special delight, being heavily decorated with murals commemorating the stay of a former occupant, Tzar Alexander III. The Golden Lion was situated at 40 Harju Street, but sadly, this large and palatial hotel is no longer there having been destroyed during the bombing of the city on 9 March 1944. In Ransome's time the hotel advertised itself as:

> THE OLDEST AND ONE OF THE BEST HOTELS IN REVAL - SETTLED AT THE CENTRE OF THE TOWN INCLUDING 50 COMFORTABLE FURNISHED ROOMS, ELECTRIC LIGHT - PRICES FROM 1 TO 5 ROUBLES.
> THERE IS A RESTAURANT, 2 BILLIARDS AND GOOD COOKING.
> BEER FROM BARRELS, BEST WINES, BATHS.
> TELEPHONE 341

Convalescence followed, after the doctor who had treated him suggested a house in Lodenzee (Klooga area) with a quiet room in which to write. A letter home from Reval dated 2 December 1919 reveals how he feels:

> My dearest old Mother,
> I am now quite recovered from my illness, and am fat in the face, cheerful (moderately), and very much better in every way with a peace of mind that I have not had since I came to England in March. I know I have done what I had to do. So there can be no argument about it...
> Well, my dear, Goodnight, and please remember that I am still the same old rapscallion
> I always was, and, as ever,
>
> Your loving son.

Above, Reval - Golden Lion Hotel. Ransome recuperated here after the October 1919 trip to Moscow as diplomatic emissary. The building is no longer there having been destroyed by bombing during the Second World War.
Below, 1914 advertisement for the Golden Lion (translation in text).

Shortly after sending this letter, Ransome moved down to Dorpat to observe the conference between the Russians and Estonians, which he had helped to bring about. Also present was a Lieutenant A. Agar RN., the Naval Representative appointed by Sir Walter Cowan, Commander of the British Baltic Fleet. He recorded meeting Ransome in the waiting room of the datcha where the negotiations were being held:

> From the windows of my room I could see much coming and going through gates where the sentries were posted, but the colonel asked me not to be seen too much. He knew all about the other Englishman mentioned by Professor Goode. It was no less a person than Arthur Ransome, the well-known writer, and it would be arranged for me to visit him in the evenings after dark. No one could possibly have been kinder to me then than Arthur Ransome.
>
> I spent my evenings with this talented man playing chess and talking, with the inevitable samovar close at hand, from which we drank innumerable cups of tea sweetened, for want of sugar in this land of poverty, by acid drops out of a tin he had brought with him. We had a common love of boats and sailing, in which he excelled, and I learned much from him in Dorpat of all places, about Russia and the life of the peasants.
>
> (From *Baltic Episode* by Lt. Agar)

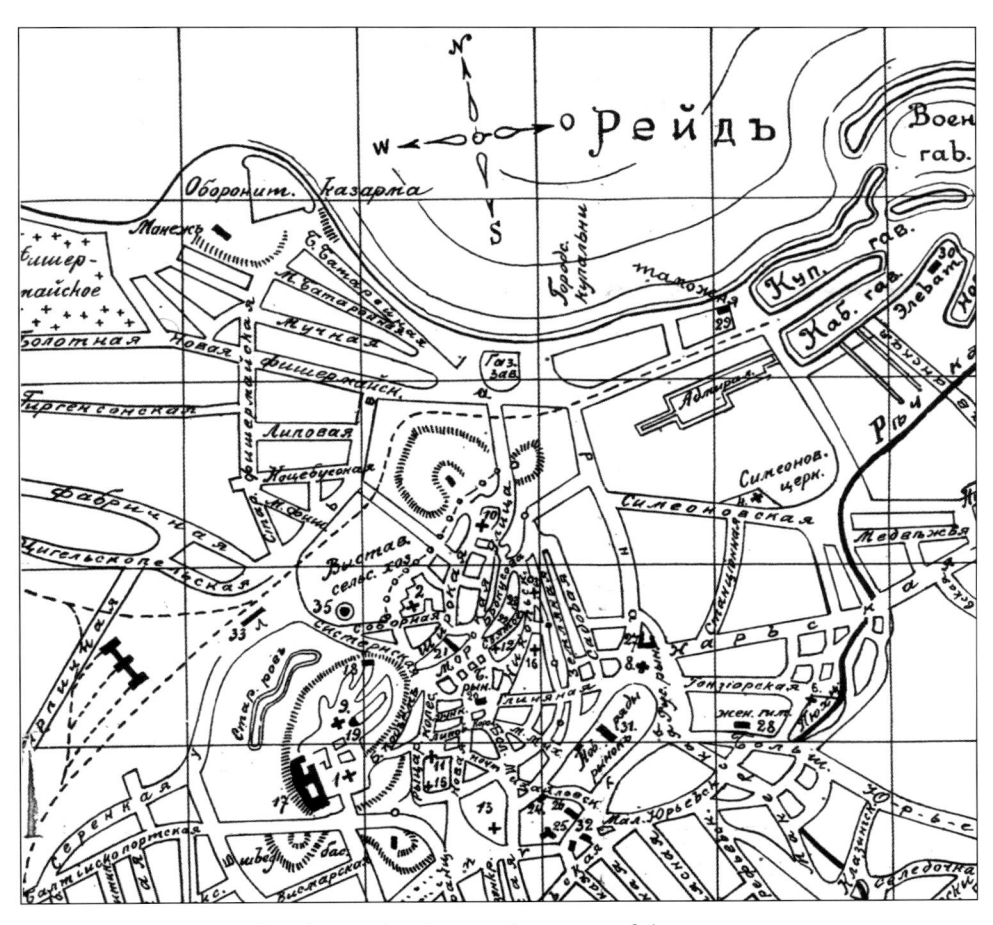

Reval map showing northern part of the town.
Guide to Reval and its Environs 1908.

They moved out to the new lodgings at Lodenzee at the head of Lahepe Bay in late winter and spent most of 1920 there. The nearest railway station was at Klooga on the main line to Baltic Port (Paldiski). This location afforded the best of all possible worlds: a forest to roam in, a lake to fish in, and the bay for swimming and boating in. It was indeed, a happy and idyllic place.

The datcha Wiegand was of medium size and had other lodgers. Arthur and Evgenia appear to have had one room to themselves with the use of other rooms as necessary. The house is no longer there, but according to Alan Lawrence (a member of the Arthur Ransome Society), who has investigated the location, the house was dismantled and reassembled some distance away, and therefore, is still in existence. (*Mixed Moss*, Winter 1997)

In early spring of 1920 Ransome found himself on a fact-finding trip to Moscow. It was essential to keep in touch with the Russian political situation in order to provide *Manchester Guardian* readers with informed up-to-date

Ransome in Russia

Ransome and Evgenia, body shape cartoon of themselves.
Reads '1917 Petrograd; 1918 Stockholm; 1919 Reval'

reports. Living in Estonia afforded a certain freedom not previously found during the years formerly spent in Russia – the censor seemed kinder! On the return journey via Petrograd, he called at his old Glinka Street rooms and did not like what he discovered. In a letter home dated April 19, he describes what he found and his reaction to it:

> ...In Petrograd yesterday between arrival and departure I rushed round to see what had become of my old rooms. The infernal idiots had made a search there. They found my collection of newspapers, every copy of every paper issued in Petrograd from Feb.1917 to Feb.1918, an absolutely priceless and irreplaceable collection which I had intended for the British Museum. THEY BURNT THE LOT amid the protests of my old landlady, who, however, succeeded in saving my favourite fishing rod, a few pictures and my Turkish coffee mill. Boots, felt winter boots, the files of my old telegrams*, cameras, practically everything of value stolen. I was very angry for a moment when I heard of it, and saw my bare and ruined room, and then I grinned a deep and solid grin. It is after all only just that I as a bourgeois should suffer like the rest, and now at least I have the necessary feeling for the chapter on that subject in my history. I had such contempt for the Russian bourgeois that I had difficulty in thinking of him without impatience, and found it hard to take him seriously when he complained of losing his piano and what not. I despise him as much as before, but in describing his mental state

---

A file of these are held at the Brotherton Collection in Leeds.

142

after the revolution I have now the best of subjective material. Devil take it. I forgive them for stealing my boots, which were no doubt wanted for the army, but to burn that collection of papers, to destroy such material for the chronicling of their own revolution, and to BURN it (if they had collared it for their own archives I should not have cared a damn)... but to burn it... Forty thousand million dancing devils with pink tails and purple stomach aches.

Also missing were most of his books and paintings, including a drawing for the proposed book on the revolution, by Mitrokhin.

It must have been quite a debilitating experience to discover his store of carefully hoarded written material had been burnt, and other possessions stolen. This is, however, not all it seems, particularly when one considers the odd time lapse here from the last time he visited. More than fourteen months earlier when Evgenia and he returned with Vorovsky's party from Stockholm, he had spent the night at the Astoria Hotel in Petrograd. Knowing at that time that all accommodation was now controlled by the state, and being only ten minutes walk along the Moika Canal from the hotel, why didn't he go and find out about his flat and possessions when there was still a chance to do so? Precisely when the raid on his flat took place is not recorded, but he would have stood a far better chance of salvaging his belongings from his landlady, or doing something about them then, rather than leaving

Old Reval. Street Scene.

things to chance and complaining later. It does seem very strange to take this view, especially after a lapse of two years during which time he could not have been paying any rent.

All during the Revolution period, Ransome had been making notes, saving newspapers, and various other supporting material with a view to writing a book about these earth-shaking times once it was all over. He even commissioned a picture of the Litovsky Castle on fire, from Mitrokhin, which he planned to use for the cover of the book. When the police raided the flat, everything was either destroyed, stolen, or went missing – or so it was thought. While this may be true for most of Ransome's things, it was not the case for the picture painted by Mitrokhin. Numerous recent searches

Above and Below, Dorpat (Tartu).
Venue for the Russian/Estonian conference

and enquiries at the various state institutions revealed that the original painting was to be found in the collection of a St. Petersburg curator working at the Hermitage. A photograph was taken of it, and permission granted for its use on the cover of this book.

Hundreds of books have been written about the time of the Russian Revolution and the period straight after. In few of these books are there references to Arthur Ransome, his presence as a witness, or what he reported, in spite of him having unrivalled access to ministers and being one of the best informed of any foreign observer. One can only conclude that this sad state of affairs exists because Ransome was unable to write the book he planned on this momentous period. It can only be pure speculation that such a book, had it been written, would have been the definitive work, and would have established for him a far more prominent position in the chronicle of events than has unfortunately turned out to be the case.

Ransome and Evgenia now had less commitments than at any time during the previous two years and yearned for a more settled existence. They wanted to use some of their free time to engage in outdoor pursuits. Ransome had always been interested in the water, and wanted a boat that they could sail or use for fishing. One day in the summer, whilst walking along the beach near

Reval, he spotted a wooden boat for sale. He liked it, asked the price, and without a survey, bought it. The next day, he and Evgenia, with only a pocket compass and a small map, set out early at 6 30 in it for Lahepe Bay, some 50 kilometres to the west. Ransome wrote in his log with some expectation: 'I hoisted the sails. There came a breath of wind and slowly, slowly, so slowly that there and then we christened her *Slug*, she moved into the bay and we were looking at the Rock of Reval from the sea, as I had so often promised that we would.

It was a hot day with light variable winds from all directions, so when the wind died away altogether, Ransome jumped overboard to cool off. In spite of a bottle hanging over the side in the water tethered with a piece of string to indicate any movement, he failed to notice the boat drifting off with a little breeze towards Finland! With Evgenia shouting at him to come back, he swam as fast as he could and just caught her up! Then he found that he couldn't get aboard – the sides of the boat were far too high. At last, with the wind rising he made a great effort and finally clambered up by way of the bowsprit and flopped down in the bottom of the boat exhausted. Attempts to repeat this boarding in shallow water never succeeded. Perhaps the absence of fear of being left at sea had something to do with it! Setting a course of west-north-west, they made for the Island of Nargon about eight miles away.

Finding a little bay south west of the point, they grounded the boat,

WAR : *Men of the Pen who Have Won Distinction.* (See p. 180.)

Mr. Arthur Ransome

Special correspondent of "The Daily News" in Russia. He has travelled extensively both in that country and in France. Mr. Ransome is a well-known contributor to "The Fortnightly," "The English Review," and other periodicals

Slug on the beach at Lahepe Bay. Ransome's first boat in Estonia.

landed, made a fire and boiled up some tea. After a few hours, the appearance of dark clouds over Reval moving westwards suggested it was time to pack up and get going. With a rising wind, they decided to run towards the Surop Lighthouse on the Estonian coast. A stiff breeze pushed them along, and at one stage, they nearly capsized in a sudden squall, with water pouring over the gunwale as a result of the stone ballast shifting. After some distance, the storm blotted out Nargon Island astern as they then set course west south west. At midnight, with hardly a breeze, they were able to establish their position when the Packerort Lighthouse became visible.

To get home, they had only to round Cape Lohussar into Lahepe Bay. With the aid of the pocket compass, Ransome headed *Slug* southwards in the hope of seeing the silhouette of the land. At about two in the morning, when all sensible folk are in bed, they heard loud barking. Drifting in towards the shore, the anchor was dropped over the side finding bottom at two metres. Tired right out, and far too tired to talk, they made a tent out of the mainsail and fell instantly asleep in the bottom of the boat. They woke-up later in the morning, and found just enough wind to take them home to the south-west corner of the bay where, after stripping, they towed her into shallow water and anchored. This little experience gave them both confidence in the boat, and not a little in themselves.

Lahepe Bay was not a good place to keep the boat afloat. *Slug* could be reached only by swimming. An improvised raft was used as a dinghy, but it had a bad habit of tipping sideways into the water and as a result, jettisoning any possessions that it carried. Much to their annoyance and inconvenience, *Slug* twice sank at her moorings. Overall, they had a lot of fun with the boat that summer, but knew she was only a makeshift towards something better. Evgenia had never been sailing before, but in spite of the spills and frights, she was not deterred in any way and remained enthusiastic.

It is generally assumed that *Slug* was the first boat that Ransome could call his own, and therefore, the first of eight (not including any dinghies).

However, there is some mystery here because, there are some references to having had another boat earlier, one with a deep keel and possibly moored in Southampton? The references, mostly from letters home, imply that the craft was acquired sometime during, or before 1916. We know that Ransome visited Oulton Broad in the autumn of 1914, but there is no mention anywhere of having bought a boat while he was there. Indeed, there is no mention anywhere else at anytime of having a boat, or getting rid of one. Nor does he record visiting it on trips home from Russia. Without some hard evidence, one is forced to conclude that this boat, if it ever existed, was more a question of what he would like to own rather than a tangible asset. Information wanted!

Apart from the regular reports for the *Manchester Guardian*, Ransome devoted some of his spare time this year to learning navigation.

Ransome on a train somewhere in Russia 1922

Some books on the subject were acquired, with evenings and odd moments devoted to studying the art in anticipation of being able to take himself to places without specialist help. He did become reasonably proficient at coastal navigation, which was all that was needed around the Baltic coasts, but he never mastered the art of astro navigation in any meaningful way – not that Ransome ever made a voyage where such skills were needed. A sextant did form part of his on-board navigation kit for most of the time that he had *Racundra*, but this was probably more for pride of ownership or anticipation of voyages he would like to make, rather than anything else.

Well into the autumn, they packed up the lodging at Lodenzee, and moved back to a room at the Golden Lion Hotel in Reval as it was more convenient to see out the winter from there.

Panorama of Reval Port

BALTIC SAILING

After Christmas 1920, Ransome made a flying visit to Moscow to fulfil a series of engagements. Interviews with Litvinov and other Bolshevik leaders on trade, relations and other mutual areas of interest followed. He was soon back in Reval turning his thoughts towards how he might get Evgenia home to England, and in a manner which would prove socially acceptable. He was still married to Ivy, but desperate for a divorce. To this end, he sent his mother in the January a request that she look for a cottage for them. His request is clear in this short extract:

> What is wanted is a cottage very cheap, with in it three bedrooms, so that I can file my books round the walls and really get down to work... Therefore cottage, I would suggest a letter of enquiry to a Lowestoft house agency, or Harwich or Ramsgate or likeliest Norwich asking for small cottage on the Broads...

Obviously, only somewhere at a safe distance from Hatch would do, but nothing became of this and in late January, Ransome left for a six week 'follow up' assignment to Moscow. There were further discussions on trade with

Reval Panorama

Litvinov as well as interviews with Radek. There was also up-to-date information required on Lenin's health. The visit was rounded off by covering the Russian Turkish Conference and attending the Parade of Communists. He stayed as before at 46, Povarskaya, but this time, was obliged to share the room with four other occupants, such were the changed times now that all accommodation was controlled. The experience was less than agreeable.

In early April, they gave up their Reval hotel address and moved out to lodgings in Klooga (these are thought to be the same lodgings as Lodenzee). These lodgings have not been identified.

With the approaching spring, Ransome was anxious to prepare for a boating summer. *Slug* had whetted their appetite for a better boat – possibly one with a cabin. A five metre craft with a tiny cabin was found in Reval Harbour. On 25 March, he bought the boat paying £10 of the £25 asking price, and named her *Kittiwake*. She would do for the 1921 summer in Baltic Port, where they planned to base themselves. Because of the boat's size and draft, a tender was required. However, because of the poor economic situation, it was impossible to get anyone to build them a suitable dinghy.

Ransome solved the problem by securing the services of a local undertaker! The result was the equivalent of a coffin with shaped ends, and once in the water, was totally unstable. Ransome said that it was liable to capsize if he moved his pipe from one side of his mouth to the other. The bunks in the new boat were very narrow, and in order to be able to make use of them, they fitted wider mattresses to enable them to sleep aboard if necessary. Other new kit put on board to enable them to make longer voyages included, a primus, a kettle, a saucepan, a frying pan, a couple of plates, two mugs, knives, forks and spoons etc. To make the *Kittiwake* more homely, Evgenia made some curtains for the portholes.

Early trial sails in her showed that she was unstable even with two reefs down. Additional iron ballast was added, but it did little to keep her on an even keel. They were very disappointed and soon lost their confidence in her. In May, they left for Baltic Port, spending the first night anchored off the Reval Yacht Club. More than twenty-four hours of being flung about by wind and sea brought them to the entrance to the harbour. After finding their way to a suitable quay, they tied up alongside and Ransome went ashore to book rooms in the little hotel kept by the harbour-master and his wife. The genial harbour-master greeted him with a cup of hot coffee, but after twenty-five hours at the tiller, Ransome fell asleep with his head on the table, the drink untouched. The rest of the summer was spent sailing about and enjoying themselves around Baltic Port.

Reval Port - Fishing Harbour

Neither *Slug* nor *Kittiwake* seemed to fulfil the Ransome's nautical aspirations. Both appear to have been spur-of-the-moment purchases and poor sea-boats, which resulted in risky trips being undertaken. They did not take either craft out for a trial sail before purchase to establish their sailing abilities, or whether there was sufficient stability for coastal work. The fact that they had managed to make two small coastal passages without mishap, was down to good luck, rather than judgement. They had some fun with these craft, but they were very limited, and performed a lot less well than they would have liked. Ransome, the eternal optimist, had some big ideas. He was now looking to capitalise on their experiences with the possibility of building a proper sea-going yacht.

A famous Estonian yacht designer, Otto Eggars, was recommended to them. He had a reputation for building fast yachts with fine sailing lines. He was also the consummate salesman, who managed to bowl them over with his ideas for the perfect go-anywhere boat, one even that could be sailed to England, if required. Such a vessel would be capable of being lived on, able to be sailed single-handed, and big enough and stable enough to go to sea when other vessels were putting back into harbour because of bad weather. At this point, Ransome became worried about being persuaded to invest in a boat which could put him into debt, but the enthusiasm of Eggars carried him off his feet and pounds out of his depth! Or so he said, but Ransome's earnings in the last couple of years had been substantial, with not all the agreed allotment going to Ivy. Years later he wrote to her explaining that he didn't pay her the full amount so that she would not get used to having so much, when in different circumstances he might have to pay her less.

The dream produced an agreement for *Racundra*. Otto Eggars, who lived at 29 Sihminde Strasse, Reval (an address to which Ransome was a frequent visitor) no longer had his own boat construction yard in Estonia, where, had it been possible, Ransome would have preferred his yacht to have been built. But towards the end of the year, plans were produced, and construction for this special craft commenced in a shed on an island in the mouth of the Dvina River [now Daugava River], in Latvia.

During the winter, Ransome made frequent journeys across the ice to watch the building progress. Construction was slow – very slow. There were delays and by the summer of 1922 the boat was still not ready in spite of many promises. His diary is littered with many frustrations and the disappointments experienced with the builders over many months, such that any pleasure of expectation of completion and ownership had long ago evaporated by the time he finally took delivery.

Klooga Station - Ransome alighted here for Lodensee.

Meanwhile, this happy sailing summer of 1921 came to an end in the middle of August, when the *Manchester Guardian* ordered Ransome to move to Riga, Latvia. Riga had become one of the main centres of information for Eastern Europe. It attracted all sorts, White Russian emigrés, Tzarist Officers, a variety of military men of all nationalities, and a large international intelligence community. Both the British and US Governments, not having Missions in Moscow, received much of their information from there. Most

Arthur swimming in Estonia.

newspapers wanting access to where the information was likely to be, prudently kept their correspondents there too.

Late August saw the Ransomes, complete with Evgenia's cat Tom, settled at 23 Stralsunder Strasse, Kaiserwald – a suburb on the north west outskirts of the city. In the *Autobiography*, Ransome mentions that rooms had been rented in a small house on the shores of the Stint See, a lake beside the forest, convenient for fishing and boating. A visit in April 1999 revealed that most of the houses in the area were not that small, that 23 was no longer there, and that it would have been at least a kilometre from the lake shore. The name of the road has been changed to Stokholmas iela, and that of the district to Mezaparks. The Kaiserwald area should be viewed as a not very dense pine forest adjacent to the lake with houses scattered about amongst the trees.

Ransome refers to the lake as the 'Stint See'. This Germanic name was applicable for only a short period in Latvian history, and no one consulted at the History Museum of Riga appeared to have heard of it (see coloured map of Riga). This lake today is known as Kisezers [Keesherzers] and is approximately 7 kilometres long and 2 kilometres wide. With sandy bays, the lake area is more than twice that of Coniston Water. The surrounding land is

Evgenia

flat [as is most of Latvia] and with no Lake District hills to play havoc with the wind it is a beautiful place in which to sail. Ransome clearly displayed his special gift for picking out suitable places in which to live while he was in the east – places both conducive for reporting work and for enjoying himself.

Occasional trips into Russia for journalistic purposes continued, including a special trip in September to view and film the mass starvation in the Volga region. It was a trip which produced what is thought to be the only movie film ever taken of Ransome. The clip, which shows Ransome standing with George Ercole (cameraman) and others by a train, forms part of a news programme issued by Pathé News. This silent film has a caption, which adds: 'Arthur Ransome, noted journalist on his trip across the Latvian – Russian border.'

In early November, Ransome left for a five week trip to England. Although he made the usual round of visits to his friends, the main objective was to try and reach some arrangement with Ivy over their relationship. He was desperate to be free of her, but unfortunately to Ransome's great disappointment, no progress was made at all. He arrived back in Riga two days before Christmas. In March 1922, he made another visit to England, spent mostly in Manchester. There was also a few happy days with the

Collingwoods, as well as trying to move things forward with Ivy. This whole business was becoming so frustrating, and once more the visit ended with no meeting of minds. In between visits to England, he spent a large part of February in Moscow on a reporting assignment for the *Manchester Guardian*. There were interviews with Trotsky, Litvinov and Chickerin, as well as a round of meetings with numerous other Bolshevik ministers.

To add to his woes, the boat construction was falling behind schedule, and it was beginning to look as if they would not get delivery on time, in spite of it being promised for 15 May. They had a dinghy and had to content themselves with sailing it around the Stint See. For added interest, they joined the Riga Yacht Club, to which they could walk in about twelve minutes. Membership was a welcome pleasure, as it was a friendly, homely and cosy place. It was also an active club, and a popular meeting-place for local sailors, ice-yachters and skaters. Ransome records that the food they most enjoyed was pork chops, sometimes apple tart to follow, and always coffee. The kind, motherly woman who managed the club was equally ready to cook the food, as look after babies too young to go sailing. It is sad to report, that this Riga Yacht Club, whose membership they so much enjoyed, no longer exists.

Kittywake. Ransome's second command

The delays continued, and in desperation, because the sailing season was well advanced, Ransome launched the shell of *Racundra* on the 28 July and removed her to the little harbour of the Stint See. An old sailor looking after dinghies there offered to help. As the 'Ancient Mariner', complete with long white beard, blue trousers and sweater, and red stocking cap, he became part of the crew and the model for the fictional 'Peter Duck'. (Arthur Ransome Society member John Cowan in correspondence with descendants of the 'Ancient Mariner', discovered the origin of the name *Racundra*. Ra (Ransome), c (Carl [Sehmel - The Ancient], und (and), ra (Evgenia - who was not yet a Ransome).

The three of them worked hard to complete the fitting out, the painting and preparations for sea. Evgenia painted and concentrated on the inside, while Ransome secured some of the major fittings and adjusted the complicated centreboard arrangements. Finally, they were able to take their dream yacht *Racundra* for sea trials. Her sailing ability was set out in a letter to his mother on 17 August:

> She is very easy to manage, and so slow on her helm that I have plenty of time to run about and do things while she takes care of herself. Our motion has a stately leisuredness about it that is reminiscent of the Middle Ages.

And towards the end of the letter:

> Lamp in the cabin fixed. Mattresses now going down. Sweet peas on the cabin table and his Brittanic Majesty's Minister coming to tea on board this afternoon.

The summer of 1922 was slipping by. On 20 August they finally left Riga on their first voyage. Up the Latvian and Estonian Coast they sailed, and crossed the Gulf of Finland to Helsingfors [Helsinki] before returning by much the same route to Riga.

In a letter home to his Mother after the voyage, Ransome mentions that the 'greatest joy was in the navigation… It made all my mugging up of books seem really worth while. The voyage had been undertaken a bit later in the season than Ransome would have liked, so that when they got back almost all the other boat owners had taken their boats on to dry land and under cover for

Above, Old Riga Port on the Divina
Below, Old Riga City

the winter. This voyage produced a book entitled *Racundra's First Cruise*. It became a classic nautical tale and has been reprinted many times. Its lasting appeal must be in the engaging style of writing, and because the voyage took place in a picturesque part of the world that is, perhaps, little known.

During the period of the voyage they were not married, and for reasons of delicacy, Evgenia is always referred to in the book as, 'the Cook'. As it was late in the season, they quickly stripped the boat of all the odds and ends, bits of loose equipment, compass, mattresses, anchors, books, charts etc and removed them to their lodgings about one kilometre away.

During February 1923, Ransome went on another reporting trip to Moscow. While he was away, their large wooden house caught fire and burnt down. Evgenia only escaped because her cat Tom woke her up. They lost almost everything: new evening clothes, papers, the family clock, sextant, all the equipment from *Racundra* being stored in the house for the winter, even wire rigging and the tiller. Walking about among the ruins he picked up two shackles and the bottom of his beloved cabin lamp. Anything that was not burnt was stolen by the fire-brigade who saved camera cases from which the cameras had disappeared. A neighbour reported seeing them smashing open

Racundra on the Divina

the sextant box with a hatchet and breaking the sextant as a result. Ransome ended a letter to his mother reporting the fire, 'I am too gloomy to write anything at the moment...Your affectionate but rather unlucky son.'

They were almost immediately re-housed a short distance (200 yards) along the road from the burnt-out house at 15 Stralsunder Strasse. This second house also no longer exists (April 1999). The space that would have been occupied by the dwelling is now part of a very large garden to number 13 Stokholmas iela – an altogether more modern construction.

The first house was positioned on a corner between a major and a minor road. Following the fire it was not rebuilt, and 76 years later, in April 1999 the area was still waste ground with some bushes and a footpath going across it as a short cut. On a visit in September 2001, however, a large modern house had been built on the site. It was occupied and complete with lawns, all the original trees and surrounded by a low wall with fence on top.

Period picture of Stint See.

In general terms, one can see that the older wooden dwellings in these woods are slowly being replaced by modern brick structures, so that in a few years time there is the possibility that the traditional sort of wooden house that Ransome lived in will no longer exist.

There were two return trips to England in 1923. Ransome had hoped to get the fire-damaged family clock repaired, but it turned out to be impractical and he was very disappointed. He also continued to put pressure on Ivy for a settlement, hoping that she would relent and give him his freedom, but they could not agree on details and only a little progress was made towards a solution.

In May, Ransome made an important trip into Russia and found a first-class crises in Anglo-Russian relations brewing. Lord Curzon was Foreign Minister, and he had sent a note to Moscow to be delivered to the Russians. The note had the appearance of an ultimatum, which although it might not bring war, would certainly result in breaking up any such trading relations that existed.

The note, couched in straight language, made a number of what was thought by the Bolsheviks to be unjustifiable demands. What was more serious was that R.M. Hodgson, the head of the Mission, was instructed to deliver the note without any discussion or comment. Ransome visited in turn

Stint See from where Ransome kept Racundra (2001).

Litvinov, Bukharin, Zinoviev and Chicherin a number of times, all of whom were convinced that the British Government was determined to bring about a rupture in relations.

Ransome spent many hours in the Kremlin consuming gallons of tea while talking with the Russian Leaders. Eventually, he was able to persuade Litvinov to walk in an agreed park at a time when he would find Hodgson, who similarly 'just happened' to be out for a walk. Both expressed their appropriate surprise on meeting each other and got down to a delicate discussion without malice. The situation was not resolved immediately, but eventually it was, and no break in relations took place. Although Ransome took no credit for this, it is clear that without his knowledge and acceptance by the Russian leaders, the outcome would have been somewhat different.

The sailing season for 1923 was delayed due to the urgent Russian reporting trip in May, and the follow up visit ordered by the *Manchester Guardian* in June. Eventually *Racundra* was prepared and provisioned for cruising. In the middle of July, somewhat later than they would have liked, they set off for their sailing holiday. A similar route was covered to the previous year, but on the outward journey they stopped at Reval for a break. The following day Ransome finally received a telegram from Ivy indicating there was some movement in her conditions for the settlement of their divorce.

Harbour on the Stint See where Ransome kept Racundra (2001) (as marked on the Stint See map on the colour section).

Leaving Evgenia and 'the Ancient' in charge of *Racundra*, Ransome set off within a few days by steamer for Stettin. He completed the rest of the journey via Berlin and arrived in London 24 hours after leaving the ship. Consultation with Ivy produced some shift towards a settlement, but not enough for Ransome. It was, a breakthrough in that there was some movement and a recognition by Ivy that her husband was serious and prepared to be flexible. For

Old Riga - Above, business quarter. Below, shopping area.

many years she had been hoping he would cave in and return home, but it was now beginning to dawn on her that he was many years past any decision of that kind. At some point a settlement would have to be agreed. A couple of further days were spent visiting his mother at Kemsing before making the return journey via Helsingfors to Reval.

The sailing holiday resumed with a crossing to Helsinfors. A pleasant week was spent sailing amongst the Finnish Islands and fishing. The last two days were marred by westerly gales with *Racundra's* anchor dragging during the night. Eventually they gave up and sailed back across the gulf. On their return to Reval, Ransome received an urgent telegram from the *Manchester Guardian* to go to Russia again. With a series of southerly gales setting in, a decision was made to close the voyage for this year and to lay *Racundra* up for the winter at Reval until the following spring. Ransome had *Racundra* unrigged, all the stores and bedding removed, and the hull lifted out of the water onto a cradle. The boat was then roofed in to protect her from the elements, especially the heavy winter snows. Evgenia and the Ancient set off for Riga by train, while Ransome headed east for Moscow.

Racundra's First Cruise was published later in the year. The very first words of the first chapter of this book about the building of *Racundra*, give us a particular insight into the kind of person that Ransome was; how he saw himself, especially in relation to youth and growing up. He started the book:

> Houses are but badly built boats so firmly aground that you cannot think of moving them. They are definitely inferior things, belonging to the vegetable not the animal world, rooted and stationary, incapable of gay transition. I admit, doubtfully, as exceptions, snail-shells and caravans. The desire to build a house is the tired wish of a man content thenceforward with a single anchorage. The desire to build a boat is the desire of youth, unwilling yet to accept the idea of a final resting-place.

This interesting piece of philosophy characterized Ransome throughout his life. He was always on the move from one house to another, or thinking about how he could justify having another boat; and it never ceased!

Three weeks were spent on the usual round of reporting interviews with Bolshevik leaders in Moscow. Before the year was out, he had made another quick trip to England in search of a settlement with Ivy, and another trip to Russia to prepare an interview which Litvinov gave for the *Manchester Guardian*. Exhausted, he arrived home on Christmas Day. The middle of January saw Ransome back in Moscow again. A few days later, and quite unexpectedly, Lenin died. Although ill, he had been getting better and his demise was not thought imminent. He passed away on 21 January 1924, having suffered ill health during the preceding two years, as well as the effects of long periods as a refugee and the assassination attempt in 1918. For Ransome, who had known Lenin, it was a great shock and disappointment. As events were to prove, all Lenin's colleagues in the revolution would lose their lives one by one, as Stalin consolidated his power – not that anyone at that time could possibly have foreseen how these events would unfold.

Lenin's funeral was on Sunday 27 January, and Ransome was present to cover it. On 2 February, Hodgson went to the Commissariat for Foreign Affairs in Moscow to deliver a note, which gave British recognition of the Soviet Government – nearly six and a half years after it had been formed. As early as April 1919, an official Russian military journal carried an article on Anglo-Russian relations and said, 'English Press raising question of recognition of Soviet Government,' and gave extracts from *Daily News* and *Chronicle* and ambassador Buchannan's speech. 'Russia has heard all this sort of thing before and if England really wishes actively to help Russian people she had better follow advice of *Daily News* and recognize Soviet Republic...' Ransome never understood why it took so long.

The recognition was legal and welcome, but it was only grudgingly done by keeping the representation to a Chargé d' Affaires. Odd, when one realizes that the Russian Government controlled one sixth of the world. Intervention had been a disastrous policy for those countries who had taken part in it; it had helped to consolidate a civil war which otherwise, might have fizzled out as soon as it had started. Recognition of the Soviet Government finally brought a recognition that the Intervention policy was now dead. Ransome records in the *Autobiography*:

> 'It was a happy day for me. 'My war', which had lasted for more than five years after the Armistice of 1918, was over. I was free to struggle back as best I could to my proper job.'

Marriage Settlement

The death of Lenin and the associated events gave Ransome, whose health was often questionable, a bit of a relapse. He was laid up in his hotel for three days before departing from Moscow on 9 February. Four days after returning to Riga he sailed for England. The ship, *SS Baltriger*, sailed from Libau (Liepâja) but became stuck in ice near the island of Bornholm. The few passengers were happy to play cricket on the ice while running out of food. The German cruiser *Brunswick* appeared, and offered assistance by cutting a channel through the ice, but the results were only temporary. The *Baltriger* turned back to try a passage through the north channel, but became fast again. Eventually a Danish ice-breaker arrived and escorted the vessel to Copenhagen. The full journey to London having taken eleven days instead of the normal three to four!

Ransome always looked forward to his journeys home, but on this occasion his intent was decidedly more serious. He had come to prepared for a show down with Ivy over their marriage. He saw his lawyers in London and with some urgency asked them to arrange the best deal possible. In the meantime, he went off to Manchester to visit his paper and Coniston to see the Collingwoods. He visited his mother in Kemsing and spent the rest of the time fishing.

To get an agreement, Ransome had, more-or-less, to submit to Ivy's demands. He was bitterly disappointed by her inflexible attitude, but in the end a deal was concluded. Ivy was an abandoned woman – hardly a dignified position at the best of times, but even worse in the Britain of the 1920s. Although retaining some sort of affection for her husband, she was conscious of her up-bringing, and thought it right to hurt him as much as she could.

The problem was that Ransome had few distrainable assets. The final arrangement was not one entirely satisfactory to either party, but it was one that gave him his freedom. Ivy was to keep such possessions of his as she had, including, much to his eternal regret, his library. The library was not that valuable, but if by keeping it she could hit him where it hurt, she would do so. In later years, the correspondence between the two of them over this library would become quite acrimonious. Ransome, of course, eventually realized that he should, as Lascelles Abercrombie (distinguished poet and critic) said years earlier, have removed his books and himself at the outset, when there could not have been any doubt over his intentions. More than thirty years later when Ransome was drafting the *Autobiography*, he touched on this relationship in a note to his literary executor:

> I am sure that I was just as far from being a husband of the kind she would have chosen as she was from being a suitable wife for me. It is unfair to tell any such story from one side only. I hope to write the thing again on these lines, with NO reference to matrimonial difficulties unless of the very mistiest kind.'

In spite of the above, in the published *Autobiography*, Ransome does describe at quite some length how he saw the relationship. The only concession that Ivy made, was to allow Ransome to keep his father's gun and his own writing desk. He reluctantly signed the documents on Tuesday 8 April. And on the 11th he left London, and arrived in Riga, via Berlin on 14th. He was at last, a free man.

They lost no time. A quick trip was made from Riga to the British Consulate situated at 17 Lai Street, Reval, Estonia to make arrangements for their impending marriage. Evgenia moved out to Klooga, with Ransome following a day later. On 8 May the Master and owner of *Racundra* married the Cook under the flag of the Cruising Association. Ransome set out the situation graphically in a letter to his mother:

British Consulate in Reval, 1924

Correspondent in The Baltic States

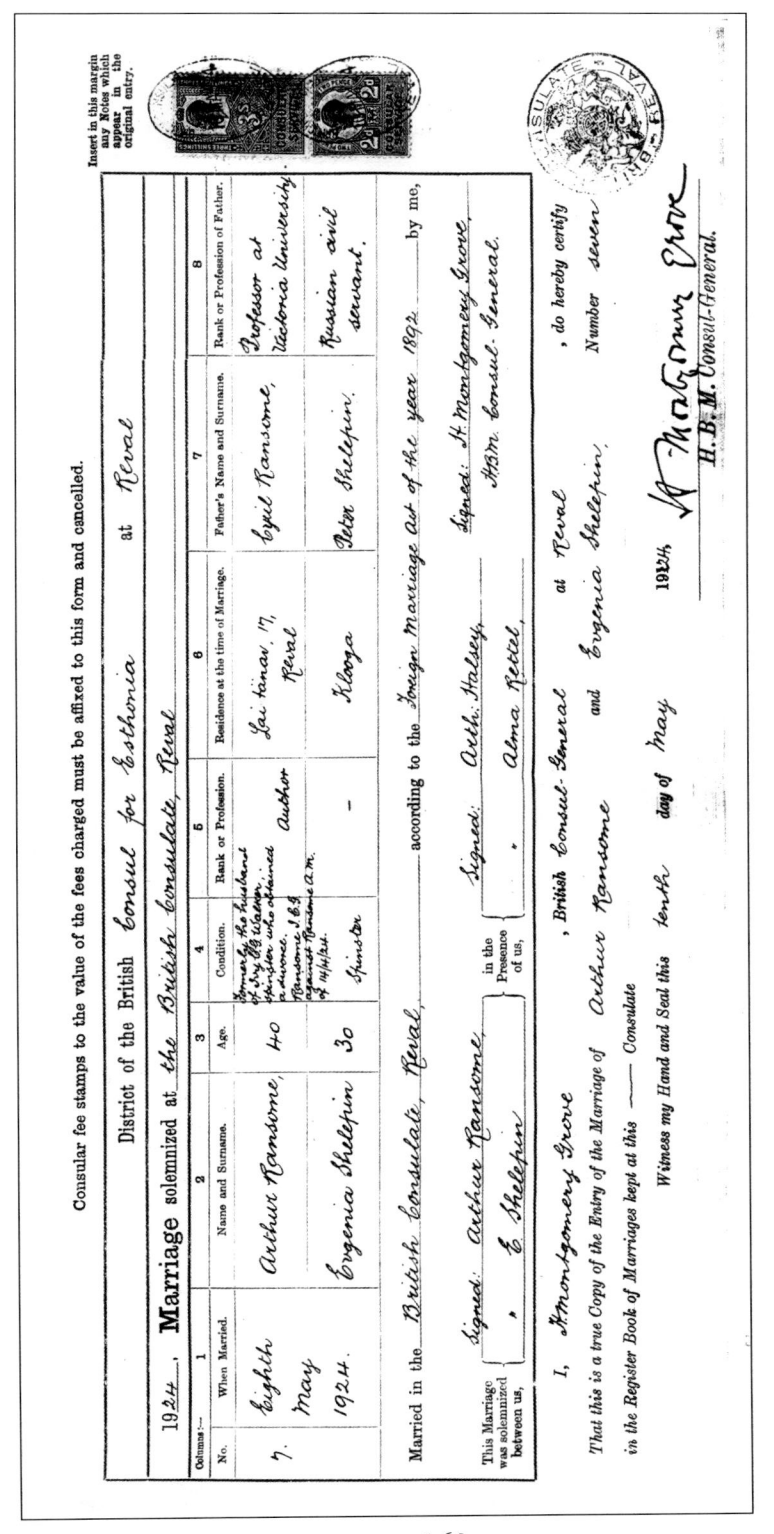

Columns:—	1	2	3	4	5	6	7	8
No.	When Married.	Name and Surname.	Age.	Condition.	Rank or Profession.	Residence at the time of Marriage.	Father's Name and Surname.	Rank or Profession of Father.
7.	Eighth May 1924.	Arthur Ransome	40	Formerly the husband of Ivy Elsy Walker, whom he obtained divorce, 18.5 Ransome v Ransome of 14/4/1924. Spinster.	Author	Lai tanav 17, Reval	Cyril Ransome	Professor at Victoria University.
		Evgenia Shelepin	30	Spinster.	—	Klooga	Peter Shelepin	Russian civil servant.

Married in the British Consulate, Reval, according to the Foreign Marriage Act of the year 1892, by me,

Signed: Arthur Ransome,   Signed: H. Montgomery Grove,
        E. Shelepin.   H.B.M. Consul-General.

This Marriage was solemnized between us, in the Presence of us, Signed: Arth. Halsey, Alma Kettel.

I, H. Montgomery Grove, British Consul-General at Reval, do hereby certify That this is a true Copy of the Entry of the Marriage of Arthur Ransome and Evgenia Shelepin, Number seven in the Register Book of Marriages kept at this Consulate

Witness my Hand and Seal this tenth day of May 1924.

H. Montgomery Grove
H.B.M. Consul-General.

At the British Consulate, Reval, the Master and Owner of *Racundra* was married to the cook!

Special Collection, Leeds University. By kind permission of the Lupton family.
Marriage certificate – Office for National Statistics – © Crown Copyright.
Reproduced with the permission of the Controller of HMSO and the Queen's Printer for Scotland.

My dearest Mother,
It is done. As a matter of fact it was done on May 8 at the British Consulate, by H.B.M. Consul Grove, who was extremely nice and welcomed Evgenia into the community of British subjects with a really sweet little speech. After the ceremony we went upstairs to Leslie's room, where Leslie had left a bottle of champagne for this special purpose...
   Always, my dearest mother
    Your affectionate & grateful son.
      Arthur.

It will be remembered that, for a couple of years just after the Revolution, Evgenia was certainly persona non grata as far as England was concerned. Ransome had tried desperately to get papers which would allow her to land and live in England, but without success. Ever since they crossed the Red/White Russian lines into Livonia/Estonia in the autumn of 1919, Ransome had been aware that, should circumstances allow him to be able to get Evgenia into the UK, it was likely she would have to sign a declaration renouncing any political affiliations she might have with the Bolsheviks. In the Golden Lion Hotel, Reval on 21 November 1919, she signed the following:

Dear Arthur,
I hereby promise you on my word of honour that I will undertake no political commissions in England from the Bolsheviks or any other political party and further that I will engage in no conspiratorial work whatsoever without first expressly informing you that I consider this promise no longer binding.
   Signed: Evgenia Petrovna Shelepina.

It is more than likely that Ransome, after advice from the Consulate, drafted this item for Evgenia to sign. In a sense, this was a formality carried out to allay any fears that might be lurking in Foreign Office minds. In practical terms, however, it had very little validity since Evgenia had long given up on politics of any sort. Indeed, throughout the fifty years that she lived in the United Kingdom, she showed not the slightest hint of interest in politics at any time. The same, in a way, could be said for Ransome. Their interest in the politics of the Russian Revolution stemmed almost entirely from being caught up in the developing situation at the time. Had there been no Revolution, Evgenia could well have remained at the Ministry of Trade and Industry and married a Russian.

The honeymoon, if it is appropriate to call it that, consisted of getting *Racundra* out of the Reval winter storage, into the water, rigged and stored for cruising. All this took nine days before a start could be made on the return voyage to Riga. This leisurely cruise would appear to have been enjoyable and without any mishap, and lasted six days. They were accompanied on the trip by Lieut. Commander Gordon Steel, V.C. as an extra hand. On arrival in Riga and to jolly-up his time in port, Ransome bought an accordion, and Steel left to return to Reval. *Racundra* was returned to the Stint See and stripped out. Perhaps Ransome didn't think there would be any more sailing that year.

In early June, and for the first time since leaving in October 1919, Evgenia accompanied her husband on a reporting trip back to Moscow. It also afforded her an opportunity to see her mother and sister, which as events turned out, would be the last time for many, many years.

On 1st August they took the re-stored *Racundra* for a cruise in the Dvina River, up and down the River Aa and up Bolderaa to a romantic area consisting of a maze of narrow channels between tall, strong reeds. The area gives the impression of extending for hundreds of square miles, so claustrophobic are the narrow channels, but in reality it is not that big, although you could, if you were self sufficient on a modest boat, lose yourself in the area for a long time. They were gone for almost a month and a half, with Ransome managing to get many of his writing commitments completed. Food was a bit scarce, but with eggs and the fish they caught, they managed to survive quite well. Returning to the Stint See, *Racundra* was stripped out for the last time and everything removed to their lodgings. Ransome laid *Racundra* up for the winter, and unfortunately, she was never sailed by him again.

On 14 November, they said their farewells to *Racundra*; a little ship which had given them so much pleasure, and to the city of Riga, and sailed direct to London on the *S.S. Gourko*, thus bringing to an end the eleven momentous years that Ransome had been involved in Eastern Europe.

CHAPTER VIII
EVGENIA SHELEPINA AND THE OCTOBER REVOLUTION

HER STORY

Evgenia Petrovna Shelepina was born on the 10 April 1894 in the small town of Gatchina, situated, some twenty-five miles south south-west of St. Petersburg. Her father, Peter Shelepina, was thought to be a gardener in the Tzar's service, but his precise occupation was unknown. So with this in mind, searches were made of all the Tzar's archives of residences covering the Gatchina area in the hope of finding out exactly what the nature of his occupation was, and where the family may have lived at the end of the nineteenth century. His details were eventually found by Greg Palmer and Tatiana Verizhnikova at the St Petersburg archive and they revealed that he was not a gardener, even though this was one of his interests, but was the curator of the Tzar's Imperial Hospital and Charity Institute under the Imperial Court at Gatchina. This was quite an important position and carried entitlement to accommodation. The family occupied a large flat conveniently located in a side road adjacent to the hospital, and from there, it was only a short walk to the centre of the town.

Peter Shelepina's appointment document to the Institute Charity Hospital.

The hospital building is still in existence (1996). The interior of the front middle section consisted of a hall with a balcony around part of it, which was sometimes used as a church, while the main section behind and in the wings housed the hospital part. There is a small woodland in front of the building these days, such has been the tree growth in the last hundred years, but in Shelepina's day, it was gardens.

The Shelepina family grew up in Gatchina, and both Evgenia and her sister did their schooling here. They were privileged in being able to attend the local grammar school – one of the best grammar schools of the period, and both graduated under the Empress Maria – Governess of

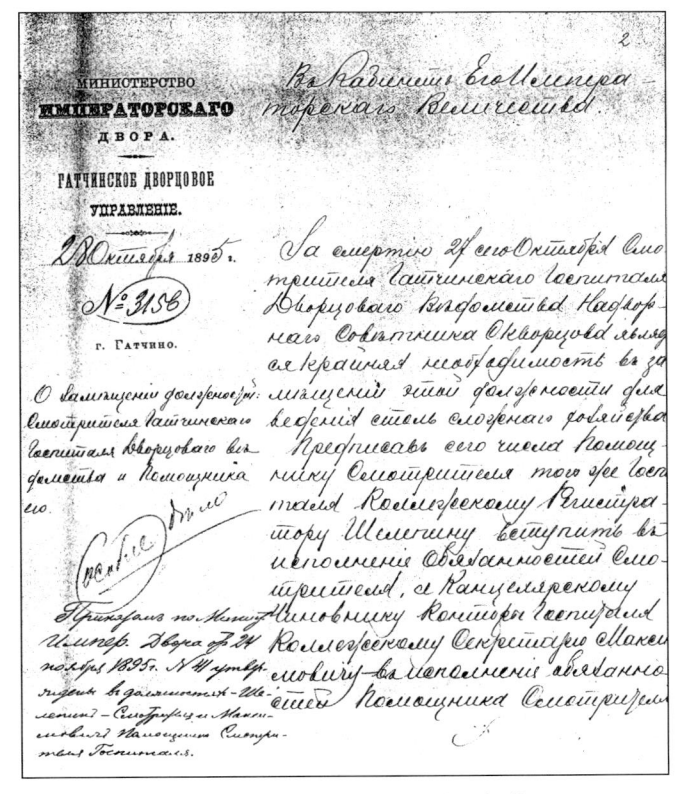

Peter Shelepina's handwritten Oath of Allegiance to the Imperial Court.

the school. The school quite amazingly, still survives in its original building.

As the years went by and the girls became of an age, their thoughts turned towards the kind of careers open to them for possible employment. When they finally came to look for work, it seems probable that a close neighbour of the Shelepina's, who worked in one of the main Government ministries in St Petersburg, may have advised or assisted the two girls into their first Government jobs!

Evgenia's first address on leaving home, as we can see from her passport at Abbot Hall, was at Sadovaya 65, Petrograd. This location was within walking distance of the railway station for journeys home, but quite a long tram ride away from the Stenography College at 106 Nevsky Prospect, where she was a student. This college advertised itself as the only institution in the Capital providing courses suitable for students who wanted to be correspondents, work in local government, state councils or the Duma etc. etc.. The college year, which was spent at this address, was from September through to May, but some weekends, the period June to August and any short holidays, were spent at home in Gatchina.

St Petersburg. Above, Evgenia's first lodgings at 65 Sadovaya.
Below, Her stenography college 106 Nevsky Prospect.

Petrograd. Above, Evgenia's second lodgings at 52, Line 11
and below, her third at 49, Line 8.

In early 1915, and now working for the government, Evgenia moved north of the Neva River to another flat on Vasilievsky Ailend, Line N11, house 52, (flat number unknown). It was on a direct tram route into the city. She was now aged 21. Her last address, before the Bolshevik Government vacated Petrograd in March 1918, was a little further up the road, still on Vasilievsky Ailend, at Line N8, house 49. She took possession of this flat, which was shared with her sister, on the day before the October Revolution. Ransome was certainly a visitor to this last address, but almost definitely not to the previous two.

In the period leading up to the Revolution, Evgenia worked for the Ministry of Trade and Industry as a clerk/typist – the only form of employment she had had since leaving secretarial college. Although not

Institute Charity Hospital, Gatchina to which
Peter Shelepina was appointed.

strictly a political person, she did, as sometimes happens with young people, have an open approach to politics. Her ideas, probably formulated during the 1916 – 1917 period, pointed her towards the direction of the Bolshevik movement: a movement which she thought, from their propaganda, was the one most able and capable of providing fair government for all the people. Of all the political groups, they were the most committed towards wanting peace with Germany. In sympathy with their objectives she joined the party. It is not known how long she had been a member at the time of the Revolution, or whether this interest was shared by others in her work place, but it seems unlikely that many in her Ministry would have shared her strong Bolshevik view of politics. Government departments still carried on as if the old order still existed, and this, in spite of the Tzar abdicating earlier in the year and the weak coalition in the Duma.

In 1918, when the Government moved to Moscow, Evgenia went too. Trotsky was appointed to a new position as Minister for War, while Evgenia remained within Foreign Affairs under the new minister, Chicherin. Either just before the move to Moscow or just after, Evgenia set down in various notes her experiences and feelings about the early days of the Revolution and her subsequent employment as Trotsky's secretary. These notes dated Moscow 18 March, together with those about the subsequent journey to Brest were written down to be a record and intended as information for Ransome. These notes were created on Ransome's own typewriter which suggests that she dictated and he typed. The originals are mixed up and out of sequence, perhaps they were written down as she remembered each event. With a few slight adjustments they form the basis of what follows. (Please note - the style and punctuation are exactly as in the originals). Ransome, in handwriting on the front of these notes records, 'Very good account of what it looked like to a young honest Russian.'

Rue Bogooutovskaya, Gatchina c1900. The Shelepinas lived here after giving up their flat in the road road adjacent to the Charity Hospital.

Gatchina – Evgenia's school.

Evgenia's Story

Eroida (sister) and I were still living then at Gatchina with mother, and the question of each day was, would it be easy or not to get a place on the train back there at night. The day before the revolution, we had taken a room together on the Vassilievsky Ostrove (Ailend 8, 49), and we sat there a little and drank tea, and thought what fools we had been not to have done so earlier, and so escape the difficulty of travelling in and out of Petrograd. But we had not moved in, and on the morning of the revolution we came in together from Gatchina as usual.

On that first day I remember seeing the sailors and workmen with their flags crossing over the bridge. Everybody crowded to the windows of the Ministry to look out. But they were not at all pleased. I was very pleased. They crowded to the window and then drew back again when they heard the shooting in the town, and were telling each other that the crowd would come in and shoot them next. They were sure that the people would come in and kill everybody in the Ministry, but they dared not leave because of the shooting.

I tried to telephone Eroida, because we had agreed to meet at the station at six o' clock to go home by train together. The telephone was not working. So I went to the station. I was never under fire. I have always had bad luck. I have never once been under fire all

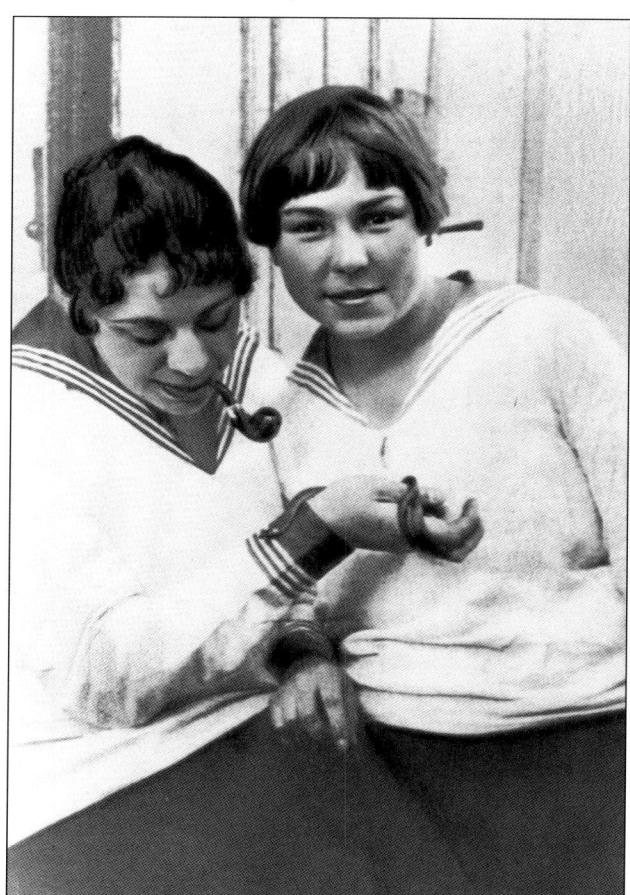

Evgenia and her sister Eroida

throughout the Revolution. Of course I heard firing all the time. Sometimes it was in the next street. Sometimes it was far away, but I got the whole way to the station without being in any danger at all. I was pleased to see the workmen and sailors and excited and happy, because I wanted them to win.

I waited at the station for four hours not knowing what had become of Eroida. Then, thinking that perhaps she might have gone home earlier, I got into a train that was just leaving and went home. I found mother in Gatchina in great anxiety. She accused me of deserting Eroida, and asked me how I could have come home without her. There were tears and cries and general disturbance. Mother had heard all sorts of rumours and no one knew what was happening. She was angry with me because I could not tell her. I did not know myself although I had come from Petrograd. I put on my coat and was for going back to town, but mother would not have that either.

Eroida got back early the next morning. She had gone to a friend's rooms when the fighting began, and the fighting had come to that very street. People were firing up and down the street so that she could not get out. It was just like Eroida to have all the experience when I really wanted to have it. At last when things were quieter, she and another girl who lived in Gatchina also, went out. Almost as soon as they were in the street they had to lie flat on the ground because someone with a machine gun was firing at anything that moved in the street. They had to lie down six times before they got to the station.

For the next three days I was ill, and then for two weeks the trains were not running between Gatchina and Petrograd. Kerensky was in Gatchina and every day we expected troops from the front, but I was hoping they would not come. We used to send messengers to the station every day to know if a train was going. Then I heard that everybody in my Ministry had met and passed a resolution not to work for the Bolsheviks, but to go on strike. I asked whether anybody had voted against the resolution, and was told that only two had refused to vote, but all the rest were for striking. I wished I had been in Petrograd so that there should have been at least one vote against striking. Ours was a very black hundredish ministry.

Nearly everybody had worked there during the old regime, and under Kerensky, and they all believed that the Bolsheviks would only stay in power a few days, and that if they went in with the Bolsheviks they would presently be left between two stools. I used to go to the station myself to ask about trains. Perhaps you will understand. Quite apart from the question of the Bolsheviks, it was painful to me to think that the machine of which I had been a part had stopped. The Ministry is just like that, a big machine, which goes on always, and if one cog goes out it is replaced by another, but the machine itself goes on always. And now it had stopped, I could not bear it.

At last we heard that a train was to leave for Petrograd. Eroida and I went to the station early in the morning, and waited there all day until late in the evening, but there was no train. The next day we went again, and did at last get to Petrograd. Eroida was working in the Commission for dealing with refugees which had never stopped at all, so she went straight back to her office and went on as before. I found my Ministry (Trade & Industry) closed up. No one was there. But I heard that at the Ministry of Labour they were taking the names of people willing to work.

When I came to Petrograd that morning, I got my friend Mara, who was secretary of the Bolshevik Party at Gatchina, to give me a document. We composed it ourselves. It said that I 'was delegated by the Gatchina Party of Bolsheviks to the Ministry of Labour,' and was signed by Mara and also quite seriously by the president of the Gatchina Soviet.

Mara was the daughter of a Baltic Baron, who was actually a chief of police. Up to the revolution she had cared about nothing but frocks and flirtations, but with the revolution she threw herself into the movement, and afterwards became secretary of the Gatchina Soviet, and is now (March 1918) a member of the Praesidium, with much influence. She is twenty years old. At first people called her 'Baroness', but in the end they got accustomed to calling her Comrade Mara. With this document given me by Mara I went to Smolny and found Shlyapnikov the peoples Commissary for Labour, in room 67 which afterwards became the room where I worked – the room of the People's Commissary for Foreign Affairs.

There were two soldiers at the door. I showed my document, and they went in and Shlyapnikov came out. I told him how I wanted to work, and how it hurt me to think of people not working. He laughed, and said, that he agreed it was very important, but that I should not have come to bother him with it, but should have gone to the Ministry of Labour where there was a committee of mobilisation which was arranging work for all the suitable people who came along. He laughed at me, of course, but so nicely that I was not offended at all, and went off to the Ministry of Labour in the Marble Palace*. So I went there, hoping that some at least of my old comrades in the ministry would be

---

* *Built for Count Grigory Orlov and situated in the Ulitza Millionaya.*

there too. I could not find one. There was a crowd of students and girl students and others, and so I waited with them.

I was asked 'What recommendations have you?'

I said, "I have no recommendations at all, but I worked in the Ministry of Trade and Industry for so long.'

I was asked, 'What can you do?'

I said, I could do anything they wanted, that I could typewrite, and take shorthand notes, and knew a little book-keeping, that I was willing to do anything they thought useful.

They asked what party I belonged to, and I showed them my card of membership of the Bolshevik party. Then they gave me some typewriting to do in the Ministry of Labour. I set to work at once, and so on the evening of the day I left Gatchina, I was already at work. The Marble Palace, which is the Ministry of Labour, had magnificent rooms, and its' beauty and the feeling of solidarity in it had a quieting effect upon me. I felt better already, as soon as I was at work there.

The person in charge of the department where I worked was a young woman, not very well educated. She knew I had worked in a Ministry before, and perhaps for that reason made a particular show of friendliness for me, though being laughably careful not to let me forget that she was in charge and that I was under her supervision, though she could make no pretence of understanding the work. Every day fresh people came in to work, and as all applications passed through the Ministry of Labour, I used to go every day to look at the lists to see if any of the people from the old Ministry of Trade and Industry had come in, because I was always hoping that I should get back to my old place and be part of the old machine that I knew, and see it working as before. But not one of them came in.

The man who was at the head of what they called the Committee of Mobilisation which dealt with the organisation of work and finding workers for the Ministries used to laugh at me for being so anxious to get back to my old post. We used to talk together, and I told him how I looked at things. One day he came to me and said, 'We want people for the Foreign Office. Do you know any foreign languages?" I said I could tell one from another, but I could not talk any of them. He said, 'That is unfortunate, but it cannot be helped, and we can get no one at all. Trotsky wants some practical sensible person for a secretary, and we can trust you, and you belong to the party.' I told him I wanted to get back to my old place in my old Ministry, and he promised that this work should be only temporary, and that I ought to do it. I was anxious

Leon Trotsky by Y Annenkov.

to do something more than write on a typewriter, so I agreed, and went off to Smolny.

I found Trotsky in that same room where I used to see him, at the end of the corridor on the third floor. It was differently furnished then. There was just one table in the corner by the two windows. In the little room partitioned off was some dreadful furniture, particularly a green divan with a terrible pillow on it. You see it had been the room of the resident mistress on that floor of the Institute when it was still an Institute for girls. Trotsky sat on one side of the table and I sat on the other. I did not hide from him that I was quite unfit for the work, but that I wanted to do anything I could.

It was settled that I should begin at once. The first work I did was to make that dreadful room into a place fit to work in. Trotsky gave me a paper to take to the Ministry of Foreign Affairs to get a good typewriter, instead of the broken one that was in the room for show, and telephoned for his motor car to take me there and bring me back with the machine and some furniture. He gave me two soldiers to help in getting the furniture. I remember we had to wait a very long time before the motor car was ready.

We went to the Foreign Office, and there found Zalkind (who was for a time assistant Commissary for Foreign Affairs, and afterwards was sent as Russian Minister to Berne) in his room, which was just as you saw it, if not worse. Zalkind was half dressed, his hair wanted combing, the room was like a lumber room. The sofa where he slept was still like the nest of a wild beast. The big table with its red felt top was dusty and piled with papers, and inkpots which had been used for ash trays, and glasses with the dregs of coffee in them, and old bits of bread from the day before. There were half a dozen people in the room, and Zalkind took the note I had brought him from Trotsky, read it aloud, and said, pointing at me, 'We have destroyed secret diplomacy and come to that.' I did not like his manner. He told me to find the sailor Markin who knew where everything was. Then I met a very neatly dressed sailor.

Markin was not at all so anxious to look proletarian in the first days as he was later. Then he was dressed very carefully in a neat uniform, and his beard properly trimmed. Markin had very little education, but had a most amusing way of saying 'surprising', 'extraordinary' and 'astonishing', not like most people say those words, but as if they were newly forced out of him by his real feeling of the sensations that they suggest. In those days he was very elegant. He took me to the room where I afterwards went to live†, where we found the machine we wanted, and a table and some good chairs, all of which I took back with me to the Smolny, so that next day room 67 was already a place where it was possible to work.

The rear of room 67 was screened off as a private quarter for Trotsky. In this room one day, there was a young girl with hair cut short like a boy. She was sitting at the table doing nothing, and afterwards went with me to the refectory downstairs. This was a big barrack of a room with sawdust and spilt soup all over the floor, and bare tables. You bought tickets at a side table, and then took your place in a long queue, and when your turn came, received a bowl of soup, very hot, and, as you passed by grabbed a wooden spoon out of a basket. The soup was very hot, the plates very deep, and the spoons so large that sometimes it was impossible to get the soup into them at all. Then there was dark coloured tough macaroni, which I did not know how to eat. I could not pick it up on the big wooden spoon, and I did not see where forks were to be had. Most of the soldiers sitting about were eating with their fingers. A few had forks, but I thought they had brought them with them, and decided to bring a fork myself next time. I asked the short haired girl what work she did, and she answered that she did no work at all. I said I thought that was bad, but she explained that she was Trotsky's daughter, and was studying. She was about sixteen, very like Lev Davidovitch, with fine eyes, and a rather malicious expression. Trotsky has been married twice, and this was one of the children of his first marriage.

---

† *Probably a room in The Commissariat of Foreign Affairs fronting Palace Square.*

Downstairs in the refectory there was a woman serving out food. I think she had served there in the time when Smolny was still an institute for girls, and she was always thinking of old times, and comparing the comrades with the noble young ladies whose places they had taken.

At first I did not know how to talk to Trotsky. I thought of him as of someone so great, and so high, all of whose time was given to the work. It was almost a shock to me to find that he had a daughter. I did not think of him having any human relations at all. I did not know how to address him. Once only I called him Comrade Trotsky. It came out very funnily, and he immediately called me Comrade Shelepina, and we both laughed. After that I always called him Lev Davidovitch, and he called me Evgenia Petrovna.

I with my long training in a Ministry under the old regime, was offended somehow, for the dignity of the Ministry, when I found Trotsky himself taking thought about the arrangement of his room. This table was to be in that place, and this chair here. It seemed to me that there ought to be a whole corps of people to think of all these things, and that Trotsky should have no attention to spare for such matters. I always remember the affair of the phonograph. He asked me if I could write shorthand. I was terribly ashamed because I could not. He said, 'In the Ministry of Foreign Affairs there is a phonograph. We will use that.' So I went off to the Ministry and found Markin, and after a long hunt we found the phonograph and brought it back.

Trotsky never used it, but we fixed it on the table by his desk. There it stood always, and had a most imposing appearance. Perhaps that was all he wanted it for. It was only just before we left Petrograd that we found out how to work it. Everything was almost packed, and we were in a cheerful mood, expecting every day that the Germans would come in and hang us all, and make a good end of it. Soldier Jukov took the phonograph, and got it to work. He shouted English songs into it. You know how he talks English. Then I shouted into it. Then we made it shout back. On that last day three young people from one of the guerrilla detachments came in to look for Trotsky. They found us playing with the phonograph, and they shouted into it too, all kinds of rubbish, songs, and German swear words. If the Germans find it and turn it on thinking to discover state secrets, they will be surprised by a funny medley of cheerful noises.

At first very few visitors came to room 67. They were mostly foreigners asking for passports to go abroad. Russians too. I used to let almost all of them see Trotsky, particularly the foreigners. I was a little more careful with the Russians. But at first I had no idea what was important and what was not. For example, I tore up and threw away all the replies of the Foreign Embassies to Trotsky's note inviting them to join in discussions of general peace.

The first real bit of Foreign Relations we had was with the King of Sweden. There came along a certain Svanstrom or Swenstrom, from the Swedish Red Cross, with a letter from Charles (Prince?) suggesting the making of a neutral zone so that the exchange of invalid prisoners could go on directly through the front instead of by the roundabout way through Torneo. Svanstrom spoke to me in French, and I was ashamed at having to reply in French, and was still more ashamed when it turned out afterwards that he could talk Russian. I was ashamed, not for myself, you understand, but for the dignity of the Commissariate of Foreign Affairs. I did not think that they ought to know that Trotsky had not been able to get a secretary who could talk French. Well, worse was to come.

Svanstrom was to leave for Sweden in two days time, and Trotsky promised an answer to take back to the king of Sweden. Well, the first day passed, and Trotsky did nothing. I could not think he had forgotten it, and I did not like to remind him. Then Svanstrom came for it, and I told him it was not quite ready but would be ready in time, and that it would be sent to him. Still Trotsky did nothing. The next day was Sunday. Trotsky wrote the reply on a scrap of paper, and gave it to me to have it properly typewritten so that it could be given to Svanstrom for the king. Our typewriter, which wrote with English or French characters was a very bad one, so I sent it to the Foreign Office.

It was Sunday and no one was there. At last very late it came back. It was written on beautiful paper, but dirty, you should have seen it. It was full of mistakes which had been rubbed out with indiarubber, and the indiarubber still showed. It was not that it was to be handed to the King that gave cause for concern. It was that any foreigner should think we were such a set of uneducated barbarians as to be unable to send out a neater looking document. I did not know what to do. So I tried to make a cleaner copy on the old English machine in room 67. Its ribbon was full of copying ink, so that it smudged, and the machine itself was filthy. It had not been used for I don't know how long. My first copy was worse than the original. The second was not much better, and I spent hours over them, because I was accustomed to write on a Russian machine, and all the letters were in different places, and I had to look at each letter, because I did not know how the French words were spelt. And I did not know how to put the accents on. Then Trotsky came in, and I told him the whole story and showed him the three copies to choose from. He chose the first, and laughed and told me to put it in an envelope. Nor was even that the end. We were to give Svanstrom a pass and also a Swedish officer who was to go with him. And we sent neither the passes nor the letter. They came for them themselves early in the morning. I nearly died of shame when I handed them the envelope, and then, to make things worse, the Swedish officer kissed my hand. It was so unexpected, for one thing, and there were a lot of people about, and I thought it would seem to them altogether like bourgeois times and the old regime. Altogether it was a most unfortunate incident. And with that began Bolshevik dealings with foreign powers.

Journey to Brest

You will remember that for several days the wire to Brest was spoilt, and there had been no news from there whatever. Of course couriers went to and fro, but that was all, and Stalin (Lenin's right hand) came into the room where I was and said, 'We must send some trusty person to bring back a report of how things really are.'

I said, "Send me", never thinking for a moment that they would. Stalin said,

"Seriously, would you go?"

I said, "Of course I would go if I were sent."

He said, "all right, the train goes at eight thirty tonight. I will speak to Lenin." Then Lenin came in and spoke to me and left me with the impression not only that I was not to go, but that no one was going.

I consequently made no preparations whatever, and was much surprised when at five thirty Stalin came in, and seeing me, said "What are you not ready?"

I said, "I understood that I was not going."

He said, "Yes, you are going." So I rushed off to get things together. They gave me a document which, unfortunately I threw away only the other day, when packing to leave Petrograd. It said that 'Trotsky's secretary was travelling to Brest as Courier Extraordinary.' I packed my night things into a big wooden box, one of those flat boxes made of thin wood for carrying dresses. Eroida put our joint allowance of bread into it, and some tea and sugar for the journey. I also took a pillow. Besides that they gave me a big parcel of newspapers for Trotsky, and a packet of cuttings and other papers. I had no money at all, but Eroida borrowed some from other people in the ministry.

I got to the station just before the train was due to start. I found the Commissar of the station, and was asking him for one of the soldiers of Field Chasseurs since one of them regularly travelled to Brest as Courier, when there came up to me a Colonel? Fokke of the General Staff and said he too was going to Brest, and was glad he had not to travel alone. I also said I was glad. The Commissar at the station knew me by sight. No one asked for our documents, and we presently found the train, where there was a coupé set aside for us.

It was a first class coupé with a sliding door in the middle, dirty beyond words, the upholstery torn to shreds, and the cushions indescribably dirty. I was glad I had brought my own pillow. Fokke talked with me a little, and made a very bad impression upon me. He had most unsuitable luggage and too much of it. I was ashamed of my own flat box, but he had an enormous cardboard milliner's packing box, with the name of some Petrograd firm on it. Beside that he had a big portmanteau, another package, and a very heavy bundle. This bundle was extraordinarily heavy, and I do not to this day know what it was. His manner was not at all the manner I thought suitable for one going, as I supposed he was, as consultant to the peace delegation (since he had been two or three times in that capacity). He was gay and seemed to laugh at everything, whereas, I as you know all that time was in a very heavy mood. Presently I decided to sleep on the upper berth in my half of the coupé, and he decided to do the same in his.

Three sailors came in and sat on the seat below me, and three or four soldiers came into his part of the coupé. The door between was partly closed. About two hours late we started. Then the guard woke me up and asked for my ticket. I had not got a ticket, and he said he had had no instructions about me, and that I must get out. A crowd of soldiers in the corridor backed him up, saying they did not see why a lady should be able to lie down in an upper berth without a ticket, and that they would prefer to lie there themselves instead of standing in the corridor.

At last, however, he was satisfied, and I slept. When I woke in the morning I found that many more had crowded in. There were two sailors sleeping on the floor below me, as well as half a dozen crowded into the lower berth. I could not get down, so I lay there on top, in a terrible mood, until about half past five that day. The soldiers changed their mood during the night, and some of them even took the trouble to bring me some hot water to make tea. We got to Dvinsk that night, and after some waiting went in an automobile to the staff of the fifth army. Colonel Fokke went in and left me in the corridor for a long time. Then we went back to the station and, in a much better train, just an engine and a carriage but a very good carriage went further. It was at this point that Colonel Fokke insisted on showing me his documents. He showed me a permission to go and visit his sister at Riga. I thought it most improper that he should travel to Brest when he was really travelling with such a purpose. I did not want to see his documents but he, perhaps because he was nervous, insisted on showing them.

At midnight we came to the neutral zone. We walked for about two versts, soldiers coming with us, and carrying our ridiculous luggage. Then suddenly there appeared a German officer with a lantern buttoned to the front of his overcoat, his hands in a little muff. He greeted us very abruptly, said we were three hours late, and without the slightest regard for us or for the German soldiers who were now staggering under our baggage (Fokke's big box was particularly awkward to carry) hurried at a great pace. We went on foot another four versts. Then we found sledges waiting for us, simple low sledges like the peasants use. The German officer sat by the driver, Fokke and I side by side behind. For some time there was more sand than snow, and I remember the unpleasant gritting of the runners. There was no moon, but it was fairly light. We came at last to the low building of white logs which they call the Casino of Berchhof. Fokke said that the manner of the Germans had very much changed towards us, and that when negotiations began they had been quite different, and very friendly.

Here we went into a sort of main room. Opposite the door there was a big stove, solidly built, and decorated with three or four little pine trees standing on the top of it. On each side of the stove was a long simple dining table. There was another such table in the corner on the right of the door, and, immediately opposite the stove was a smaller table, specially made for card playing. The walls of the room were ornamented with extremely coarse paintings, all reflecting the same kind of primitive wit. There was, for example, a Russian moujik, with a bottle of vodka, and every German, of course, had his tankard of beer. There were also pictures of women.

In this place we had supper. The German officer became more friendly here, though I did not care to talk with him. Fokke had tried to talk with him all the way. At first he had been unwilling to do

Evgenia Shelepina and the October Revolution

anything in a hurry. It appeared that the train from Berchhof did not leave until next morning. The officer asked me if I minded sleeping in a barrack. Of course it was all the same to me where I slept. We went out from the casino, and round several smaller buildings adjoining it, which I think must have been kitchens, and came behind it to the place he called the barrack. It was incredibly clean. The beds in it were made up with clean wood shavings.

He took me to a room opening out of the main barrack, and said that it was his own room and that I could sleep there. He apologised for it, but I was really astonished at it. There was everything anybody could want. A washing stand so arranged that you could pour clean water on yourself from a jug and let the dirty water run away. I wondered how long they had been in this place. It seemed to me that they had fixed themselves up as if they meant to stay there for ever. I am sure no Russian officers take the trouble to arrange for washing so pleasantly. Then there were pictures on the walls, photographs, comfortable chairs, everything as solid and nice as it could be. He said that he would have to lock the door from outside, which he did, but I was too sleepy to have any particular feeling of imprisonment.

I woke in the morning and got up at once. I had just lain down as I was with my pillow. The officer bid me good morning, and took me into the Casino, where we had tea. It was the most distasteful stuff. Then they put our things on a sledge, and we walked to the station which was quite near. I will not describe the railway journey to Brest. There were two changes, Vilna and Bielostok. We reached Brest at 11 at night, and went at once to barrack No.7 in the fortress, where the Russian delegation was housed. Trotsky laughed, when he saw me. 'When they said that a lady had come, I was sure it must be you, but I do not understand why you have come in the least.' I said I had come because I found it dull without him. Then, of course, I told him how it was that I had come. He told me to talk to Comrade Joffe, because he himself was starting for Warsaw early in the morning, so that I would not see him again.

Then I saw Madam Radek, who was very glad to see me, as I was glad to see her. We talked for a little and I went to bed, and slept. I was tired out.

Next day I went with Radek and Madam Radek and Metzkevitch (a Lithuanian) for a walk in the town. Radek had to get permission from the Commandant, for every purchase he wished to make. This had the most terrible effect upon me. I felt I was going to choke. The town was a dead town. All the houses were broken in some way or other, some with their roofs blown off, others with their walls blown in. Nothing had been done to mend the houses, but the streets had been tidied up, so that there was an oppressive orderliness even in the disorder of the broken town. There were only two or three little shops open, selling necessary things, tobacco and thread, and such things, and then there was a bookstore, over which, of course, Radek spent more time than over all the rest.

When he was buying cigarettes, I told him to buy some for me. He told me the permission given him by the Commandant did not allow him to buy any more. It was as if the Germans had hit me a blow in the face. At Brest, for the first time in my life, I really wanted to kill people. While we were walking, we met a party of Russian prisoners. They walked in rags, and a guard of armed Germans walked with them, making a sort of cordon around them. It was a terrible sight. Their prisoners in Russia, as you know, are poorly clad, but their overcoats are overcoats, at least. These poor Russians were clothed anyhow, in rags, hung together to make a pretence of warmth.

It was forbidden to speak to the prisoners, but Radek called out to them, and one of them from somewhere in the middle of the party answered him. I do not remember exactly what he said. The impression made on me by the whole scene was so terrible that I hardly noticed their words. I heard Radek speak, and I heard the others reply, but I do not know what they said.

*   *   *

So ends these very interesting accounts by Evgenia. Within a very short time after these reports were made, her political views began to change. She wanted a lower profile, and took steps to remove herself from the centre of power. By late 1919 it is doubtful whether she wanted to be associated with the Bolsheviks. Her detachment was complete once she was in Estonia and living with Ransome.

An additional snippet of information survives regarding Evgenia and her firearm. It will be remembered that, for the period Evgenia worked at the Smolny, she carried a small handgun. On going into room 67 (Trotsky's office) there were some east-facing windows on the left from the door. The second window had bullet holes through both inner and outer panes. Evgenia broke a telephone and blew a hole in the wall with a bullet when she was playing with her revolver. She had always wondered how the other bullet hole had come to be there. The hole in the inside pane was smaller than in the outside one, so she knew that the bullet had been fired from inside the room. Evgenia was very glad, when she found out that it had been made by Trotsky himself playing with his revolver, and that he knew as little about such things as she did.

Evgenia's Russian passport.

ACKNOWLEDGEMENTS

The research and writing for this book has taken the best part of three years, and has entailed a number of journeys around the North West area of Russia and to the Baltic Republics. In all of our journeys and deliberations, we have only met with kindness, very willing help, and enthusiasm.

For basic biography, chronology and some general details, we have relied to a great extent on Ransome's *Autobiography* and the biography, *The Life of Arthur Ransome* by Hugh Brogan. Without these basic sources the task would have been a daunting one. Our first thanks are to Ransome's executors John Bell, Christina Hardyment and Dave Sewart, and to Hugh Brogan.

Most of Ransome's private letters, diaries and details are held at the Brotherton Collection at Leeds University Library, our special thanks to Assistant librarian Ann Farr for her great help and knowledgeable stewardship. To the Lake District Art Gallery and Museum Trust, Abbot Hall, Kendal for permission to quote from the Dora Collingwood journals.

To the Public Record Office, Kew, for permission to quote from documents relating to Foreign Office comments and observations of the time.

The National Library of Russia, St. Petersburg, must be one of the ultimate treasure houses for researchers. We are indebted to various departments, particularly Mrs E.V. Barhatovrev of the Department of Prints for much help and advice. Also to the St. Petersburg Photoarchive of the Academy of Science for the use of period photographs.

We have received assistance from the National Libraries of both Estonia (Tallin) and Latvia (Riga), and thank them for historical notes, maps and photographs. To the Photographic Archive in Tartu Estonia for help with the pictures of Ants Piip and Otto Strandman. During a visit to Riga, Jury Melkonov and family were extremely kind and hospitable in looking after me and ensured that all the local Ransome sites were fully examined. Also for much help, especially in providing super period maps of the old city. To Sergei and Maya Melkonov for transport and guidance over a period on the Ransome trail in Eastern Latvia, and Maya especially for being a brilliant translator. A heart felt thank you to Irena Semanova for helping with information back and forth between the UK and Russia.

We especially wish to thank Roger Wardale for being extremely helpful, both with advice as an acknowledged expert on Ransome, and for undertaking the thankless task of proof reading the text at such short notice. So many useful suggestions and corrections were made that the book would have been all the poorer without.

Acknowledgements

Many other people have helped in various ways. Our special thanks to Margaret Ratcliffe for general help and with illustrations of Ransome and his mother Edith, and to the Lupton family for permission to publish. Also to John Edwards for help and information relating to the Boulton family in Australia. Special thanks are due to Cecily Ledgard for the photograph and permission to reproduce the Boulton painting 'Cows crossing a valley'. Also to John Prescott for the scanning and re-alignment of the same picture, Sonia Whitaker for the picture of the Alexandro Nevsky Monastery and Mary Pritchard for the picture of Tatiana. Hazel Vale has always been very supportive and we thank her for her kindness and for permission to use the picture of Ivy Ransome.

Claire Kendall-Price a writer and editor in her own right, undertook the mammoth task of designing and laying out the manuscript in preparation for printing. Our special thanks are without reservation for her knowledge, organisation, help and guidance in producing this book.

We have tried to identify and credit all copyright holders, but this has proved to be more difficult than we would have believed. Our sincere apologies if anyone has been inadvertently omitted due to insufficient information.

ILLUSTRATION CREDITS

Front Cover Painting – UA Rysakov's Collection, St Petersburg.
Front and Back Cover Portrait – Special Collections, Leeds University.

Black & White

Abbot Hall, Kendal, 185
Architectural Monuments of Leningrad, 79, 84 lower
Eesti Kirjandusmuuseum, Tartu, 114, 115
Lupton family, 16 upper & middle, 145, 147
Melkonov, Segey, 151
National Library of Estonia, Department of Research, 140 upper, 162
National Library of Magazine - Russia, 24 both
National Library of Russia, Department of Prints, 31, 32 upper left, 35, 38/39 upper, 38 middle 40 upper, 42, 50, 51 both, 56 upper, 60 lower, 63 upper & lower, 89 lower, 94 both, 95, 96 upper, 140 lower, 141, 143, 148-9, 150, 155 upper, 157, 166, 167, 170, 171 both
Photo Archive of the Academy of Science, St. Petersburg, 27 upper & lower, 28 both, 29 upper, 30, 32 upper right, 32 lower, 34 upper, 44, 60 upper, 64, 76 upper, 77, 88 all three, 89 upper & middle
Special Collections, Leeds University, iv, 29 lower, 83, 87 both, 132, 133, 142, 146, 152, 153, 154, 172
Stucke, family, 56 lower, 57 upper
Tabitha Lewis Estate, 21
All other illustrations from authors collections

Colour

Ledgard, Cecily, Cattle Crossing a Valley
Central library, Riga, 1920s period map
Whitaker, Sonia, Alexandro-Nevski Lavra. Trinity Cathedral.
All other illustrations from authors collections

BIBLIOGRAPHY

Afanasiev, A.N.,	*Russian Folk Fairy Tales. Vol 2: Fairy Tales of Northern Area.* (Collected) 5 volumes. (Moscow 1914)
Alexander, C.E,	*Ransome at Home.* Amazon Publications 1996 *Ransome in the Baltic.* RTC BASK, Riga 2001 *Ransome in Estonia.* RTC BASK, Riga 2003
Brogan, Hugh,	*The Life of Arthur Ransome.* Jonathan Cape 1984 *Signalling from Mars : The Letters of Arthur Ransome.* Jonathan Cape 1997
Bruce, HJ,	*Silken Dalliance.* Constable 1947 *Thirty Dozen Moons.* Constable 1948
Collingwood, Dora,	Unpublished journals, diaries and letters. Lake District Art Gallery & Museum Trust, Abbot Hall, Kendal
Christopher, A, & Gordievsky, Oleg	*KGB - Foreign Relations from Lenin to Gorbachov.* Hodder & Stoughton 1990
Edwards, J,	*Edward Baker Boulton - Forgotten Colonial Artist.* Unpublished manuscript
Gatsuk, V.A,	*Fairy Tales of the Caucasus.* (Ed) Moscow 1905 *Russian Folk Fairy Tales.* (Collected) Moscow 1910
Hammond, Wayne G,	*Bibliography of Arthur Ransome.* Oak Knoll Press 2000
Hardyment, Christina,	*Arthur Ransome and Captain Flint's Trunk.* Jonathan Cape 1984
Hart-Davis, Rupert,	*Hugh Walpole.* Macmillan 1952
Hunt, Peter,	*Approaching Arthur Ransome.* Jonathan Cape 1992
Justice, E,	*Three Years in Russia.* London 1739
Karsavina, Tamara,	*Theatre Street.* Constable 1948
Kendall-Price, Claire,	*In the Footsteps of the Swallows and Amazons.* Wild Cat Publishing 1993
Kennon, George,	*Russia and the West.* Little, Brown & Co. 1960
Kinel, Lola,	*Under Five Eagles.* Putnam 1937
King, Hilary,	*Arthur Ransome - an unsung hero in Estonia?* From *Mixed Moss* Vol 3 No 6 - Journal of The Arthur Ransome Society Winter 1999

Kochan, Lionel,	*Russia in Revolution.* Granada Publishing 1981
Lockhart, RH Bruce,	*Memoirs of a British Agent.* Putnam 1932
Marshall, Pauline,	*Where It All Began.* 1991
Mitrokhin,	*Mitrokhin.* Aurora Art Publishers. Leningrad 1977
Moorehead, Alan,	*The Russian Revolution.* Collins with Hamish Hamilton 1958
Pitcher, Harvey,	*Witnesses of the Russian Revolution.* John Murray 1994
Radzinsky, Edvard,	*The Last Tzar – The life and death of Nicholas II.* BCA 1992
Ransome, Arthur,	*Bohemia in London.* Chapman Hall 1907 *Oscar Wilde.* Martin Secker 1912 *Old Peter's Russian Tales.* Illustrated by Dmitri Mitrokhin TC & EC Jack 1916 *The Soviet Government of Russia.* Forward by Karl Radek. Moscow 1918 *The Truth About Russia.* New York 1918 *The Autobiography of Arthur Ransome.* Jonathan Cape 1976 *Racundra's First Cruise.* Jonathan Cape 1984 *Six Weeks in Russia.* Redwords 1992 *The Crisis in Russia.* Redwords 1992 Unpublished diaries, letters and manuscripts, Brotherton Collection, University of Leeds.
Reed, John,	*Ten Days That Shook The World.* Sutton Publishing 1997
Thomas, R. George,	*Edward Thomas – Biography.* O.U.P. 1987
Trotsky, Leon,	*The History of the Russian Revolution.* 1932
Tyrkova-Williams, Ariadna,	*Cheerful Giver: the life of Harold Williams.* Peter Davies 1935
Valentinov, Nikolay,	*Encounters with Lenin.* O.U.P. 1968
Verizhnikova, Tatiana,	*Arthur Ransome and St. Petersburg.* TARS Literary Papers 1995 *Harold Williams and Russia of the Russians.* St. Petersburg 1996 *Arthur Ransome and his Letters from Russia.* History of St. Petersburg, Society & Culture at Academy of Science 1998 *Mitrokhin & his illustrations for Old Peter's Russian Tales.* from The Research of New Materials Moscow 1999

Bibliography

Verizhnikova, Tatiana *cont/*   *St. Petersburg Britons - The History of the St. Petersburg British Community to Arthur Ransome.*
        The State Hermitage Museum Russian Studies Vol 3, St Petersburg 2000.

Wardale, Roger,   *Nancy Blackett : Under Sail with Arthur Ransome.*
        Jonathan Cape 1991
    Ransome at Sea: Notes from the Chart Table. (Ed)
    (Transcript of Ransome's Logbooks 1920-1954.)
        Amazon Publications 1995
    Arthur Ransome and the World of the Swallows & Amazons.
        Great Northern. 2000

Williams, Harold,   *Russia of the Russians.* Pitman 1914

INDEX

ABC of Physical Culture, 14
Abercrombie, Catherine, 15
Abercrombie, Lascelles, 15, 22, 26, 162
Acland, Francis, 46
Agar, Lt. A. 140
Albert Bridge, 12
Aladdin and his Wonderful Lamp, 46
Anglo-Russian Bureau, 60-66
Atkinson, Mary and James, 5
Anglo-Russian Bureau, 64-67

Balham, 12
Bakst, Leon, 42
Baltic Episode, 140
Bell, Aust, 4
Benois, Alexandre, 42, 43
Benois, Nadia, 43
Berenger, Guy, 59
Bergen-op-Zoom, 4, 5
Bielostok, 183
Birds Factory, 35
Black, A.&C., 16
Bohemia in London, 16, 18
Bottomley, Gordon, 15, 26
Boulton, Edward Baker, 4, 6
Boulton, George, 4
Boulton, Nithsdale, 6
Boulton, Rev. William MA, 5
Boulton, Thomas, 4
Brest-Litovsk, 171, 183
Brest-Litovsk Negotiations, 87
British Propaganda Office 65
Brown, Curtis, 18
Bruces, 34
Bruscheti, Alice, 44
Brusilov, General A.A., 67
Buchannan, Sir George, 40, 51, 63, 64, 78, 93, 160
Bukharin, Nikolai 158
Bullit, William, 104

Camperdown, 5
Cardington, 4

Carlyle Studios, 15
Cameron, Charles, 36
Campbell, Ivar, 22
Cartmel, 15
Chelsea, 12
Chicherin, Georgi V, 154, 158, 171
Child's Book of the Garden, 15
Clark's Factory, 35
Cole, Peggotty, 14
Coleman-Smith, Pamela, 13
Collingwood, Barbara, 13, 14, 18, 21, 68
Collingwood, Dora, 13, 14, 17, 18, 21
Collingwood, Edith, 13, 14, 45
Collingwood, Robin, 13
Collingwood, Ursula, 13
Collingwood, W.G., 11
Courtney, Ralph, 18
Cowan, Sir Walter, 140
Cruising Association, 162
Curzon, Lord, 157

Daily Chronicle, 39, 40, 160
Daily News, 56, 57, 74, 75, 80-82, 93, 95, 113, 160
Daily Telegraph, 59
Darling, Mr Justice, 23
Deniken, General, 112
Diaghileff, 42
Doboujinsky, 42
Douglas, Lord Alfred, 23, 24
Doumergue, Gaston, 94
Dragunevitch, 127-130
Dublin, 5

Economist, 82
Eddison, Ric, 6
Editha Mansions, 14
Eggers, Otto, 150, 151
Ellen, 4
Elite Hotel, 97, 99
Epicoene, 44
Ercole, George, 153
Fohke, Colonel, 181, 182

Garvin, J.L. 80, 81
Gellibrand, Edmund, 27, 28
Gibbs, Governor, 4
Golden Anchor Hotel, 96, 97
Golovin, 42
Goode, Prof, 140
Gordons, 34
Gould, William, 36
Grant Richards, 9, 10
Grove, Consul H.M. 164
Guchkov, A.I., 42, 74
Guerrilla War and Tactics, 98
Gwynne, Rachel Emma, 5

Hatch, 21, 22
Hamilton, Molly (Mary Agnes), 82
Hamiltons, 34
Hardy, Thomas, 22
Hanbury-Williams, General Sir John, 64
Hermitage Hotel, 31
Highways and Byways in Fairyland, 16
Hirst, Francis, 82
Hodgson, R.M., 157, 158, 160
Hollywood Road, 12, 13
Hugo, Victor, 44
Huron Weekly, 10

Ignagtovsky, 120-122

Jacksons, 3
Joffe, Adolf, 183
Jonson, Ben, 44
Judenitch, General, 112, 114
Jukov, 178
Justice, Elizabeth, 35

Kaiserwald, (Mezaparks), 152
Kalevipoeg, 113
Kamenev, Lev B., 90
Karakhan, L.M., 102
Karsavina, Tamara, 42
Kerensky, A., 78, 81, 94, 173
Kinel, Lola, 69, 70, 72, 73, 98
Kittiwake, 149, 150
Korovin, M., 42
Krupskaya, Nadezhda, 41

Krylov, 36

Lanehead, 11, 18
Lawrence, Alan, 141
Lee Brockhurst, 5
Lenin, (Vladimir Ilyich Ulyanov,1870-1924)
  references, 72, 75, 81, 86, 87,
  90, 92, 94, 97, 100, 104, 105,
  107, 115, 116, 149, 160, 161, 180
Lewis, Sir George, 24, 25
Litovsky Castle, 44, 66
Litvinov, Maxim 101, 102, 115, 116, 130,
  131, 148, 149, 154, 158 160
Lloyd George, David, 113
Lockhart, R.H.B., 63, 94-96, 99, 101,
  109, 111
Lykiardopoulos, Michael, 23, 25, 39, 48, 63

Manchester Guardian, 40, 59, 75, 111, 113,
  118, 141, 147, 151, 154, 158-160
Markin, 177, 178
Markino, Yoshio, 13
Mara, Comrade, 174
Maria, Empress, 167
Mariinsky Theatre, 37
Martens, Conrad, 4
Masefield, John, 13
Metropole Hotel, 97
Michael Palace, 43
Miliukov, P.N., 41, 74
Milner, Lord, 94
Mitrokhin, Dimitri, 42-45, 143
Mixed Moss, 141
Morning Post, 40
Morris, William, 9
Moscow Arts Theatre, 23

Nabokov, Vladimir, 36
Nekrasov, 36
Nibthwaite, 7
Nicholas II, 78
Night in Luxembourg, 23
Nisbit & Co, 46

Observer, 80, 81
Old College - Windermere, 7

193

Oldmeadow, Ernest, 10
Oldenburg, Sergei, 41, 74
Old Peter's Russian Tales, 42, 43, 49, 50, 51, 55, 68
Owen Mansions, 16, 18

Palmer, Greg, 166
Pares, Bernard, 61
Partisan War, 98
Pasternak, Boris, 44
Peel Island, 11
Peter, General, 119
Peters, William, 59, 60
Philips-Price, Morgan, 59, 94, 95, 105, 111, 113
Piip, Ants, 114-116, 118, 119, 130, 131, 137, 139
Pochin, of Barkby, 19
Pockim, Catherine, 56
Poe, Edgar Allan, 44
Pokrovsky, Prof.M., 116
Pond and Stream, 15
Pushkin, A.S., 36

Radek, Karl, 86, 87, 97, 99, 116, 149, 183, 184
Radek, Rosa, 87, 183
Ransevet, 42
Racundra, 151, 154-156, 158-160, 162, 164, 165
Racundra's First Cruise, 156, 160
Ransome, Arthur M., family, 3, Australian connections 4-6; School 7-8; London 10-11; Chelsea 12; met Ivy 18; Marriage 19; Douglas court case 23; to Russia 31; Tzar's appearance 40; Moscow 49; *Old Peter's Tales* 50; Vergezha 56; operation 55; early correspondent 59; the Anglo-Russian Bureau 62-65; Revolution 74-78; FO relations 93; Vologda, 95-7; Stockholm 100-01; Scotland Yard 104-5; civil war trip to Moscow 114-136; Baltic correspondent 139; Dorpat Conference 140; Glinka Street raid 142; marriage to Evgenia Shelepina 162
Ransome, Cecily, 3
Ransome, Cyril, 3, 6, 7
Ransome, Edith, 3, 5-8, 10, 16, 112, 139, 164
Ransome, Evgenia, (Second wife neé Shelepina), First Meeting 83, Relationship 84-5; Smolny office 91-2; Moscow 97; Stockholm 99-101; return to Russia 102; passport application 112; across war lines 116-118, 130; journey 131-135; diamond smuggling 137-8; Baltic existence 139-41, 143-4, in *Slug* 145, in *Kittiwake* 150, flat fire 156, 159; marriage 162; declaration 164; early life and lodgings 166-67, 170
Ransome, Geoffrey, 3
Ransome, Joyce, 3
Ransome, Ivy (first wife, née Walker), introduced 18; marriage 19; references 30, 31, 46, 53, 55, 58, 68, 148, 154, 157, end of marriage/divorce, 158-162
Ransome, Susan, (Great Aunt) 7
Ransome, Tabitha, (Daughter) 20, 24, 52, 53, 58, 85
Ransome, Thomas, 3
Rasputin, Grigory, 79, 80
Remizov, 42, 97
Rennet, Frederick, 57
Repin, Ilya, 34
Reuters, 59
Reval Yacht Club, 150
Riga Yacht Club, 154
Robins, Raymond, 95
Rodzianko, M.V., 41
Ross, Robert, 23
Rouse, Dr.W.H.D., 8
Rugby, (Public School) 7

Russia of the Russians, 39
Russian Tales, 50

Scale, Major, 100, 101
Scheglov, M., 50
Scott, C.P., 93, 113
Secker, Martin, 23
Sehmel, Carl, (The Ancient) 154
Sept Médailles, 44
Shelepina, Iraida, 84, 172-174, 180, 181
Shelepina, Peter, 166, 167
Shlyapnikov, 174
Six Weeks in Russia, 102, 103, 112, 113, 116
Slug, 145, 146, 149, 150
Sokolov, Dr., 55, 56
Somoff, Konstantine, 42, 43
Soudeikin, 42
Souls of the Streets, 14
Stalin, Josef, 42, 87, 97, 108, 109, 160, 180
Steel, Lt. Comdr. Gordon, 165
Steffens, Lincoln, 104
Stolen Turnips, 68
St. Petersburg Archive, 166
Strandman, Otto, 115
Strindberg, 26
Struve, Peter, 41
Stucke, George T., 56
Stucke, Dr. L.S., 55, 56
Svanstrom, 179, 180

Tales from the Caucasus, 50
Tales in the North of Russia, 50
Tchargra, Lydia Andreena, 44
Teliakovsky, 42
Temple Bar Magazine, 15
The Blue Bird, 48
The Cherry Orchard, 48
The Elixir of Life, 49, 58
The Gold Bug, 44
The Mexican Rebellion, 98
The Secret City, 65
The Soldier and Death, 68
The Tales of Russian People, 50
Things in Season, 15
Thomas, Edward, 11, 14, 19

Thomas, Helen, 15, 19
Thompson, Sir Basil, 93, 104, 105, 113
Thornhill, Colonel, 64
Times Book Club, 23
Trotsky, Leon, 2; detention 81, 83; meeting A.R. 86, 87; Smolny 90-92; war books 98; meetings 107 interviews 154, War Minister, 171, wants secretary 175-76; relations 177-78; at work 179-81; Brest-Litovsk, 183, 184
Tzarevich, 79
Tumanov, General Prince, 77
Tyrkova, Arkady, 41
Tzar Fedor, 48

Unicorn Press, 10, 11
Ustinov, Peter, 43

Vergezha, 47, 53, 54, 57
Verizhnikova, Tatiana, 166
Victorov, 48
Vilna, 183
Volkov River, 53
Vorovsky, V.V., 83, 86, 99, 101, 143

Walcha, 4-6
Walker, George, 19
Walker, Sophia, 20, 23
Walker, E.B., 66
Wall Nook, 15-17
Walpole, Hugh, 42, 48, 64, 66
Weirguari, 4
Wellington Valley, 4
Wells, H.G., 41
Wem, 5, 6
Wem Grammar School, 5
Whishaw, Norman, 29, 49
Whitelaw, Robert, 8
Wilcox, E.H., 59
Wilde, Oscar, 23
Williams, Ariadna, Vladimirovna, 41
Williams, Harold, 39-41, 45, 47, 53, 55, 56, 58, 59, 62, 64

Wilson, Sir Henry, 94
Wilton, Robert, 59
Winter Palace, 40, 45

Yeats, W.B., 13
Yorkshire College, 8
Yusupov, Felix, 80
Yusupov, Palace, 67, 80

Zalkind, 176, 177
Zinoviev, 158